EDUCATION

CHARTISM

To Mark

J. T. Ward

Senior Lecturer in Economic History
University of Strathclyde

CHARTISM

B. T. BATSFORD LTD London

First published 1973
© J. T. Ward 1973

Made and printed in Great Britain
by C. Tinling and Co. Ltd, London and Prescot
for the publishers B.T. Batsford Ltd,
4 Fitzhardinge Street, London W.1

ISBN 0 7134 1383 2 (hardcover)
ISBN 0 7134 1384 0 (paperback)

Contents

Introduction

'It is extremely unlikely that any competent or satisfactory narrative of a stupendous national crisis will ever now be given to the world', W. E. Adams wrote of Chartism in 1903. Despite such deterrent counsel, however, historians have become increasingly fascinated by the story of the first working-class political party. Most of those who have published their views have dealt with aspects of the movement. The present volume is an attempt to re-examine Chartism as a whole. In presenting such a study, one is aware of the still controversial nature of much Chartist history. Over the years writers holding very different views have looked at the movement and provoked and participated in controversies over its nature.

In the nineteenth century the first general history of the movement held the field. R. G. Gammage, soured by his experiences during Chartism's closing years, published his book in 1854; it was revised forty years later and was supplemented only by occasional personal reminiscences and biographies. British historians in general tended to write off Chartism as a proletarian failure, a temporary aberration from the Victorian saga of progress through the operation of liberal capitalism and self-help. Thus, writing of the events of 1848, Spencer Walpole decided that the 'discovery [of fraudulent signatures to the Petition] turned the whole thing into ridicule . . . and the cause of Reform was for years arrested by the abuse of the machinery devised by the Reformers'.

From the end of the Victorian age a succession of foreign studies started a revival of interest in Chartism. From Germany in 1898 John Tildsley showed how the socio-economic background affected the movement's course. Fourteen years later, from Paris, Edouard Dolléans enhanced this view with his study of *Le Chartisme*. And in 1916 three American scholars at Columbia University, H. U.

Faulkner, F. F. Rosenblatt and P. W. Slosson, produced seminal
studies of aspects of Chartist history. Marxist writers also started to
examine the movement. The Russian Yuri Kovalev's anthology of
1956 is the largest collection of Chartist literary efforts—largely
forgotten productions ranging from humble cottage verses to radical-
romantic poetry in the tradition of Byron and Shelley.

During the first Great War two writers worked on general narrative accounts of Chartism. Both died at a tragically early age,
leaving their manuscripts to be completed by others; consequently,
neither work can fairly be regarded as an expression of the author's
final judgment. Mark Hovell of Manchester University was killed as
an infantry officer in 1916, and his work was completed by Professor
T. F. Tout. Julius West, a Russian exile and Fabian official, died in
1918, leaving his work to be seen through the press by J. C. Squire.
Both books became classics. Half a century later, any writer on
Chartism is conscious of a debt to such pioneers.

It would be arrogant to claim to supplant the narratives of Hovell
and West. But after half a century it seems reasonable to re-assess the
Chartist story, taking account of the many studies which have appeared since the last syntheses were published in 1920. This inevitably
involves deciding between rival viewpoints propounded by modern
writers. One cannot hope to please them all.

Political doctrines have considerably influenced much modern
writing on Chartism and the Chartists. Several authors, for instance,
have seen Chartism as an ancestor of their own philosophies and
movements. In 1929 a young Oxonian, Hugh Gaitskell, taught the
Workers' Educational Association that 'Chartism, in its beginning
the last and most violent protest of the new proletariat, reveals in its
conclusion the triumph of a new bourgeoisie'. But in the same year
Theodore Rothstein attempted to delineate a connection *From
Chartism to Labourism,* and in 1938 Reg Groves asserted *But We Shall
Rise Again.* The present volume does not suggest any particular
group as the legatee of Chartism or see Chartism as part of some
amorphous 'Working Class Movement'. It is simply a history of
Chartism and Chartists and their forebears. It does not share that
sentimental regard for 'good old days' which affected many Chartist
reminiscences. Thomas Cooper, writing in 1872, presented a fine
example of such Chartist regrets:

'In our old Chartist times, it is true, Lancashire working men were in rags by thousands; and many of them often lacked food. But their intelligence was demonstrated wherever you went. You would see them in groups discussing the great doctrine of political justice—that every grown-up, sane man ought to have a vote in the election of the men who were to make the laws by which he was to be governed; or they were in earnest dispute respecting the teachings of socialism. Now, you will see no such groups in Lancashire. But you will hear well-dressed working men talking, as they walk with their hands in their pockets, of 'Co-ops' (Co-operative Stores), and their shares in them, or in building societies. And you will see others, like idiots, leading small greyhound dogs, covered with cloth, in a string!

More important to Chartist studies than most 'political' or 'sociological' tracts have been two lines of historical works. A new era was opened by David Williams's study of John Frost in 1939 and by G. D. H. Cole's *Chartist Portraits* of 1940. The biographical approach has added new dimensions to the subject. Students of Chartism have subsequently learned much from other works on prominent Chartists and their colleagues—notably from Cecil Driver's biography of Richard Oastler (1946), John Saville's of Ernest Jones (1952), A. R. Schoyen's of Julian Harney (1958), Donald Read's and Eric Glasgow's of Feargus O'Connor (1961) and Alfred Plummer's of Bronterre O'Brien (1971).

A second modern branch of Chartist researches was immensely encouraged by the publication of Asa Briggs's *Chartist Studies* in 1959. More than anyone else, Professor Briggs and his colleagues taught us the vital importance of local investigations. Chartism was not the monolith of the elementary text; its contours were shaped by much more than the six radical 'points'. In recent years many further studies of the varieties of Chartism in the districts have filled in many gaps. Further local studies will greatly enhance our understanding of the movement.

Over the years many people have given me generous help—by advice, by loans of material, by conversation—in the work which led to this book. I cannot hope to thank them all. But my debt to that kindest of teachers, the late Mr F. R. Salter, OBE, of Magdalene College, Cambridge, is unforgettable. Dr G. Kitson Clark of Trinity College, Cambridge, and Professor Asa Briggs of Sussex University invaluably corrected some of my earlier notions. For advice and loans

of papers or transcripts, I am indebted to Mr J. M. Y. Andrew and
Mr Lionel Munby of Cambridge University; Dr W. H. Chaloner and
Dr Alex Wilson of Manchester University; the late Colonel G. W.
Ferrand, OBE, of Oving; Canon J. C. Gill of Worthing; Sir Fergus
Graham, Bt, KBE; Mr Frank Jacques of Cambridge; Dr Norman
McCord and Dr D. J. Rowe of Newcastle University; the late Pro-
fessor David Owen of Harvard University; Miss G. M. Phillips of
Mingle End; Mr A. G. Rose of Manchester; Dr J. D. Walsh of Jesus
College, Oxford, and Mrs C. M. Lyman of New Haven. I am also
grateful to many librarians and their staffs who have helped me at
various times—at Aberdeen, Ashton-under-Lyne, Ayr, Bingley,
Bolton, Bradford, the British Museum, Bury, Cambridge University,
Derby, Dewsbury, Dundee, Dundee University, Edinburgh,
Glasgow, Glasgow University, Halifax, Harrogate, Horsforth,
Huddersfield, Keighley, Kilmarnock, Knaresborough, Leeds, Leeds
City, London University, Manchester, the National Library of Scot-
land, Oldham, Paisley, Preston, Rochdale, Rotherham, Sheffield,
Stockport, Todmorden and Wakefield.

Those with whom I live or work have inevitably suffered most
from my growing obsession with Chartism. Some of my colleagues
in Strathclyde University—Professor S. G. E. Lythe, who kindly
commented on part of the text; Dr J. H. Treble, who generously
lent me much material; and Dr J. Butt and Dr W. H. Fraser, who
gave me advice—provided much encouragement. I am also grateful
to Miss Sandra Currie and Miss Maureen Jones who typed the book
and to Mr J. P. H. Connell, of B. T. Batsford, a most considerate and
patient publisher. But kind friends are no more to be blamed for any
deficiencies than are my wife and son, who tolerated a long period of
writing.

J. T. Ward

1 *The Antecedents*

Many strands went into the making of the first great working-class political movement in the history of the world. For a brief period in Britain during the fourth and fifth decades of the nineteenth century, Chartism held an umbrella over a host of causes. It appealed to a wide spectrum of protest, though it never contrived to produce a consensus among protesters. Its varied groups and assorted policies made heady appeals to many working people. It sought to correct ancient abuses and it dreamed of a fairer society. It had fire and excitement, along with sober temperance; it offered to contemporaries a variety of panaceas for a range of complaints. But Chartist policies were scarcely new; however novel convinced votaries consider successive schemes, in Britain 'radicalism' rarely achieves any unprecedented 'breakthrough'. Indeed, one of the endearing characteristics of British radicals (at least after their initial publicity) has been their tendency to search for historical justification of their actions. Radical history is strewn with appeals to the real or imagined past.

In a traditionalist country even the most 'advanced' radicalism develops its traditions. 'The time will come when Chartists will discover that in a country so aristocratic as England even treason, to be successful, must be patrician', declared Disraeli in a celebrated speech in 1840. His remark constituted more than merely a pre-'Young England' *bon mot* or Tory sneer against Lord John Russell. There was some point in the comment that[1]

> Where Wat Tyler failed, Henry Bolingbroke changed a dynasty, and although Jack Straw was hanged, a Lord John Straw may become a Secretary of State.

Chartism—despite the genealogical claims of some of its leaders—

was never patrician. But its message was often, inevitably, traditionalist. Its appeal was largely successful among those inclined to lament the passing of older forms. Its call for parliamentary reform had been heard in Elizabethan parliaments and, more dramatically, during the constitutional struggles of the mid-seventeenth century, as 'radical' and 'conservative' attitudes and philosophies were being formed. And demands for various versions of 'social justice' had an even larger ancestry. They had probably been made 'when Adam delved and Eve span' and certainly had provoked a lengthy discussion before Adam's mediaeval descendants mused over the problem of 'who was then the gentleman'.

The multi-coloured hues of Chartism were further tinted by multifarious local experiences. Local and regional variations in Chartist activity, organisation and philosophy were partially delineated by the varied experiences, recollections, traditions, customs, folklore and mythology of a people with intense regional loyalties and widely differing social relationships. Chartism was never the monolithic movement demanding up to half a dozen 'political' points, or the united phalanx of social revolutionaries reported by some contemporaries and transcribed into 'history' by some later writers. Current hopes and contemporary distress in an industrialising society inevitably affected some Chartists' immediate aims, policies and practices. But these factors intermingled with varying degrees of sometimes sentimental traditionalism. Chartism's boundaries were moulded by a real or alleged past as well as by a myriad of complaints about the present and a host of dreams for the future. As a result, the Chartist empire was vast. Its sun for a time flickered over millions of working people.

I

Notions of short parliaments, roughly equal constituencies and an extended suffrage may be traced to the Army debates on constitutional reform in 1647. Henry Ireton's *Heads of the Proposals* then envisaged biennial parliaments sitting between 120 and 140 days and representation 'according to some rule of equality or proportion'. Ireton further proposed

> to render the House of Commons (as near as may be) an equal representative of the whole, and in order thereunto, that a present consideration be had to take off the elections of burgesses for

poor, decayed, or inconsiderable towns, and to give some present addition to the number of Parliament members for great counties that have now less than their due proportion.

John Lilburnes' Levellers inevitably wanted more—a republic, a single chamber and manhood suffrage. Such democratisation was premature and stillborn: neither the Commonwealth nor the restored Monarchy cared to test Colonel Rich's warning that under the rule of 'those that have noe interest in the kingdome . . . there may bee a law enacted that there shall bee an equality of goods and estate'. In general, Ireton's belief that 'an absolute naturall right . . . is noe Right att all' was accepted, and practical men long continued to disregard the mumbo-jumbo of abstract theorists. Above all, Ireton's insistence that

> noe person hath a right to an interest or share in the disposing or determining of the affaires of the kingdome and in chusing those that shall determine what lawes wee shall bee ruled by heere . . . that hath not a permanent fixed interest in this kingdome

became part of accepted constitutional theory.[2]

The arrangements which appealed to the majority in the Council of the Army, including a redistribution of parliamentary seats, were briefly adopted under the Commonwealth. But republican rule involved the disappearance not only of Crown and Church but also of Parliament itself. What survived in politicians' minds was the connection between the ownership of property—that 'permanent fixed interest in this kingdome'—and political citizenship. And the 'Restoration Settlement' attempted to implement the philosophy of the Anglican divine Richard Hooker by limiting the exercise of full English political rights to men who were at least nominally practising members of the Church of England. The relationship between Church and State thus became increasingly an intrinsic part of any and every constitutional debate. From 1689 the 'Revolution Settlement' was more concerned to protect the rights of private property, for which the philosopher John Locke provided a vital, rational, Whiggish justification.

After the revolution of 1688 against King James II—arguably more aristocratic and 'oligarchic' than the bourgeois and squirearchic revolt of the 1640s against Charles I—the 'permanent fixed interest' became increasingly important. The Triennial Act of 1694 yielded to the Septennial Act in 1716. From 1710 MPs were subjected to a means test by property qualifications; landed property must produce £600 p.a. for knights of the shire and £300 for borough Members. Aristocratic 'patrons' exercised increasing control over many borough and some county seats, and many small constituencies became even more venal and corrupt as small self-perpetuating electorates sold their 'independent' votes to the more affluent candidates.[3] And affronted religious nonconformists, at least nominally excluded from public life and public service, could do little to improve their position; but their isolation from the mainstream of political life encouraged both an extensive involvement in eighteenth-century industrial entrepreneurship and a growing 'radicalism' hostile to the Church and State establishment. The ubiquitous, expanding quarrelsome dissenting sects were to provide bases for many different radical beliefs and traditions.

During the second half of the eighteenth century English radicalism developed in many fields. But radicalism properly so called was intermingled with many varieties of protest and many voices of reform. Meal mobs, machine-wrecking riots, anti-papist pogroms, Church and King loyalist demonstrations—spontaneous popular upsurges—competed for public support with varied movements favouring political and constitutional reform. And much of the demand for parliamentary reform came from men who saw themselves as conservatives of old arrangements and 'original' intentions rather than as radical pioneers of a new political order. The ideas and ideals of Whig activists directly descended from seventeenth-century notions of Liberty, particularly from tyrannical executives. Thus the rascally John Wilkes fought not only for the right to criticise King George III (as exercised in the celebrated 45th issue of the *North Briton*) but also against the government's power to issue general warrants and against the Commons' decision to expel him and to void his successive victories in the popular constituency of Middlesex. The cry of 'Wilkes and Liberty!' did more than arouse metropolitan mobs to violent demonstrations. Prosperous London merchants were roused to make their own protests; freeholders in many counties felt impelled to defend their ancient electoral rights; and from 1769 the Society of Supporters of the Bill of Rights demanded reform, annual parliaments and free elections.[4] By 1774 Wilkes was Lord Mayor of London and again MP for Middlesex. He excited wide support among London craftsmen and county voters alike. But his calls for shorter parliaments, more equal constituencies, redistribution of seats, the exclusion of placemen and greater control over

Members by electors were not new, but were part of a traditional reformism. And Wilkes ended his political life as a Pittite Tory.

Wilkes's achievement was to arouse public interest in the question of parliamentary reform. Among those prominent in his defence was the active, philandering Anglican priest John Horne (later known as Horne Tooke), a founder-member of the pioneer society of 1769, which was initially concerned to relieve Wilkes's debts. In 1771, after a public row with the arrogant and extravagant Wilkes, the equally arrogant and extravagant Horne led a secession to form the Constitutional Society. The remnants of the original body went on to draw up a declaration to be placed before parliamentary candidates binding them, if elected, to support eleven items of reform—a dangerous form of delegacy against which Edmund Burke delivered the classic condemnation. And in Parliament itself some brave spirits, like John Sawbridge, William Dowdeswell, Earl Stanhope and sections of the aristocratic Whig coteries, kept alive the reform proposals inaugurated by William Beckford.

These activities of the sixties and seventies were predominantly middle class in origin and attracted considerable aristocratic support both in the Lords and the counties. This tradition continued. In 1776 John Cartwright, a minor Nottinghamshire squire, published *Take Your Choice*. The earnest, eccentric and honest militia major had already shown his sincerity by losing his naval commission through supporting the American colonists against Lord North's administration. He now propounded a thorough-going radicalism, including such ingredients as annual parliaments, equal representation, manhood suffrage, the secret ballot and some payment of MPs. But any revolutionary intent was expressly denied. True to English radical form, Cartwright insisted that

> Making our Parliaments *annual* and our representation *equal* can neither of them in any sense, nor without a direct falsehood, be styled innovations. *Both of them were the antient practice of the constitution.*

This delusion was, indeed, maintained in the title of his proposed 'Grand National Association for Restoring the Constitution'.[5] Such an argument had at least some attraction for an honest Whig, appalled by allegations of mounting court influence since the days of Lord Bute and by the denial of free elections in uncorrupted Middlesex. That real radical change went too far for the closely connected conservative and dynastic network which made up the Whig alliance only gradually became apparent.

For a time, the Marquess of Rockingham's Whigs held the reform stage at Westminster, with their plans for 'economical reform' to restrict opportunities for electoral influence and corruption by the executive. Sir Philip Clerke proposed to exclude government contractors from the Commons; the Duke of Richmond suggested reductions in the King's civil list and all public emoluments, in the interest of 'true Oeconomy'; Burke demanded considerable savings in public expenditure and a concomitant reduction of the Crown's electoral influence.[6] But the Rockingham Whigs could scarcely hope to succeed without much external help. 'If the people are not true to themselves,' declared Burke in December 1779, 'I am sure it is not in us to save them'.

'The people'—that is, those county politicians who for long represented the bulk of the reform interest—acted quickly. Another absentee Anglican priest, squire and prolific pamphleter, Christopher Wyvill, started a major campaign for wide reform in Yorkshire. At a great county meeting in December 1779 eight peers, seventeen MPS and a host of gentlemen and freeholders petitioned for 'rigid frugality . . . in every department of the State' and for a reduction in the 'great and unconstitutional influence' of the Crown. From this gathering emerged the celebrated Yorkshire Association of 1780, demanding shorter parliaments and more equal representation. The Yorkshiremen were soon followed by other organisations in the shires. To the consternation of traditionalists, a network of associations 'unconstitutionally' demanded triennial elections, additional county representation and extensive 'economical' reform.[7] Parliamentary sympathisers generally concentrated on promoting the last theme, carrying John Dunning's famous resolution 'that the influence of the Crown has increased, is increasing and ought to be diminished'. Again Burke proposed wide retrenchment, while Richmond hopelessly urged the Lords to 'restore' universal suffrage and annual parliaments.

The alliance between economical and constitutional reformers was an uneasy one. Certainly Burke, the brilliant champion of economy and enemy of corruption, wanted no massive constitutional upheaval. Nor, for less philosophic and more personal reasons, did 'liberal' lords of broad acres seriously favour any major change. But the ever-active Cartwright attempted to draw the two reforming wings together in the Society for Promoting Constitutional Information, founded in April 1780. The Society's social gentility was guaranteed from the start: the president was the Pittite reforming squire Sir Cecil Wray and the minimum subscription was a guinea. Cartwright's recruiting activities were backed by Capel Lofft, a Suffolk lawyer-squire, and John Jebb, successively Anglican priest, Unitarian minister, medical practitioner and (in 1779) advocate of a national convention. Members included the Duke of Richmond, the future Dukes of Norfolk and Roxburgh, the Earls of Effingham, Derby and Selkirk, Lord Sempill, Sawbridge and fourteen other MPs, Stratford Canning, R. B. Sheridan, General Fitzpatrick, the Scottish agricultural improver John Sinclair and the radical Unitarian preacher Richard Price, along with several businessmen. This highly 'respectable' body attempted to enlighten public opinion by publishing papers favouring annual parliaments, universal suffrage and the ballot. 'It is remarkable', as that pioneer assessor of early reformers, G. S. Veitch, wrote, 'that the least circumspect among its members was the heir to a dukedom'—the gross sensualist and drunkard who moved from the ranks of the Whiggish Cumbrian gentry to become the 11th Duke of Norfolk.[8]

The Society's beliefs were anathema to most Rockingham Whigs, who bravely persisted with their 'economical' campaign. Defeat in America, the fall of Lord North and the formation of Rockingham's ministry in March 1782 at last led to some Rockinghamite success. Contractors were excluded from the Commons; revenue officers were disfranchised; several sinecures were abolished; pensions were somewhat reduced; and official influence was marginally curtailed. Such cautious measures, freeing the political system of a considerable amount of alleged corruption (though often by reducing electorates) but preserving the system itself, were the limit of the Rockingham men's involvement with reform.

'Economical' reforms inevitably did not satisfy the grave Society men—let alone the future Norfolk, who in 1798 was publicly to toast 'Our Sovereign's Health: the Majesty of the People'. But if the Rockinghamites were generally unsympathetic, some other parliamentarians were increasingly friendly to parliamentary reform. There was the honest Sir George Savile, Member for the great Yorkshire constituency. Lord Chatham himself had favoured triennial parliaments in 1771, and the Earl of Shelburne had followed him. And although Chatham's reformism was slow and hesitant—to him, 'Representation . . . was not of person but of property'—his followers included important allies of the reform campaigners. In particular, his second son, the brilliant young William Pitt, accepted the parliamentary leadership of the campaign in 1782.[9]

In May 1782 Pitt proposed an enquiry into 'the present State of the Representation' and was defeated by only 20 votes. The tide seemed to be flowing for the reformers. Thus encouraged, a few days later Richmond, Surrey (the future Norfolk), Lord Mahon (future Earl Stanhope), Wray, Pitt, Cartwright, Wilkes, Wyvill and other widely varied reformers assembled in the Thatched House Tavern, under the Lord Mayor. They resolved to organise nation-wide petitions for 'a substantial Reform of the Commons House of Parliament'—possibly the most specific demand to be expected from such an assembly. In July the Constitutional Society for the first time condescended to address its social inferiors—'particularly . . . those who subsisted by honest industry'—on their political rights and the need for unanimous support. The Yorkshire committee also canvassed opinions on a national scale. Parliament faced the results of these activities in 1783, when it was inundated with reform petitions. And Shelburne's accession to the premiership in July 1782 (with Pitt as his Chancellor of the Exchequer) augured well.

Reformers' hopes were dashed when the apostate reformer Charles James Fox allied with his old enemy North to defeat the ministry. A Fox–North coalition of old politicians, nominally led by the Duke of Portland, was established in April 1783. The apparently unprincipled alliance scandalised 'honest Englishmen' of many shades of opinion and enraged reformers. But Pitt's attempt to revive reform resolutions in May was easily defeated. However, in December the King dismissed his unpopular ministers. When Pitt bravely accepted the invitation to form a new ministry many reformers rejoiced at an impending victory.[10] Most of the noblemen, squires and professional men whose miscellany of imprimaturs had long guaranteed the reform campaign now looked to the old hero's son to provide success.

II

As a royal choice—and particularly as the choice of a monarch periodically described as a 'tyrant' in some radical circles—Pitt inevitably did not appeal to every reformer. On the other hand, Fox, however Whiggish his professions, was difficult to forgive both for his alliance with North and for his India Bill, which appeared to presage an extension of government influence. Parliamentary reformers in both Houses generally preferred Pitt. In March 1784 the Yorkshiremen by a majority followed the same course when they petitioned for a dissolution; and as the coalitionists resigned Wyvill's Association became a Pittite body. Following his electoral victory in March, Pitt promised Wyvill to stake everything on reform—and Wyvill indiscreetly made the pledge public. Backed by many petitions, in April 1785 Pitt sought to introduce what Wyvill described as 'a plan of reformation, the most extensive and effectual, and at the same time the most mild and practicable which had been devised'. County representation would be increased; small boroughs would be bought out through a sinking fund; London and the new large towns would gain seats. The premier's motion was defeated by 74 votes.[11] This reverse ended Pitt's career as a parliamentary reformer. His involvement had been brief, but the fact that Pitt henceforth accepted Parliament's decision scarcely justifies allegations of insincerity. To him and many of the 'new' politicians the consequences of making the issue a matter of 'confidence' were too serious to merit consideration.

After this major disappointment the reform campaign largely subsided. Pitt remained widely popular. The gentry were satisfied at cutting royal expense and influence; Parliament generally lost interest in reforming itself; and Yorkshire Association and Constitutional Society alike subsided. Only occasional activity demonstrated that 'reform' was not entirely forgotten: in 1786 some hitherto apathetic Scottish counties petitioned against the scandalous state of the representation of North Britain; inquiries were unsuccessfully proposed at Westminster in 1786 and 1787; and in 1788 Mahon gained a (quickly repealed) Act on county electoral registers. But a new lease of life for reform movements arrived with the centenary of the 'Glorious Revolution' of 1688–9. A crop of 'Revolution societies' rapidly blossomed in many towns. The purposes of such bodies varied considerably. Some were simply boozy convivial groups of celebrating diners; some existed to propagate assorted versions of King William III's achievements; some were frankly radical in their hopes for the future. In most societies a kedgeree of varied purposes was served. The most dangerous aspect of most of them was the potential implication of their title.[12] Most importantly, the London Revolution Society organised something more than an annual orgy of 'Whiggish' toasts. Under such men as Stanhope, Price, Lofft, Sawbridge, the wealthy Thomas Brand-Hollis and the Unitarian Dr Joseph Towers, the Society proclaimed the sovereignty of the people.

Abuse of authority justified resistance to authority; free elections, a free press, freedom of conscience and trial by jury were basic British rights. Such liberal postulations proved heady stuff to some provincial reformers. And as this new enthusiasm developed it was further excited by the news from France.

In the summer of 1789 events moved quickly in Britain's ancient and now near-bankrupt rival. The first States-General since 1614 met in May; the 'third estate', with some aristocratic and clerical support, declared itself a National Assembly in June; and in August the nobility yielded its feudal rights. The symbolic storming of the Bastille, the liberal declaration of the Rights of Man and the start of what sometimes appeared to be an effort to create a constitutional monarchy in France immensely cheered many English reformers. In November the London Revolution Society, under Stanhope, congratulated the National Assembly on its triumph. Price then delivered his famous sermon on 'the Love of our Country'—a discourse which provoked Burke's superb combination of retort, warning and philosophic assertion of conservatism, in 1790.[13] To some sympathetic Britons France was simply following a way traversed by Britain a century previously. To Protestant dissenters the French were providing splendid precedents for humiliating proud ecclesiastical establishments. For many young intellectuals the Revolution was excitingly moving, heralding a blissful dawn of a newer and freer society—the purposes of which were subjected to no detailed examination. The largest literate section of British people probably considered that the Bourbon kingdom deserved its new troubles; and a patriotic, francophobe mass appears to have agreed with this view. For the generality of ordinary folk, toiling in the fields, events in France—if they ever heard of them—were irrelevant tales from foreign parts. And on a slowly growing intellectual 'Right' Burke and his little band of devotees condemned the Revolution as a disaster which menaced European civilisation, contemporary standards of decency and the whole notion of tradition.

Burke's impassioned, prophetic, morose *Reflections* provoked a host of answers, ranging from Tom Paine's best-selling radical assertion of *The Rights of Man* (1791) to William Godwin's turgidly intellectual *Political Justice* (1793).[14] The general effect of French events was to provoke wide discussion of abstract 'rights' of natural justice, extending reform propaganda from diatribes on Crown corruption and rotten boroughs to at best philosophical discourses and at worst rubbishy theoretical tracts. Consequently interest in

THE ANTECEDENTS

France simultaneously strengthened and weakened English reformers. Henry Flood's suggested reform Bill was easily halted in
the Commons in March 1790. And despite considerable sympathy
with and satisfaction at French progress, the first signs were appearing that some politicians feared the contagion spreading from the
Continent. Certainly Pitt's government triumphed at the elections.
But the Revolution Society—whose title was to cause some confusion in both France and Britain—commenced a verbose correspondence with many French political societies (including the ever-
shifting Jacobins), expressing much mutual congratulation, pacific
sentiment and 'progressive' generality.[15]

Old Dr Price and his colleagues, bumbling through their enthusiastic panegyrics, understood the public mood of neither France
nor Britain. French developments, together with the literary argument between Burke and his critics, increasingly polarised British
opinions. The subtle but speedily gathering change in French attitudes after King Louis XVI's unsuccessful flight in June 1791 was
an important factor. Dissenting bigots might welcome the secularisa-
tion of the French Church; increasing insults to the trapped French
Royal Family might please republicans; the growing power of the
Parisian mob might encourage some violent spirits. But such factions
represented a declining proportion of British public opinion. It was
not only 'reactionary' Whigs who followed Burke when he publicly
broke an old friendship with Fox in May 1791. It was not only in
ancient universities and public schools that young radicals were
reprimanded. The English mob, whose improvement had so often
been planned at expensive 'public' dinners and in select clubs by its
social and intellectual superiors, was not particularly grateful.
Indeed, in common with most 'orders' of society, it distrusted an
academic liberalism which it never understood. Instinctively, it
preferred a Burke to a Mary Wollstonecraft, with her *Vindication of
the Rights of Man* (1790) and *Rights of Women* (1792), a James Mackintosh with his *Vindiciae Gallicae* (1791) or even a Paine; it read none of
them. Its basic, elemental patriotism led it to an intuitive defence of
'Church and King' against the dissenting intellectuals following
Price. Consequently, a section of the 'lower orders' assailed
Dr Samuel Parr at Norwich, Dr Joseph Priestley at Birmingham
and other Unitarians at Manchester; and in many other towns it
exercised a noisy power in defence of 'good old' English
institutions.

The pious platitudes, semantic casuistries and intellectual snobbery of unitarian and other middle-class reformers provided little defence against growing public hostility. The reformers put their case in a plethora of forgotten pamphlets, but they represented a narrowing bridgehead among the 'political classes'. When Tooke (who had bravely contested Westminster against Fox in 1790) revived the Constitutional Society as a Crown and Anchor dining club in March 1792, his supporters included the radical Lord Daer and the clever young Mackintosh. But the Society's strength lay with men from very different backgrounds—the republican staymaker Paine, the playwright Thomas Holcroft, the shady lawyer Joseph Gerrald, the bookseller Clio Rickman, the engraver William Sharp and the eloquent and mysterious Maurice Margarot. Almost simultaneously a grander, Whiggish 'Society of the Friends of the People' was founded by the Earl of Lauderdale and Charles Grey. Fox cautiously refused his support but did not restrain such men as Lords Buchan and Kinnaird, Sheridan, W. H. Lambton, Samuel Whitbread, Philip Francis and Henry Erskine from joining, along with Cartwright and Daer. The Society proposed 'to restore the freedom of election and a more equal representation', together with more frequent elections. But times were difficult for high society dabblers with reform. When Cartwright urged an alliance with 'the people' (a race scarcely known by his colleagues) the Society refused to talk with Paineites. And when a move to expel Cartwright failed, such respectable men as Lord John Russell resigned.

The astute Tooke had long shed any vestigial regard for Foxites. He broadened the Constitutionalists' membership and further approached 'the people' by helping the most novel and celebrated reform group, the London Corresponding Society of January 1792. The LCS represented a major breakthrough in 'reform' history. Hitherto, the cause had been propounded by country squires and professional men, 'advanced' aristocrats and remote divines. Working people had occasionally been involved on the periphery, but their reactions had been fickle and unpredictable. Now Thomas Hardy, a Stirlingshire shoemaker working in Piccadilly, persuaded seven companions in the Bell Tavern to establish an entirely new body. The LCS favoured universal suffrage, annual elections and equal constituencies. It collected weekly pence rather than annual guineas. It met weekly for sober discussion in divisions of thirty members rather than occasionally for tipsy orgies. It proposed to correspond with other groups, maintained a reasonable and moderate policy and largely followed the proposals enunciated by the Duke of

Richmond; but its recruitment of self-educated artisans and small tradesmen made it unique.[16]

The fortunes of the assorted reform societies, genteel and plebeian, revolutionary and conservative, ranging from the slopseller Favell's Southwark Friends of the People to aristocratic cliques, increasingly depended on events in France. Pitt coolly watched developments while ensuring that detailed reports reached him from his ambassador, special agents and spies in France. He was equally well informed, no doubt, on the activities of the Southwark, Aldgate, Manchester, Birmingham, Sheffield, Norwich, Derby, Leicester, Stockport, Warwick, Edinburgh and other 'Friends of the People', 'Friends of Universal Peace' and 'Constitutional', 'Patriotic', 'Reform', 'Revolution' and 'Political Information' societies. Certainly Henry Dundas, the Scottish political manager, closely watched the newly awakened Scottish reformers. The pioneering Friends of the People was headed by men who was respectable enough— Major Maitland, Captain Johnston, Colonel Dalrymple and Colonel Macleod—but also included the brash young self-made lawyer Thomas Muir of Huntershill. It had London links through Daer and Tooke; it organised a Scottish 'convention' of 140 delegates in December 1792, adopting a title used by burgh reformers in 1784; and it appeared a frightening innovation in hitherto easily controlled Scotland.[17]

As official and public attitudes hardened, many reformers weakened or deserted. But the Constitutional Society continued to support Paine and, despite the peaceful nature of its naïve propaganda, supported Jacobin calls for a wider revolution. With the LCS, it ignored the alarm signals. In February 1792 the Holy Roman Empire and the King of Prussia allied to maintain order and contain the revolution, and in April France declared war on the Hapsburgs seeking to protect her Hapsburg Queen. British authorities then started to take action against suspect groups. Bow Street runners and magisterial agents were infiltrated into the radical societies; taverns refused accustomed accommodation for meetings; and in May the government issued a proclamation against seditious gatherings. In November the Canadian lawyer John Reeves founded his Crown and Anchor Association to 'protect Liberty and Property against republicans and levellers'. It was in vain that the societies professed moderation.

British opinion was saddened by the French King's suspension in August and the declaration of the Republic in September and outraged by the October pledge of aid to other revolutionaries, the autumn massacres and the killing of Louis XVI in January 1793. Politically silly men like Priestley might accept honorary French citizenship, bitter men like Paine might slander 'loyalists' from a safe distance and crazy men in obscure clubs might mislead French politicians over English enthusiasm for their activities. But British feelings hardened against revolution and organic change at home or abroad. And slowly a government which desired neither war nor civil disturbance started to move. Paine was prosecuted for seditious libel; the intelligence department was augmented; loyalist journals were subsidised; charges were preferred against various minor radicals. William Cowper summarised moderate opinion in January 1793, when he told William Hayley

> I will tell you what the French have done. They have made me weep for a King of France, which I never thought to do, and they have made me sick of the very name of liberty, which I never thought to be.

III

What radicals came to regard as their persecution began before the start of war with France in February 1793. Apart from the inevitable prosecution of Paine, whose behaviour and writings made his defence by Thomas Erskine virtually impossible, most English cases in 1792 were small. Prosecutions grew in 1793. William Frend was expelled from Cambridge for welcoming early French reforms. Tooke's friend, the francophile attorney John Frost, was imprisoned for some drunken republican remarks. And a certain arbitrary laxity appeared in the selection of subjects for prosecution and in jury decisions. At Exeter an unpopular dissenting minister, William Winterbotham, whose offence apparently amounted to sermonising in the 'high-brow', 'liberal' manner of his kind, was fined £200 and imprisoned for four years. But in London Daniel Eaton, a notorious publisher of such 'seditious' works as Hog's Wash (1793–4) regularly defeated prosecutors. While the London Morning Chronicle printers escaped, Daniel Holt—a Newark printer—was fined £100 and imprisoned for four years. And Godwin's 'treasonable', seditious, republican, socialistic, almost anarchist—but expensive and very dreary—work did not attract prosecution.[18]

Such events scarcely justified later accusations of a concerted, planned, vindictive ministerial tyranny backed by the courts. Indeed, the freedom allowed in a nation at war is surprising to a modern observer. Historians reared in the security of Victorian liberalism were scandalised by the bumbling attempts of the government to silence its enemies in the courts; few of them lived to witness the illiberal efficiency of modern governments in similar situations. But in one area later liberal accusations were correct. Following the defeat of the Jacobites and the persecution of Episcopalians, eighteenth-century Scotland was a poor, dour Calvinist land, with a largely absentee upper nobility, a backward agriculture, a corrupt political system, four moribund universities, a range of petty burghs and a system of serfdom in its collieries. Later in the century Scotland was changing. Mercantile dynasties were creating a new Glasgow, aided by the scientific interests of its university; Edinburgh, backed by its university philosophers, was becoming a northern Athens; innovating lairds were developing a new agriculture. And there was growing resentment among men reared in presbyterian theology at the scandalous condition of Scottish politics, whether in the close, self-perpetuating burgh corporations or in the nonsensically determined parliamentary electorates. The Scots intelligentsia—from Professor Dougald Stewart of Edinburgh to Lords Kinnaird, Lauderdale and Sempill, from exciseman Rabbie Burns to puritanical Glasgow and Dundee merchants—wanted change. Henry Dundas, the great Scottish minister and manipulator, and the Scottish judges —especially that latter-day Jefferies, Lord Braxfield—did not agree. Their alarm developed as seemingly militant societies of tradesmen and artisans blossomed. Various little men—publishers, printers and pamphleteers, some of whom fled abroad—were prosecuted before bigger game was hunted down. In May 1793 another more militant convention led to further action.

Sleepy Scotland had awakened quickly, and its 'democrats' were a thorough-going group. At their head was Muir, an astute orator whose extreme radicalism was cloaked by admonitions about moderation. On returning from France and Ireland, Muir was arrested on a charge of sedition in August 1793. He foolishly defended himself before Braxfield, was sentenced to fourteen years' transportation and thus entered the mythology and martyrology of Scottish radicalism.[19] A month later Thomas Fyshe Palmer, an Old Etonian and former Cambridge fellow who was oddly placed as Unitarian minister at Dundee, was tried at Perth for issuing a seditious address on behalf of local Friends of the People; he was transported for seven years. His real offence was Robert Dundas's conviction that he was 'the most determined Rebel in Scotland'.[20] Ignoring the trials and the Commons' rejection of Grey's reform motion by 282 votes to 41 in May, Scottish radicals went ahead with plans for a third 'Convention of the Delegates of the Friends of the People associated to obtain Universal Suffrage and Annual Parliaments' in Edinburgh. London radicals elected Gerrald and Margarot as delegates; the Constitutional Society sent Charles Sinclair; and the player Matthew Brown represented Sheffield and Leeds reformers. The Convention met in October and November, unwisely debated reform and was closed by the authorities. Further Scottish trials followed. The Convention's secretary, the farmer William Skirving, was transported for fourteen years, as were Margarot and Gerrald. And a former government spy, Robert Watt, was hanged for treason. Henry Erskine managed to save Sinclair.[21]

London radicals protested at the Scottish sentences and planned further conventions. In May 1794 the cabinet decided to act against such English reformers. Hardy of the Corresponding Society and Daniel Adams of the 'Constitutionalists' were arrested, followed by eleven others including Tooke, Holcroft and the poet John Thelwall; and the Commons set up a committee of secrecy to investigate allegedly subversive plots. After hectoring examinations by the Privy Council, the prisoners were tried in the autumn. They denied any treason and were brilliantly defended by Thomas Erskine. Above all, they faced more sympathetic and less sycophantic English juries. When Hardy, Tooke and Thelwall were found not guilty, the Government gave up the other prosecutions. Provincial cases also started to turn sour, although the reckless young Henry Redhead Yorke was fined £200 and gaoled for two years: he married his gaoler's daughter, turned against reform and became a barrister.[22]

After their triumph in the courts, the English reformers were further divided. The Corresponding Society bravely continued its work; the 'Friends' and 'Constitutionalists' less courageously disintegrated. And the government strengthened its hands with legislation restricting the freedoms of speech, publication and assembly. In March, 1796 two 'Corresponding' missionaries, John Gale Jones and John Binns, were arrested but escaped conviction. The naval mutinies of 1797 were more serious. No real connection between mutineers and reformers was satisfactorily proved, but a Commons which rejected Grey's latest Reform Bill by 256 votes to 91 was deeply concerned. As the war situation worsened and the government became increasingly worried, anti-reform measures were tightened by virtual censorship and the suspension of *habeas corpus*. In 1798 George Mealmaker, a militant Dundee weaver and leader of the radical 'United Scotsmen', was transported for fourteen years. 'Corresponding' and 'United English' leaders were also arrested, and Fr. O'Coigley, leader of a faction of revolutionary 'United Irishmen' (who organised an armed rebellion in 1798), was hanged for treason. In 1799 further legislation suppressed the last, lingering remnants of the reform societies. By this time the government had ridden out the peace demands of reformers and others, serious riots against recruiting methods and food prices, dangerous mutinies and a full-scale rebellion in Ireland under Wolfe Tone.[23] And despite many reverses and the loss of many allies, it was determined to maintain the war against the regicides-turned-imperialists—against what Burke appropriately called in 1796 'an armed doctrine'. Particularly after Pitt's peace manoeuvres failed and Buonaparte's aggressions grew, most remaining British liberals became patriots, taking their politics from the witty pages of George Canning's *Anti-Jacobin*.

IV

In the gloomiest of days for reformers, when reform was widely equated with treason, some brave spirits kept alive a cause which now had its myths and its martyrs. Old Cartwright never gave up hope. The eccentric Thomas Spence hawked his cheap tracts on egalitarian republicanism in Tottenham Court Road. And Pitt's resignation of 1801 and Henry Addington's subsequent peace with Buonaparte inevitably pleased liberals. But the reformers' image was further tarnished in November 1802 by the sensational arrest of Colonel E. M. Despard for planning to kill the King and lead a London proletarian revolution; Despard and six others were executed in 1803. And reformers remained largely out of touch with a public opinion hostile to French aggrandisement and to Napoleon's assumption of the French Imperial title in 1804.[24]

Pitt returned to the premiership in April 1804, to lead a willing nation in an already resumed war. But the prematurely exhausted minister died in January 1806. William Grenville's coalition which succeeded was largely Whiggish and gave office to several sympathisers with reform. But even the francophile Fox, as Foreign

Secretary, lost his hopes of peace before his death in September; and Grenville failed to persuade the King to accept a lightening of Roman Catholic disabilities. The Grenvillite collapse in March 1807 and its replacement by the Duke of Portland's second ministry made little difference to reformers, except to those who hoped for liberalism in Ireland or resented court power. The government's one triumph had been the carrying of the Pittite William Wilberforce's motion to abolish the slave trade.

Portland's unimpressive government received overwhelming support at the election of June 1807. But a new radicalism was now starting to make its voice heard. Francis Place, a London tailor who had learned his reformist principles from the Corresponding Society between 1794 and 1797, put them to use at the Westminster election in behalf of Sir Francis Burdett, apparently a new Wilkes. And William Cobbett, the former sergeant-major who had returned to England from America in 1800 determined to disseminate patriotic propaganda against republican 'fanaticism and infidelity', was gradually drawn into a highly personal espousal of the reform cause.[25] The flamboyant combination of tradition and reform revived the hopes of the veteran Cartwright and Tooke but had little immediate effect, beyond the election of Burdett. Indeed, the government briefly gained popularity in 1808 during rejoicing over the risings of the Spanish patriots against French imperialism. But this gain was dissipated by the rows over the commission-selling activities of Mrs Clarke, the current mistress of the commander-in-chief, the Duke of York—against whom a sustained campaign had long been mounted. The parliamentary Opposition and metropolitan 'radical reformers' again concentrated on rooting out examples of nepotism, corruption and excessive public expenditure. However, it was military failures—in Spain, Italy and Walcheren—that brought down Portland's government in September 1809. Ministerial divisions were openly displayed when Canning, the Foreign Secretary, fought a famous duel with the War Secretary, Lord Castlereagh. The Whigs being divided, as usual, the earnest, underestimated but resourceful Spencer Perceval formed a seemingly weak cabinet which survived until his murder in May 1812.[26]

Meanwhile, some of the old-style extra-parliamentary reformers had resurrected the London debating and dining clubs. The Whigs, under Grey or Grenville, had largely lost interest in either parliamentary or 'economical' reform, though Samuel Whitbread bravely maintained his support. Some Whigs, no doubt, relied on the King's recurring illnesses to lead to a regency under the Prince of Wales with his Whiggish sympathies and contacts. More radical reformers indulged in various forms of sedition and libel. In 1810 Gale Jones was imprisoned for libelling MPs; Cobbett was sentenced to two years' imprisonment for protesting at monstrous floggings of mutineers among Cambridgeshire militiamen in his *Political Register*; and Burdett was sent to the Tower for doubting Parliament's right to imprison Jones. Sir Francis instantly became a popular hero to the London mob, which demonstrated for him in unprecedented numbers, hindered his arrest and accompanied him to the Tower; and he subsequently brought an unsuccessful action against the Speaker. Again the demand for parliamentary reform was vocal, among City businessmen, county leaders, some Whig MPs and the old radicals.[27]

Reforming hopes rose when a renewal of the King's malady forced ministers to turn again to the 'Foxite' Prince Regent. But 'Prinny' without Fox gave little joy; he liked neither Grey nor Roman Catholic emancipation. And in general reform remained a gentlemanly affair, periodically supported and as often deserted by liberal Whigs. In 1811 Cartwright and Place were among the founders of a new group of 'friends to parliamentary reform' (which became the Union for Parliamentary Reform according to the Constitution in 1812) under Sir John Throckmorton. This 'Union Club', demanding 'representation co-extensive with direct taxation' and annual parliaments, recruited such members as Lofft, Wyvill, Cobbett, the popular liberal naval commander Lord Cochrane, Burdett, the farmer-Whig T. W. Coke and 'Orator' Henry Hunt (who had already commenced a career of provincial demagogy). Its 'radical' platitudes soon drove out Whiggish supporters, despite its 'moderate' methods. In 1812 the Hampden Club was still more 'respectable', insisting that members should own or be heirs to land worth £300 p.a. in order to qualify for attendance at its two expensive dinners: Norfolk, Cochrane, Lord Byron and the Earl of Oxford were among its members. But however socially exclusive such societies were, they favoured wide enfranchisement and annual elections, and Cartwright subsequently aided the foundation of much less aristocratic Hampden societies in the provinces.[28]

An entirely different tradition from that of the wealthy liberals was created by Cobbett's *Political Register*. Cobbett's was a popular radicalism, Tory, traditionalist and sentimental in its biting attacks on placemen, economic theorists, the National Debt, paper money, Jewish financiers and the 'great wen' of a sprawling metropolis. Its appeal was to an idealised 'olde England' of rural communities, sturdy yeomen and honest paternal squires. Cobbett, indeed, was a species of 'radical' Burke, expressing a peasant reaction against social, economic and industrial change; the political reform which he advocated was designed to protect an already undermined old order. Vastly different again was the radical utilitarianism slowly developed by Jeremy Bentham and his intellectual and highly articulate coterie. Bentham provided for generations of influential radicals a philosophy and psychology of change, resting upon the aim of 'the greatest happiness of the greatest number'. The test of utility was seminal in any examination of laws, institutions or morals, and Bentham became (in the words of his friend James Mill's son, John Stuart Mill) 'the great questioner of things established'. One section of (generally educated and bourgeois) radicals was thus taught to justify wide reform by appeal to alleged science rather than to imagined tradition or theoretical 'natural rights'. The hedonistic calculus provided a 'scientific' basis for legislation, and Bentham's version of 'common-sense' would organise new mechanisms for change, ignoring appeals to tradition, religion and sentiment.

Lord Liverpool eventually succeeded Perceval and began his fifteen-year Tory rule amidst a panicky situation. The Regent at least attempted to aid his old Whiggish friends. The late premier had been murdered by a dementedly brooding failed merchant. But against a background of militant oratory in London and Ireland and of very real violence among Yorkshire woollen croppers, East Midlands stockingers and Lancashire cotton workers, whose machine-wrecking campaigns had mounted since 1811, it was easy to imagine the existence of a nationwide revolutionary plot. Certainly worried magistrates in the disturbed industrial districts were inclined to see recurring signs of such a conspiracy. Partly an organised movement to protect ancient handcrafts from the introduction of labour-displacing machinery, partly a spontaneous and traditional reaction to a variety of complaints and partly composed of apolitical criminal elements, the Luddite wreckers in fact demonstrated few signs of any widespread plot master-minded by a central body. But when machine-smashing and arson yielded to occasional murder, and as battalions urgently needed by the Army in Spain were required for policing action, Luddism took on a grave and menacing aspect.[29] Only the widespread use of spies (whose piecework rates and productivity bonuses sometimes encouraged the emergence of *agents provocateurs*) and a number of hangings dampened enthusiasm for this form of 'radical' activity. And only many years after the events did historians revive the suspicions of contemporary authorities and discover oral traditions justifying violence as an alternative form of negotiation.

Parliamentary reformers continued to support anti-'Establishment' causes. Inevitably, they made the most of the Regent's marital scandals. The immoral Prince's treatment of his immoral wife made the gross Princess the recipient of popular addresses. And hopes of Roman Catholic emancipation still stirred liberal Members into periodic activity through the post-war decade. Meanwhile, petitions poured into Parliament against any action on the 1813 Select Committee's recommendations in favour of a protective Corn Law. There were doubts over the renewed war of 1815, after Napoleon's return to France, and over the principles of the monarchically-dominated peace settlement. And after all the fireworks and loyal addresses, the long dreamed-of peace brought further problems. Military demobilisation after the long war deepened the pool of unemployment. Traditional-style meal rioters were now inclined to blame the new Corn Laws for high food prices. Working people in many areas made varied protests, sometimes barely coherent but sometimes backed by long literary and folklore traditions. 'Whilst the laurels were yet cool on the brows of our victorious soldiers,' recalled the Lancashire radical Samuel Bamford,[30]

> ... the elements of convulsion were at work amongst the masses of our labouring population; and ... a series of disturbances commenced with the introduction of the Corn Bill in 1815, and continued, with short intervals, until the close of year 1816.

Over this fermenting situation presided a much-reviled government, an amalgam of Pittites and 'new' men which initially appeared to be a temporary compromise arrangement but which gradually attracted to its underestimated standard a formidable host of defenders of 'law and order'. Much of the credit for this achievement belongs to Liverpool himself; but he was backed by such able men as Castlereagh, Canning, Eldon, Sidmouth, Wellington, Robert Peel and William Huskisson during his long premiership.[31]

V

A new patchwork of agitations developed in reaction to post-war problems in the provinces. In the cotton districts of Lancashire groups of Anglican priests, humanitarian merchants and doctors and operatives supported Sir Robert Peel's campaign for a restriction of factory children's working hours. From New Lanark another great cotton entrepreneur, the ever-active, eccentric and anti-radical 'socialist' Robert Owen, supported this and assorted other 'improving' causes. Radicals continued to complain of Home Office spies, the military establishment and bleak industrial conditions, while foreign visitors marvelled at British freedom, moderation and industrial progress. And sentimentalists on the Left and the Right of the political spectrum continued to romanticise a golden age of a rural Britain with a socially cohesive hierarchy of ranks and interests.[32] 'Gentlemen then lived as they ought to live,' wrote Bamford. '... The gentleman transacted his own business, he met his farmer or labourer face to face.' The resulting message was an old one. 'We want *great alteration*,' declared Cobbett, 'but we want *nothing new*.' It was on similar grounds that S. T. Coleridge supported Peel's Bill: 'the labourer's health, life and well-being ... belonged not to himself alone, but to his friends, to his parents, to his King, to his Country, and to God.' And Robert Southey taught Tories the same message:

> How large a part of your population are like the dogs at Lisbon and Constantinople, unowned, unbroken to any useful purpose, subsisting by chance or by prey, living in filth, mischief and wretchedness; a nuisance to the community while they live, and dying miserably at last!

Tories and radicals of this type were linked by much more than equally roseate views of a largely mythical past and aesthetic or purely emotional dislike of the industrialising present. They shared also an organic view of society and a hostility to the new economic and political doctrines of individualism. Many of them still preferred those social classifications to which they were accustomed, basically resting upon a vertical division of 'interests'—landed, mercantile, colonial and so on—rather than the stark horizontal division between 'classes'.[33]

Certainly, there was a political 'Left' which went much further in its hostility to existing society. Two broad streams may be distinguished. Firstly, there were various forms of socialism. Thomas Spence propagated a municipal and parochial ownership of land and a government based on communes, whose sole income would arise from rents, from 1775 until his death in 1814, making a handful of eccentric converts. In a way, Spence merely developed the notions of Robert Wallace and William Ogilvie; his socialism was irrelevant to a developing industrial society. Dr Charles Hall, a bankrupt medical practitioner, led some socialists to oppose industrial capitalism with his study of the *Effects of Civilisation* (1805). Yet, despite all the bitter condemnation of the rich, with their luxuries arising from unearned incomes, Hall also was deeply rooted in the eighteenth century; he was opposed to capitalism and to industry itself and was basically concerned to nationalise the land. Robert Owen, as a great industrialist, inevitably led socialists into rather different paths—mainly into a haze of utopian, millennial nonsense in a search for a new moral world of paternalism cum co-operation. Socialism's 'realism' developed from more surprising beginnings. Patrick Colquhoun's *Treatise of the Wealth, Power and Resources of the British Empire* (1814), intended as a statistical panegyric, was capable also of a socialistic interpretation. 'It is by the labour of the people,' wrote Colquhoun, '. . . that all ranks of the community in every condition of life annually subsist, and it is by the produce of this labour alone that nations become powerful in proportion to the extent of the surplus which can be spared for the exigencies of the State.' His statistics on the distribution of incomes underlined this view.

Colquhoun saw nothing 'wrong' in his conclusion. 'Every state', he had asserted in his *Treatise on Indigence* (1806),

> is supported by the poverty of the community composing the body politic. Without a large proportion of poverty, there could be no riches, since riches are the offspring of labour, while labour can result only from a state of poverty.

The 'classical economist' David Ricardo's *Principles of Political Economy* (1817) also treated labour as the measure of value and capital as a form of accumulated labour. But Ricardian dislike of the landed interest led this form of pessimistic *laisser-faire* economics into attitudes which provided ammunition for its opponents.[34] It was easy for socialists to use Ricardo to justify their belief that labour alone created value, and that therefore the worker had the right to the full product of his labour. Ricardo, the mouthpiece and economic philosopher of industrial capitalism, thus became an unintentional justifier of socialist theories. Thomas Hodgskin, a fomer naval officer, developed the labour theory of value in his *Labour Defended against the Claims of Capital* (1825) and lectured on it to the London Mechanic's Institute—though he eventually joined James Wilson's liberal journal *The Economist* of 1843. William Thompson condemned capitalist 'theft' in his *Inquiry into the Principles of the Distribution of Wealth most Conducive to Human Happiness* (1824), postulating a utilitarian theory of social policy. In his *Labour Rewarded* (1827) Thompson answered Hodgskin, by advocating co-operation as the means of abolishing capitalism; by this means 'Labour [as] the sole parent of wealth' would receive its due reward. And John Gray's *Lecture on Human Happiness* (1825) condemned private ownership and competition, also following an Owenite line on co-operation though later concentrating on currency reform. But socialist theory—except, briefly, the version advocated by Owen—made little impression on the generality of working people.

Apart from Cobbett's literary effusions, the principal means of propagating popular radicalism was the speeches of that quarrelsome extrovert Henry Hunt. 'Orator' Hunt, after an adventurous youth, had been converted to radicalism by Horne Tooke and developed an immense popularity, though always highly independent in his approach. Together, Cobbett and Hunt taught masses of people to support parliamentary reform as a means of securing an improvement of their present lot. And behind them was ranged a host of lesser propagandists, bravely or recklessly evading those 'taxes on knowledge' the newspaper duties or the prohibitions of 'seditious' meetings. Thomas Jonathan Wooler produced the *Black Dwarf*—which largely filled the gap left by Cobbett when he fled to America in 1817. The London bookseller William Hone issued his *Reformist's Register*, and on the far Left, where radicalism merged with militant anarchism, Thomas Davison published *Medusa, or Penny Politician*. Richard Carlile fought on a variety of fronts, reprinting Paine's works, propagating republicanism, regularly entering prison, condemning religion and propounding through bleak years a self-defeating radical individualism. 'Let each do his duty,' proclaimed this brave, muddled ex-tinworker, 'and that openly, without reference to what his neighbour does.' All in all, the plethora of radical publications provided a confusing range of 'reformists' choices. But their combined impact was not very substantial in an innately conservative Britain. Cobbett's *Political Register*, surviving under various titles from 1802 to 1835, was the most influential; and the old soldier always retained an element of Tory traditionalism.

From 1811 Major Cartwright had toured the provinces, determined to link the wealthy London reformers with the people of provincial England, of whom they often spoke but whom they rarely chose to meet. In his paternalistic, avuncular way the major was shocked by 'the actual conditions of a starving people,' though he also noted that 'they preferred confiding their interests to persons of more consideration than themselves, and that they generally evinced a jealous dislike to raise those of their own standing to stations of importance'. The London Hampden Club had rapidly declined; indeed in March 1815 Cartwright dined alone. But Hampden principles were disseminated among working people by the major's tours and a network of little Hampden clubs developed. Thus the heady doctrine of universal suffrage reached such Lancashire weaving folk as young Samuel Bamford. The Hampdenites— 'meeting and *talking* about what they are to *talk* about next time'— seemed useless to Cobbett. They were also too moderate for the hectoring, vainglorious Hunt. But to the government they seemed part of a dangerous conspiracy.

It has often been asserted that real revolutionaries were simply figments of governmental imagination. But there were some fanatical psychopaths with crazy plans for a bloody uprising. They had read Spence's journal *Pig's Meat, or Lessons for the Swinish Multitude*, they knew something of his plans for agricultural communism and from 1814 they had joined East End tavern sections of Thomas Evans's generally innocuous Society of Spencean Philanthropists. Foremost in this back-alley gang were the eccentric Dr John Watson, his mad son and the rash, rakish Arthur Thistlewood, an illegitimate Lincolnshire man whose grievance against society probably began with the rapid disappearance of his several inheritances. The Parisian Terror exercised enormous fascination for such men.

VI

1816 was a bad year. Bread riots in East Anglia ended only with the execution of five men. The decline in military orders and a poor harvest caused widespread troubles. Anxious magistrates and squires reported bitter strikes among cotton workers in Bolton, Stockport,

Manchester, Preston and Ashton, iron and coal workers in South Wales, the Midlands and West Cumberland and sailors in Workington and North Shields. From Sheffield and Nottingham came reports of new Luddism; from Birmingham of serious riots; from Joseph Nadin, the active deputy constable of Manchester, of a menacing 'general union of the lower orders throughout the kingdom'. Sidmouth and many local authorities increased their networks of secret agents and informers. There were dangers in such measures. Subsequently, agents often paid by 'results' were accused of being *provocateurs* of the more violent radical enterprises. John Castle was blamed for the Spa Fields riot, Oliver (W. J. Richards) for the Pentrich rising, George Edwards for the Cato Street conspiracy and A. B. Richmond for the Scottish 'insurrection'. Yet in the absence of a police force and faced by a potentially menacing situation, it is difficult to see what else the Home Office could do.

In August a mixed bag of London reformers, including Lord Cochrane and Burdett, the radical Member for Westminster, and such Benthamites as James Mill and Place, urged provincial radicals to organise massive petitions for parliamentary reform. Through the autumn the Hanpden clubs energetically whipped up enthusiasm and selected their delegates for a mammoth assembly in the Crown and Anchor in January 1817. And on 15 November Hunt addressed an excited London rally in the Spa Fields, demanding universal suffrage, annual parliaments and the ballot and soliciting support for himself and Burdett as London's delegates. But aristocratic, fundamentally Tory Sir Francis preferred the moderate demands of the philosophic radicals to the 'democratic' passions of Hunt: he declined the honour as he would 'not insult the Prince Regent'. Hunt bitterly condemned a 'fickle and faithless leader' and himself twice unsuccessfully tried to present the London petition to the Prince. His own resolve was soon to be tested. On 2 December London radicals again rallied in Spa Fields, to protest against the rejection of their demands. Hunt arrived late, but in time to find the crazed Watsons busily organising a metropolitan uprising. The murderous venture was suppressed within hours and five leaders were charged with high treason but freed because of the ambiguous evidence of Castle.

The revolutionaries not only increased Sidmouth's vigilance. 'I am led to believe that there has been some endeavour to excite a general rising on that day [2 December], which from some cause has failed,' General Sir John Byng reported from Pontefract two days later. Local justices were increasingly perturbed by the Hampdenite delegates soon tramping to London. And London radicals were bitterly divided over universal or household suffrage, the leaders generally regretting Hunt's (albeit accidental) association with men of violence. The respectable provincial delegates, earnestly convinced of the need for universal manhood suffrage, knew little of the London in-fighting. They did not know that the Hampden Club virtually existed only in name. They were dismayed when its chairman, Burdett, was absent. And then Cartwright spoke for household suffrage, supported by Cobbett, who now declared universal suffrage 'impractical'. The bewildered delegates found more convincing spokesmen in Hunt and young Bamford of Middleton. They carried their resolutions and cheerfully, hopefully, escorted Cochrane and their petition, with 500,000 signatures for universal suffrage, to Parliament.

That morning someone shot a missile at the Prince Regent as he drove to open Parliament. To an already anxious cabinet it was the last straw. Committees of both Houses were convinced that parliamentary reformers were dangerous to the maintenance of law and order. The Government quickly passed four Acts suspending *habeas corpus* and prohibiting seditious meetings and attempts to radicalise troops. Behind this policy still lay ministerial recollections of French excesses, recently reinforced by the Watsons' call for the seizure of the Bank and the Tower and their banner announcing that 'The Brave Soldiers Are Our Friends'. But legislative speed did not prevent further protests. In March the 'blanketeers'—principally cotton weavers—started a 'hunger-march' to London to petition the Prince Regent for some alleviation of their conditions. This pathetic venture started badly, when the Manchester magistrates arrested the leaders. Troops and constables seized more at Stockport, Macclesfield and Leek. The authorities were not alone in suspecting that the 'march' was part of a wide revolutionary plot. Bamford feared the influence of the Spenceans on some of his Hampdenite colleagues. And wild talk of 'making a Moscow out of Manchester' led to the arrest of several Lancashire leaders, including the misled 'Ardwick Bridge conspirators' and Bamford: the real militants, William Benbow and Joseph Mitchell ('missionaries' connected with the London Jacobins) and John Knight (the veteran leader of the Oldham Union Society) briefly escaped. Worse was to come. In that year of dismay for moderate radicals, when Burdett had retired to the country, Cobbett had fled to America and Bamford had returned from London to Middleton for the second time (after interrogation by the Privy Council) a sadder but wiser man, some wild spirits still plotted among the militants. Dr Watson was awaiting trial for high treason, while his son, Camille Desmoulins Watson, was hiding. But their violent preaching had perhaps had some effect—on such men as Charles Pendrill, a London shoemaker; Thomas Bacon and William Turner, Derbyshire hosiers; John Cope, the Butterley iron-worker who planned to 'roast [Castlereagh's] heart', and little groups of semi-armed men who felt themselves part of a nationwide con-spiracy (and, indeed, in a vague disorganised way, probably were), awaiting only a sign from London, that home of Hampdenism to which Cartwright had taught them to look. In the obscure village of Pentrich in Derbyshire a group of rural workers decided, in June, to wait no longer. Jeremiah Brandreth, 'the Nottingham Captain', raised perhaps 300 villagers to march on Nottingham as the first stage of a national revolution. There would be mammoth national support—and 'roast beef and ale' and rum. The wet night of 9 June dispirited the thirstiest of revolutionaries among the pike-bearing stockingers, ironworkers and labourers who roamed the Notting-hamshire lanes in support of the 'provisional government' which promised such provisions. The failure to seize Butterley ironworks next morning deterred many others. The appearance of a troop of cavalry ended the 'revolution'. Yorkshire clothiers who had com-menced a similar revolution around Huddersfield dispersed even more rapidly.

Almost simultaneously, 'liberal' public opinion was shocked by Edward Baines's sensational revelations in the *Leeds Mercury* of the operations of 'Oliver the Spy'. W. J. Richards (otherwise 'Oliver') appears to have been no pioneer OGPU agent; rather, this book-keeper turned informer was a curious mixture of thoroughly incompetent 'patriot' and courageous 'detective'. He had only recently proferred his services to Sidmouth, but quickly worked himself into the ultra-radical network. His advice to 'fellow'-conspirators seems to have been to postpone the 'great day'; 'depositions' by assorted radicals after Baines had published his exclusive revelations scarcely con-stitute proven evidence. Indeed, Oliver's amateurishness was proved by his contrived (and easily discovered) escape from a radical assem-bly at Thornhill Lees on 6 June, when Byng's soldiers arrested most delegates. Oliver's second northern tour ended with a bolt for his life (via a dangerous meeting with already suspicious Nottingham men next day). Cobbett's later explanations that

Oliver drew towards London, leaving his victims successively in the traps that he had prepared for them

and that the Home Office 'wished, not to prevent, but to produce those acts' have had a long vogue. Baines's 'revelations' had been read everywhere, and Oliver became a pantomimic Sir Jasper for radical folklore. The saga of Oliver's *provocateur* role played its part in the defeat of the prosecution cases against Watson, the Yorkshire 'insurgents' and some Glasgow plotters. It did not affect the case against the Pentrich men. In November Brandreth (who had killed a man), Turner and Isaac Ludham were hanged and beheaded at Derby; twenty-four of their followers were transported and ten were acquitted.[35]

The principal result of the operations of Oliver was scarcely the role traditionally ascribed to him of contriving within a few weeks to arouse a semi-revolutionary situation in the North. But a spy scare quickly spread among radicals. More important, perhaps, was the effect of a fine harvest in 1817. The following year witnessed considerable industrial strife and the start of 'general union' development with the brief existences of the Philanthropic Society in Manchester and John Gast's 'Philanthropic Hercules' in London. But radical activity was minimal. Cause and effect seemed clear. 'Our situation and prospects at home are improving,' Sidmouth told Lord Exmouth in 1817. 'The materials for disaffection to work upon are less abundant and less susceptible than at the corresponding period last year.' Low wages rather than high bread prices or constitutional idealism provoked Lancashire's troubles of 1818; indeed, John Bagguley's attempts to engraft radical demands on to the strikers' aims were violently rejected, in addition to earning him two years' imprisonment.[36]

The situation soon changed. For one thing, the cotton strikes— most bitterly fought in radical Stockport—were largely unsuccessful. Defeated by defaulting treasurers, the arrest of their committee for conspiracy and the firmness of the masters, the spinners were forced to return to work on the employers' terms (including the reduced wage levels of 1816). The weavers, still conscious of a superior social position (despite already lower and still declining earnings) organised an entirely separate strike. Despite some slight and temporary local gains, they also were generally defeated. The lesson seemed obvious: under the Combination Acts, however laxly administered but always providing a final sanction for magistrates, trade union action was both potentially dangerous and probably unsuccessful.[37] Secondly, the harvest of 1818 was a disaster: food prices were bound to rise in the following year. Thirdly, the industrial expansion led to over-optimism, to over-production and to price falls. To men who had tried unsuccessfully during a period of growth to improve their lot by industrial action, and who now faced a slump period, it was logical to return to political action as a last hope of protection. So, at least, with hindsight, one can rationalise the changing allegiances of many North Western workers.

Certainly, a new phase of radical organisation commenced in the winter of 1818. The Lancashire Hampden clubs revived as Union societies, largely composed of operatives, led by such men as the Rev. Joseph Harrison of Stockport, Joseph Mitchell of Manchester, John Knight, W. C. Walker, P. T. Candelet, the quack medico Joseph Healey and their (generally minor middle-class) kind. The radicalism of the societies varied, as their organisation spread north and south. It generally included a programme of universal male suffrage, annual parliaments and the ballot; some of the Unionists wished to go much further in their plans for social as well as political change. The strength of the political revival was demonstrated on 18 January 1819, when Hunt addressed 8,000 workers on St Peter's Field, Manchester, and secured the adoption of a thoroughly radical remonstrance and declaration to the Prince Regent. 'The only source of all legitimate power is the People, the whole People, and nothing but the People,' asserted the declaration:

> All Governments not immediately derived from, and strictly accountable to the People, are usurpations, and ought to be resisted and destroyed ... All men are born free, equal and independent of each other ... Taxation without Representation is illegal, and ought to be abolished ... Every individual, of mature age, and not incapacitated by crime or insanity, has a right to a vote ... Annual Parliaments and universal suffrage were formerly, and ought now, to be the Law of the Land ... It is both the right and the duty of the People to possess arms ... The Crown is a sacred trust and inheritance, held only by the free consent and for the sole welfare and benefit of the People ... The keeping up of large standing armies, during times of peace, is unconstitutional. ...

And so the document continued, with references to Magna Carta and condemnations of 'innovations' such as the employment of troops and spies, the Corn Law ('obtained under false pretentions and passed at the point of the bayonet . . . a vile conspiracy between the great Landholders and the Ministers'), paper money ('a fraud upon the real property of the nation, and a flagrant breach of . . . honour and confidence'), penal laws and recent restrictive legislation. The remonstrance drew attention to 'the *cruel*, illegal and unconstitutional acts of the corrupt and wicked Administration' and 'reminded' Prinny that

> it was no exclusive attachment or predilection for the private virtues or personal merits of the family of Brunswick, that induced our ancestors to go to Hanover for a King, and transplant them from the obscurity and poverty in which they found them, to the splendour and dignity of the English throne . . .

'Briefly', the Lancashire radicals wanted[38]

> the impeachment, and if found guilty, the condign punishment of the present Ministers—A change of measures, and an immediate abolition of the odious and accursed Boroughmongering system— A radical, and such a complete Reform, as will secure to the People the exercise of that great and incontrovertible principle, that every human being is entitled to an equal participation in the sacred blessings of political freedom; and every industrious labourer, manufacturer and mechanic, has a right to reap the ample and substantial fruits of his virtuous and USEFUL TOIL.

Similar sentiments were expressed at Stockport rallies in February and April, by a new crop of Yorkshire and Lancashire Union societies and at an Oldham conference of delegates from twenty-eight towns on 7 June. When the weavers held a rally on St Peter's Field on 21 June to petition for either urgent relief or an official emigration scheme, the radicals J. T. Saxton and W. C. Walker took over the meeting, carrying resolutions favouring a national conference and a boycott of exciseable articles. A week later Sir Charles Wolseley told (reportedly) 20,000 people at Stockport that, having not been 'idle on [the] glorious occasion' of the fall of the Bastille, he would 'not be inactive in endeavouring to annihilate those dungeons of despotism' in Britain. Sidmouth's refusal to pass the Manchester resolutions to the Regent, insisted Harrison, constituted 'a barrier of corruption and the people must blow it up or blow it down'. At a great Birmingham rally on 12 July Wolseley was elected as the town's 'legislatorial attorney'. Meanwhile, on the 1st Burdett had introduced another radical motion in the Commons, while

Joseph Johnson commenced the planning of a mammoth Manchester meeting for 9 August. Similar tactics, presumably designed to demonstrate the national strength of radicalism, were adopted in many areas. The Glasgow weavers' attempt to petition for subsidised emigration on 16 June was converted into a demand for annual parliaments and universal suffrage.

Inevitably, those responsible for the maintenance of law and order, in London—but more particularly in the disaffected areas—professed growing alarm. It is important to recall that they were supported by a considerable body of 'loyalists', largely 'Church and King' Tories, whose activities have never been recorded: certainly, not every spinner, labourer, collier or weaver was given to threatening the Regent or imagining a Saxon freedom before the descent of a Norman yoke. But Whigs and liberals made political capital out of the government's troubles. 'Every one should be suspected henceforth as a spy, or an informer, or an incendiary,' declared Baines of Leeds, 'who talks of any force but that of reason.'[39] The liberal message, though carefully ambiguous and ambivalent, amounted to advice to put radical demands under the discipline of liberal (even Whiggish) organisers. Increasingly concerned and angered supporters of the established order (by no means all of whom enjoyed high social positions, possessions, prerogatives and perquisites) not unnaturally turned their initial hostility towards those opponents who enjoyed but apparently condemned privilege. Squire Wolseley and dissenting minister Harrison had never toiled in a spinning mill or at a loom; caps of liberty and tricoleurs were inappropriate badges for them; prison sentences, however, seemed appropriate for educated men who had taken advantage of the lapsing of the 'gagging' Acts in 1818. Middle-class 'revolutionaries' have rarely realised what figures they cut—for fun or contempt—among many working people.

VII

In accepting the Patriotic Union Society's invitation to visit Manchester on 9 August 1819, Hunt called for 'the *largest assemblage* . . . that ever was seen in this country'. Publicity was arranged through James Wroe's briefly influential *Manchester Observer* and London journals and at a series of rallies. Despite General Byng's coolness, the magistrates became increasingly alarmed at reports of radical arming; loyalists indented for arms; the Manchester and Salford

Yeomanry sharpened their sabres; Wroe was prosecuted for seditious libel; the meeting was declared illegal. The government itself banned seditious assemblies and drilling on 30 July. The radicals merely changed the purpose of their rally: instead of electing a local 'legislatorial attorney', they would petition for reform, on 16 August. Resenting the refusal of increased military assistance and rejecting Home Office cautions, the despairing magistrates continually discussed what most of them regarded as a terrifying predicament.

The climax of radical preparation and loyalist fears came on a warm, sunny day. Yeomanry, hussars, horse artillery, infantry and special constables took up position as long processions of marching reformers, with bands and banners, converged on St Peter's Field. The marchers were in festive mood, in their best clothes, and their orderly bearing as they tramped through the Lancashire and Cheshire countryside has been movingly described by sympathetic contemporaries. What proportion of them strictly observed Hunt's orders to leave offensive weapons at home is debatable. ' "CLEANLINESS", "SOBRIETY", "ORDER", were the first injunctions issued by the committees,' recalled Bamford, the Middleton marshal, 'to which, on the suggestion of Mr Hunt, was subsequently added that of "PEACE". But among the plethora of banners and placards was Saddleworth's demand for 'Equal Representation or Death'—which subsequently seemed dangerous. And certainly not all organisers were as careful to disarm their contingents as was Bamford.

What happened has often been described. Between 50,000 (according to the magistrate William Hulton) and 153,000 (according to the *Observer*) people assembled on St Peter's Field. The magistrates, overlooking the proceedings, decided, as Hunt arrived to tumultuous cheers, that the affair must be stopped and ordered deputy constable Joseph Nadin to arrest him. Nadin found it necessary to ask for military help, while Hunt uttered his first controversial sentences. A troop of much-taunted yeomanry, under the Tory cotton manufacturer H. H. Birley, escorted Nadin to the hustings and arrested Hunt and Johnson. But the amateur troops became embroiled in the crowd, and the authorities anxiously ordered up the experienced hussars to clear the crowd. A screaming, terrified audience ran to escape from the hussars' prodding and nudging and the yeomanry's wilder slashing. Within minutes the crowd had fled, four hundred people were injured (about two thirds of them by crushing) and eleven killed or mortally wounded and the authorities were collecting loads of stones and sticks dropped or thrown by the allegedly unarmed crowd. Forty-one persons were subsequently imprisoned and the legend of 'Peterloo' was born.[40]

The consequences were considerable. Radical propaganda made the most of the story of peaceful folk assailed by yeomanry and cavalry for many a year. Whigs hastened to reassert their position (as Earl Grey put it) as the 'natural protectors' of the people; and the outspoken Earl Fitzwilliam was dismissed from the lord lieutenancy of the West Riding.[41] Radical leaders went to prison for their incitement—and Burdett for protesting at events. And the Regent's government thanked the Lancashire authorities for their 'prompt, decisive and efficient measures' and in the winter passed the 'Six Acts' against drilling and bearing arms, restricting meetings, deterring libels and taxing journals. Reformers' reactions inevitably varied. Manchester on the night of 'Peterloo' was bitter and sullen: 'all the working people', insisted Bamford, 'were athirst for revenge'. Riots and threats in Lancashire kept loyalists in a state of alarm well into the winter, but thereafter radicalism again started to decline. Hunt and Wooler called for abstinence from taxed goods and prosecution of those responsible for the 'massacre'. Dr Watson and Richard Carlile urged a nationwide day of simultaneous rallies. Cobbett, newly returned from America together with the remains of Paine, talked of currency reform; Byron sardonically commented

> In digging up your bones, Tom Paine,
>   Will Cobbett has done well:
> You'll visit him on earth again,
>   He'll visit you in hell.

But radical England largely deserted English radicalism. For one thing, there was the rival attraction of the growing scandal over the relationship between 'Prinny' (King George IV from January 1820) and his Queen: in this prolonged contest between two gross sensualists, 'progressive' opinion took Caroline's side.

There remained, however, some coteries of desperate men. During 1820 they indulged in two melodramatic ventures. In London there was the 'Cato Street plot', still largely mysterious but apparently largely hatched by Thistlewood, the foolhardy Jacobin. Thistlewood had suffered for his principles and his financial recklessness. Imprisoned for challenging Sidmouth to a duel, ruined by his own impetuosity, regularly disappointed in attempts to create a national revolutionary network and infuriated by Hunt's suggestion that he was a spy, he resolved (as he said) 'that the lives of the instigators of massacre should atone for the souls of murdered innocents'. He concocted a crazy plot to murder the cabinet while dining at Lord Harrowby's house. In 'Spencean' pubs he met his equally poor aides, such as James Ings (who had failed successively as butcher, landlord, coffee-house proprietor and pamphlet-seller), Richard Tidd (military deserter, shoemaker and fellow Lincolnshire man), John Thomas Brunt (revolutionary shoemaker), William Davidson (Jamaican cabinet-maker and alleged sex 'offender')—and George Edwards (Spencean artist and Home Office spy). The plan to create an English republic under president Thistlewood collapsed when Bow Street runners and soldiers violently arrested some of the plotters on 23 February and the ringleaders were hanged on 1 May. West Riding 'revolutionaries', apparently misinformed about metropolitan events, made brief nocturnal marches and then hastily disbanded. Only in Scotland did a tiny group of men have the courage to declare some sort of revolution. A 'provisional government committee' organised a sizeable Glasgow strike in April, followed by a minute 'uprising' when a handful of men briefly fought a few soldiers at Bonnymuir seemingly while attempting to attack the Carron ironworks. Three leaders were executed and eighteen men were transported for their part in this foray.[42] In general, radical reformers had shot their bolt by 1820.

2 *The Background*

By 1820 the classic saga of the Industrial Revolution was well advanced in several industries and areas. Water-driven cotton spinning mills in remote Scottish, Pennine and other areas were yielding to larger steam-powered establishments in urban districts. Handloom weavers, croppers, combers and other traditional craftsmen in textile and other industries were already facing increasing competition from the new technologies. The factory system, so long in gestation, was established and rapidly expanding. The consequences impressed foreign visitors, awed by Britain's mechanical and organisational achievements and marvelling at the size of her bustling industrial plants and the measure of their mounting productivity.[1] Few of them noted the subtler social consequences. The sprawl of Northern and Midlands cities was obvious, and the squalor of their poorer districts was nothing new. But the concentration of large numbers of people at work and at home was producing and provoking new social attitudes. In place of the old hierarchy of interlocking pyramids of 'orders', 'ranks' and 'stations' there gradually developed the notion and vocabulary of 'classes', differentiated by economic interests rather than hereditary caste. Inevitably, this change of outlook occurred with varying speed and intensity in different trades and districts. But it was becoming a fact of life, with potentially vast results on social and political attitudes. 'As long as freedom and civilisation exist', asserted W. A. Mackinnon, in 1828,[2]

> property is so entirely the only power that no other means or choice is left of distinguishing the several classes, than by the amount of property belonging to the individuals of which they are formed.

Property existed in different forms. There was that 'land monopoly' against which later bourgeois radicals were to fulminate. Strict entail, primogeniture and regular enclosure had ensured the continuing strength of the squirearchic and aristocratic families. In 1873 the New Domesday survey of land ownership showed that about 80 per cent of the United Kingdom was owned by fewer than 7,000 families.[3] The paramount position of the land in a predominantly agricultural country had led such early radicals as Robert Wallace, William Ogilvie, Thomas Spence, Tom Paine and Charles Hall to advocate agrarian reforms. The ideal of communitarian land schemes was to exercise considerable influence well into the industrial age. Ricardian 'exposures' of the role of rent provided valuable support. The long tradition of food riots against high prices made many working people inclined to see grasping landlords as the villains of contemporary society. They were consequently in a receptive mood when predominantly middle-class propagandists assailed the Corn Law of 1815. Colonel Perronet Thompson's *Catechism on the Corn Laws* (1826) announced the pleasing doctrine that

> There can be no conflict on a wrong. When the question is of a purse unjustly given, it is a fallacy to say we must reconcile conflicting interests, and give the taker half.

On this issue sections of the middle and working classes could periodically combine, against the landed interest.

Industrial property was closer to the experience of the new operatives, engineers and labourers. Ricardian labour value theories, as developed by Charles Hall, Thomas Hodgskin, William Thompson and John Gray, led to the growth of co-operative theory. The attraction of co-operation in place of capitalism was that the new machinery would be used for social benefit rather than private profit. And the attraction was real and strong to many who had never read the works of the early socialist writers. Co-operation would ensure employment, social justice and prosperity; and it combined the principle of a return to the land with the replacement of capitalist control, a new social morality with a revival of agrarian communitarianism. 'The grand ultimate object of all co-operative societies, whether engaged in trading, manufacturing, or agricultural pursuits, is community on land,' declared the London Co-operative Congress in 1832. The dominant and most influential pioneer of a plethora of bodies—co-operative retail shops, producers' co-operatives, market exchanges, agricultural communities and so on—was Robert Owen, with his mission to change the world.[4] But reactions to industrialism took many different forms.

I

Politics in the 1820s was markedly different from the tumultuous years of the immediate past. Early in George IV's reign there was old-style excitement over the Queen's Affair (which was basically concerned with her past affaires). Liverpool's reluctant attempt to deprive Caroline of her title and regal rights was only narrowly passed in the Lords, whereafter the government yielded to popular clamour and gave up the measure. But the Queen died in 1821, shortly after an absurd, drunken attempt to attend the coronation. In 1822 the hated, tragic Castlereagh died by his own hand. New lines were emerging in politics, in response to the growing force of an articulate public opinion. The King reluctantly accepted Canning, an actress's son, as Foreign Secretary; and Sidmouth was succeeded at the Home Office by Robert Peel, the son of a great cotton master. The new, more liberal policies evolved by such men went hand in hand with an improving trade situation as the post-war depression lifted.

It was a sign of more prosperous times that in 1821, despite many qualms, the Bank of England was able to follow 'Peel's Act' of 1819 and resume convertibility of paper money into gold. Subsequent price falls angered many agriculturalists and industrialists; but Ricardo, the City and the cotton industry were determined to benefit from increased overseas trade. Allies in the government, like Frederick Robinson and William Huskisson, respectively Chancellor of the Exchequer and President of the Board of Trade from 1823, further enhanced traders' opportunities. The Navigation Laws were modified, colonial trade restraints were loosened, tariffs were greatly reduced, bounties were abolished, internal and Irish trade regulations were liberalised and foreign treaties were negotiated. When over-speculation and a panic rush on gold caused a commercial and financial crisis in 1825, however, the government was largely helpless. True to its new liberalism, it considered that intervention in a crisis situation, as banks and businesses collapsed and unemployment rose, was dangerous and might worsen matters. It did, nevertheless, inaugurate nineteenth-century banking reform in 1826 by permitting joint-stock country banks and forbidding the issue of English notes of under £5.

At the same time Peel carried a major set of reforms in the anti-quated, muddled and complicated legal systems, the prisons and in 1829, the police service. Humanitarians, penal reformers, pioneer social scientists and those who simply opposed the long catalogue of offences for which the death penalty was still nominally in force had all appealed for change. Prominent among such campaigners was Bentham, now increasingly convinced of the need for wide constitutional, administrative and political reform. To him it was

> apparent that, under the British Constitution, there cannot but exist, on the one hand, such a demand for fallacies, and, on the other hand, such a supply of them, as for copiousness and variety, taken together, cannot be ... matched elsewhere.

And he launched his principal attack on 'the whole class of fallacies built upon authority, precedent, wisdom of ancestors, dread of innovation, immutable laws, and many others, occasioned by ancient ignorance and ancient abuses ...'[5]

From 1824 the Benthamite-tinged *Westminster Review* provided an intellectual radical rival to the Whig *Edinburgh* and Tory *Quarterly* reviews. The twenties were, indeed, a reading age. The growth of the metropolitan and provincial press, generally with strong partisan colouring, and of a rash of aids to literacy—Mechanics' Institutes, the Society for the Diffusion of Useful Knowledge, cheap tracts, evening classes, propagandist debating groups and the like—disturbed crusty supporters of the old order. 'Steam Intellect' societies and the 'march of intellect' among the lower orders boded ill for the established system.[6] From different angles, Eldon and Cobbett were both worried about the effects on honest Britons of exposure to the new 'educational' propaganda. Many Tories were already at least uneasy over aspects of the ministry's economic liberalism. Their unease was to grow. In February 1827 Liverpool collapsed with a stroke, and in March he resigned. And now the floodgates were open to change in many fields.

The succession of Canning to the premiership started the disintegration of the followers of Mr Pitt. It was obvious that Roman Catholic emancipation would now again become an issue of importance. Wellington, Eldon and Peel led their friends out of office, and Canning was obliged to turn to Lansdowne and other Whigs for help. But after four months in power Canning died, in August. There followed Goderich's unhappy ministry which, subject to constant bickering, collapsed without facing Parliament, in January 1828. Party attitudes again polarised when Wellington formed a cabinet of the Right: the Whigs returned to Opposition, soon to be followed by the Canningites. But reforms continued. Peel rounded off his legal reforms and created a professional London police force. The Corn Law was modified with the introduction of a sliding scale. Protestant dissenters were freed from offensive restrictions (more apparent than real) with the repeal of the Test and Corporation Acts. When, in June 1828, the Dublin lawyer Daniel O'Connell, backed by the Catholic Association of 1823, resoundingly defeated Vesey Fitzgerald in the Clare by-election, another pivot of the old 'Church and State' order was undermined. It was obvious that the Clare result could be widely repeated. Consequently, in 1829 the Emancipation Act ended Roman Catholic disabilities. Another group of Tory malcontents thenceforth opposed the leadership—some, indeed, like the Marquess of Blandford, favouring suffrage extension as a means of preserving the old constitution. But many Whigs were increasingly sympathetic towards the government; and the Canningite leader Huskisson, who periodically plotted with other Whig factions, was killed at the ceremonial opening of the Liverpool and Manchester Railway in September 1830.

The death of George IV and accession of William IV in June necessitated an August election. Despite regional unemployment and complaints, the polls proceeded quietly enough. During the election news arrived from France of the July revolution. It probably had little effect on the results in Britain, but the implications of the almost bloodless overthrow of the Bourbons were quickly appreciated. 'Is not this the most triumphant demonstration', the Canningite Palmerston asked the Whig Sir James Graham,

> of the advantages arising from free discussion, from the liberty of the Press, from the diffusion of knowledge and from familiarising even the lowest classes with the daily examination of political questions?

Such thoughts were quickly taken up by the re-grouping radicals, now emerging from a long hibernation. Peel anxiously observed that in the manufacturing districts the success of the French and Belgian revolutions was

> calling into action the almost forgotten Radicals of 1817 and 1819, and provoking a discussion upon the probable results of insurrectionary movements in this country.

But reformers were divided and seemingly weak; and a government which had already broken old bonds was widely expected to solve the constitutional question by a moderate measure of parliamentary reform. It was the blunt, honest, almost apolitical Wellington who changed the situation by declaring his belief in the perfection of existing arrangements, on 2 November. Thirteen days later the government was defeated on Sir Henry Parnell's motion on the Civil List, amid nationwide protest at the Duke's speech. At least partly in order to avoid the reform motion being prepared by Brougham, Wellington promptly resigned.

In mid-November Earl Grey formed an aristocratic ministry, including the Tory Richmond, several Canningites and many Whigs. Parliamentary reform was now a certainty: Whigs had talked of it, at Westminster and in the rural palaces of their tightly inter-related leaders, for decades. They had not, however, got down to the detailed task of planning a Bill. As resolute defenders of 'the conservative interest' they knew, of course, the necessity (in Graham's words) 'to reform to the extent necessary for preserving our institutions, not to change for the purpose of subverting'; Brougham drew on old precedent by advocating 'not revolution, but restoration'. And there was some indication of the type of people whom Whigs might admit to the body politic in the political (though not social) company which they kept. Prosperous City men and provincial manufacturers, the older religious nonconformists and rationalist utilitarians were odd bed-fellows, but they largely shared one factor: they owned property.

As the four-man committee (Durham, Russell, Duncannon and Graham) planned the reform measure through the winter, they were influenced by those considerations which Macaulay best expressed in December 1831. Macaulay supported reform for two reasons:

> first, because I believe it to be in itself a good thing; and secondly, because I think the dangers of withholding it so great that, even if it were an evil, it would be the less of two evils . . . That government is attacked is a reason for making the foundations of government broader, and deeper, and more solid. That property is attacked is a reason for binding together all proprietors in the firmest union. That the agitation of the question of reform has enabled worthless demagogues to propagate their notions with some success is a reason for speedily settling the question . . .

Macaulay viewed with alarm

the two extreme parties in this country: a narrow oligarchy above; an infuriated multitude below; on the one side the vices engendered by power; on the other side the vices engendered by distress; one party blindly averse to improvement; the other party blindly clamouring for destruction; one party ascribing to political abuses the sanctity of property; the other party crying out against property as a political abuse. Both these parties are alike ignorant of their true interest.

The nation would be saved by 'a third party, infinitely more powerful than both the others put together ... the middle class of England, with the flower of the aristocracy at its head, and the flower of the working classes bringing up its rear'.

The Whigs, then, would preserve property, law, order and national institutions by enfranchising the middle classes and creating predominantly middle-class constituencies. This was a 'safe' measure. But 'bad men ... [had] promulgated with some success, doctrines incompatible with the existence, I do not say of monarchy, or of aristocracy, but of all law, of all order, of all property, of all civilisation, of all that makes us to differ from Mohawks or Hottentots.' Ignorant, impoverished workers should not be blamed for being 'deluded by impudent assertions and gross sophisms'. Macaulay 'would withhold from them nothing which it might be for their good to possess'. He rejoiced that 'the most industrious and respectable of our labourers would be admitted to a share in the government of the State'. But to go further 'would only increase their distress ... that they may be governed for their happiness, they must not be governed according to the doctrines which they have learned from their illiterate, incapable, lowminded flatterers'.[8] Here was the kernel of the Whig attitude to reform.

II

Whigs might stress—and indeed exaggerate—the danger of revolution if reform were not carried. But on occasion they acted firmly against troublesome elements. 'Unstamped' radical journals were hounded for many years. The pitiful risings of Southern farm labourers in the winter of 1830 for the cause of 'Captain Swing' against low pay, threshing machines and near-starvation were firmly suppressed by Lord Melbourne at the Home Office.[9] But during 1831 popular enthusiasm for reform mounted through the country. The continuing depression provoked continued wide protest, as instanced by the activities of Thomas Attwood's Birmingham Political Union of 1829, with its demand for currency reform, or by the Manchester bourgeois radicals with their free trade panacea. A crop of political unions was established—sometimes, as at Birmingham, Newcastle and Sheffield, bringing together small masters and skilled craftsmen, and sometimes, as at Leeds and Manchester, breaking into distinct bourgeois and proletarian bodies. In London William Lovett and Henry Hetherington founded the National Union of the Working Classes, to represent the claims of working-class radicals (albeit largely Owenite craftsmen), while Francis Place's National Political Union claimed to unite workers with middle-class radicals. And the press flung itself into the battle. *The Times* added its weight to the reform side; the *Morning Chronicle* preached Whiggish reform; Edward Baines's *Leeds Mercury*, J. E. Taylor's *Manchester Guardian*, Thomas Thompson's *Leicester Chronicle* and their like spoke for the provincial middle classes; Archibald Prentice's *Manchester Times*, John Foster's *Leeds Patriot* and John Tait's Glasgow *Trades Advocate* represented radicalism; and an assortment of journals—notably Hetherington's *Poor Man's Guardian* and John Doherty's Manchester *Poor Man's Advocate* spoke for the Left.

What these differing groups expected from reform varied enormously. To the Cumbrian landowner Graham and his colleagues

> The Government of the country would be put upon a more solid foundation, for he knew none so safe as the extension of the suffrage to the most intelligent and industrious classes of the community.

To the Congregationalist liberal Baines 'the fruits of Reform' were obvious:

> Vast commercial and agricultural monopolies are to be abolished. The Church is to be reformed, and, we could fain hope, severed from its unchristian and mutually injurious connection with the State. Close corporations are to be thrown open. Retrenchment and economy are to be enforced. The shackles of the Slave are to be broken.

The denizens of the small workshops of the Midlands were largely content with a Bill which gave them nothing: under Attwood's benevolent leadership, recalled the militant James Bronterre O'Brien, 'the Brummagem operatives seemed really to believe that they would be *virtually*, though not actually, represented in the "reformed" parliament'. But Northern factory workers favoured a wider suffrage, as John Doherty put it, to give 'a power . . . to every men to protect his own labour from being devoured by others'. And some men of the Left undoubtedly looked to reform as the inaugurator of a new atheistic, egalitarian and republican society.

The progress of the Bill gave all elements many opportunities to express themselves. Russell's proposals of March 1831 would disfranchise the smallest boroughs, reduce others to a single member, create forty-two new boroughs and fifty-five new county seats, add nine Scottish, Irish and Welsh seats, retain the 40s. freehold vote in the counties and standardise the urban voting qualification on the occupancy of a house worth £10 annually. They passed the second reading by 302 votes to 301 but failed by 299 to 291 on General Gascoyne's amendment in committee in April. The King reluctantly agreed to a dissolution and the dangerous precedent of an election fought on a single issue. Armed with a novel mandate from the excited electorate, the Whigs returned to the battle. Russell introduced a second Bill in June; the second reading passed by 367 votes to 231, the county electorates (and landowners' influence) were extended by Lord Chandos's proposal to grant votes to £50 tenants-at-will, and the third reading passed by 345 to 236 in September.

Threatening oratory, tons of petitions and Political Union talk of refusing taxes advised the Lords to pass the Bill. But in October the peers ignored this barrage of counsel by 199 to 158. A torrent of angry abuse instantly descended upon them. Place's new NPU roused moderate London radicals, including old Thelwall and the 'infidel' Rowland Detrosier (who was subsequently attacked for deserting the true proletarian cause). And Attwood's BPU held huge rallies at which peaceful but firm resistance was urged against what Russell ill-advisedly told Attwood was 'the whisper of a faction'; its further plan of November to organise on military lines was first discouraged and then prohibited. The NUWC was shriller in its protests at the Rotunda in Blackfriars.[11] And in places where there was little or no organisational restraint the mob went wild: there were riots in Nottingham, Derby and Bristol and such anti-reformers as Wellington, Newcastle, the Archbishop of Canterbury and the Bishop of Exeter were attacked. The government's efforts either to gain a royal promise to create enough new peers to carry the Bill or to convert Tory 'waverers' made little headway, and some Tories were already noting signs of ultra-radical hostility to the Bill.[12]

Russell introduced a third, slightly modified, Bill in December and the second reading was carried by 324 votes to 162. The King gave a general pledge on the creation of peers and in April the Lords passed the Bill by 184 to 175. But in May Lyndhurst's proposal to change procedure over the debate was carried by 151 to 116. When the King refused to create at least fifty peers the cabinet resigned, and after sundry manoeuvres Wellington tried to form a ministry, which would carry a more moderate measure. Many Whigs were willing to accept this arrangement; many radicals were not. 'To stop the Duke go for gold', urged Place in London; and revolutionary murmurs mounted, euphemistically from O'Connell and more plainly from some Rotundists and others. The heady 'days of May' and (more importantly) the reluctance of Tory leaders to join the Duke prevented the formation of a Tory ministry. The King finally promised to create peers; Grey resumed office; and in June the Lords carried the third reading by 106 votes to 22.

To what extent Government, Opposition, Commons, Lords and Court were really affected and influenced by the noise out of doors remains a matter of doubt. Of course Wellington noted his broken windows at Apsley House; Peel feared for his family at Drayton and Newcastle prepared to defend his at Clumber; Bishop Gray regretted the arson at Bristol and Bishop Phillpotts avoided his diocese at Exeter. The notion that Britain was on the verge of revolution at various times during the reform debates has had a long currency. Where the revolution was to occur has never been satisfactorily explained. Editor Baines leading bourgeois jeers against the Queen in a Leeds Cloth Hall yard, banker Attwood at worst threatening mass meetings for radical reform in Birmingham, lawyer O'Connell impertinently recalling Charles I's death, retired tailor Place moderating metropolitan demands and cabinet-maker Lovett, whose universal suffrage campaign Place attempted to weaken—here was no general staff of a revolution. Of course there were some real revolutionaries, little coteries whose leaders were recorded on Home Office files and subsequently resurrected by historians. There were also some violent men, driven to 'action' either by economic despair or by personal inclination. But wrecking a (long-deserted) ducal castle at Nottingham, rampaging through the centre of Bristol, rioting in market towns, throwing a dead cat at the Archbishop of Canterbury and stones at aristocratic windows was scarcely the stuff of revolution. It naturally suited the Whig case to make the most of such incidents and to pose as 'progressive' defenders of the constitution against the illiterate mob. Whigs, always claiming to understand 'the people' (by which they now generally meant the middle classes), insisted that moderate concession to the reform clamour would constitute a final settlement. Tories largely maintained that the Bill could only open the gates to democracy and that it would certainly end that variety of 'balanced' representation which they professed to regard as a glory of the constitution. And many 'radicals' mindlessly clamoured for 'The Bill, The Whole Bill and Nothing but The Bill'.[13] A few Tories and proletarian radicals understood and condemned the implications of a nationally means-tested franchise qualification, which itself made further reform inevitable. One does not have to search for Methodist or other restraints on revolution. A revolutionary situation did not exist. Reform succeeded because its supporters were largely elected at the last unreformed election, because Wellington was unable to form a ministry, because the peerage did not care to be swamped by new creations and because careful Whig manipulation of the Bill's clauses ensured a preponderantly bourgeois electorate.

III

The terms and operation of the Reform Bill were not the only disappointment which the Whigs provided for working-class radicals. Since the late eighteenth century there had been growing concern among groups of Northern clergymen, medical practitioners and humanitarians over the working hours and conditions of operatives, and particularly of children, in the textile mills. The first attempt to legislate on the subject was the first Sir Robert Peel's 'Health and Morals of Apprentices Act' of 1802, which limited pauper apprentices in the country cotton mills to twelve hours' daily labour. The industry's general move to urban districts with the growing use of steam power made further legislation necessary, to protect the 'free' town children. Prompted by Owen and backed by a considerable campaign in the textile counties, the Tory Peel again proposed a Bill in 1815. Four years, one Commons' committee and two Lords' committees later, a truncated Act was passed, prohibiting employment under the age of nine and restricting children under sixteen to twelve hours' actual work. The measure applied only to cotton mills.

During the 1820s there were periodic attempts to extend the widely ignored Act. The Whig John Cam Hobhouse was the ineffective parliamentary leader, but behind him there was a growing though spasmodic Northern agitation, now backed by such brave working-class leaders as Doherty. Hobhouse achieved virtually nothing against the entrenched *laisser-faire* views of the generality of employers and their political supporters. An attempt by the Bradford Tory master John Wood in 1825 to organise a voluntary ten-hour day in the Yorkshire worsted industry was equally abortive. The Factory Movement really began in September 1830, when Wood talked to his fellow Tory Churchman, the land agent Richard Oastler. Appalled by Wood's revelations, Oastler wrote his famous letter to the *Leeds Mercury*, protesting that

> Thousands of our fellow-creatures and fellow-subjects, both male and female, the miserable inhabitants of a *Yorkshire town* . . . are this very moment existing in a state of slavery, more horrid than are the victims of that hellish system '*colonial slavery*'. These innocent creatures drawl out, unpitied, their short but miserable existence, in a place famed for its profession of religious zeal, . . . [and] are compelled, not by the cart-whip of the negro slave-driver, but by the dread of the equally appalling thong or strap of the overlooker, to hasten, half-dressed, *but not half-fed*, to those magazines of British infantile slavery—*the worsted mills in the town and neighbourhood of Bradford*!!!

Instead of ensuring an instant reform, as Oastler hoped, the letter sparked off a bitter controversy throughout the West Riding. Through the winter attitudes were increasingly polarised, as Yorkshire Tories and radicals joined Oastler against the Whig–liberal alliance.

In 1831 Hobhouse proposed another Bill, prohibiting employment under the age of nine and restricting children under eighteen to eleven and a half hours' daily work. The masters got up a hostile campaign, condemning (as the Halifax worsted employers put it) 'the pernicious tendency and effects of all *legislative enactments*'. From March, reformers in Huddersfield, Bradford, Keighley and Leeds started to organise a network of Short-Time Committees, composed of Tory and radical sympathisers, and in May Oastler urged workers to call for a ten-hour day at the reform election. He was the natural leader of the growing agitation and in June his position was formalised by the 'Fixby Compact', when a group of Huddersfield radicals called on Oastler: 'after a great deal of conversation they agreed to work together, with the understanding that parties in politics, and sects in religion, should not be allowed to interfere between them.' But Hobhouse not only opposed a ten-hour day but also accepted a variety of amendments which reduced his ultimate Act to a trivial measure affecting only the cotton mills.

Oastler furiously redoubled his efforts, creating a wider campaign in association with the Lancashire reformers. He squarely faced the difficulty of current liberal and reform enthusiasm. 'Don't be deceived!' he wrote:[14]

> You will hear the cries of 'No Slavery', 'Reform', 'Liberal principles', 'No Monopoly' etc. But let your cries be—'No Yorkshire Slavery', 'No Slavery in any part of the Empire', 'No factory mongers', 'No factory monopolists'.

As further information about long hours, industrial injuries, ill health, foul working conditions and cruelty to child workers reached him, Oastler's agitation took on the character of a moral crusade. A new parliamentary leader, the Leeds Tory linen merchant Michael Sadler, the Evangelical MP for Aldborough, promised more energetic action at Westminster and a series of public meetings was held over Christmas in his support.

As Parliament faced the last reform debates and tensions in the spring of 1832, the North was roused to a new enthusiasm over industrial reform by such men as Oastler, the battling Anglican priest G. S. Bull of Bradford, the Huddersfield radical Joshua Hobson, the Manchester Owenite and spinners' leader John Doherty, the Tory Leeds surgeon C. T. Thackrah and the Todmorden radical cotton master John Fielden. Backed by widespread petitioning, Sadler movingly proposed his Ten Hours Bill on 16 March, but the government insisted on an inquiry by a Select Committee: the result was a parade of operatives and others before Sadler's committee between April and August and ultimately the publication of a classic and controversial volume of evidence on factory life. At Easter the Yorkshire committee held their great 'pilgrimage' to York, when workers from all the West Riding textile towns tramped to the county capital for a mammoth rally for factory reform. But with the passing of the Reform Act and the subsequent dissolution of Parliament, Sadler's Bill lapsed. From the summer, factory reformers' energies were devoted to the first reformed elections and particularly to creating a Tory–radical alliance (composed, Baines sourly alleged, 'of operatives of that nondescript and mongrel class betwixt Ultra-Radicals and Ultra-Tories')[15] to support Sadler's candidature at Leeds.

The fight was bitter as passions mounted through the autumn. And gradually the strange alliance was forged in several textile constituencies. But factory reformers faced a difficult struggle before the new bourgeois electorates: as Oastler noted, 'the People did not live in £10 houses'. Tory and radical alike could demand factory reform: Whigs and liberals 'obstinately refused to join in procuring it', asserted Doherty. 'The attainment of the bill has been left entirely to the Tories and Radicals.' Both Tories and radicals loathed what Hetherington condemned as the 'tyrannical, infamous, hellish' Reform Act, which, said the Leeds factory reformer Cavie Richardson, 'deprived the poor of every vestige of political existence'. Ralph Taylor, another Leeds radical reformer, wondered 'what the operatives were to reap from the Reform Bill, if they and their children were to work the exact number of hours which they were *able to bear*', and condemned an Act 'whose greatest beauty was that it totally proscribed the Working Classes from the exercise of their Political Rights'. Tory and radical alike were coming to share Oastler's view:[16]

> *I hate Whig politics with a most perfect hatred* . . . [The Whigs] are the great enemies of the Factory Bill, the great supporters of the Factory System, which is fast destroying the *Landed Interest* and the Labouring Classes . . . The time is come when all must join together against the political economists, or this country cannot be saved.

But Tory and radical candidates had to solicit *petit bourgeois* votes. Proletarian marches, excited rallies and condemnations of the sins of liberal capitalism cut little ice with the newly enfranchised respectable folk. In December Sadler was easily defeated by John Marshall, the son of the local flax magnate, and Macaulay. Few other sympathetic Tories or radicals were successful in the North.

'For a season, treachery and malice and hypocrisy have triumphed', Oastler bitterly declared:

> The voters of Leeds have listened to the voice of the tempter— they have rejected the man whose eloquence was wont to be raised in Britain's senate in defence of the poor. The unoffending and oppressed factory child has lost his disinterested advocate—the starving Irish peasant has been deprived of the eloquent assertor

of his rights—the English agricultural labourer will mourn that that voice which so forcibly described his sufferings and prescribed their cure, has *by the voice of the Leeds electors* been silenced—and the poor manufacturing labourers, who have done their duty, and from distant and neighbouring towns and in Leeds itself, (having no votes themselves to give), have prayed and petitioned by tens of thousands that the *voters of Leeds* would send to Parliament the champion of their and their children's rights, will grieve to find that their prayers and their entreaties have passed unheeded, whilst falsehood and the voice of the oppressor have prevailed. They will mourn that that man on whom their hopes were fixed, and to whom their gratitude was due and freely tendered, should have been rejected by those who pretend to be the friends of liberty and freedom, and who proudly apply to themselves the epithet of 'LIBERAL'. Well, who can wonder, man is only fallen man! The Jews professed much zeal for God and love for piety—and they preferred Barabbas to Jesus.

Oastler went on to spell out a Tory–radical message—and Whig 'hatred afforded him convincing proof that he was right'. He was

> *not* of the present School of 'Political Economists', 'Free Traders', 'Liberals', so called; 'Emigration Boards and Committees' I detest —I contend that the Labourer has a *right* to live on his Native Soil; there is room enough and there may be food enough in our native land for us all ... The Altar, The Throne and the Cottage should share alike the protection of the Law ... Shall the Law refuse to protect the only property of the Poor, HIS LABOUR, because some few unjust, unprincipled men refuse to pay its value? ... I maintain the Law *must* interfere.

No man was 'more attached to the "three estates" than [Oastler], not one more opposed to change'. But Tories must learn to change: 'Will you go back? You cannot. "Stand still?" Impossible.' For

> The People have now learnt their strength, the avalanche is descending and will crush their opponents. It is not too late to guide it—it *is* too late to oppose ...

Oastler 'did not like' the Reform Act:

> I never did. I always knew it to be a 'Grey trick', nothing but a delusion ... [a] most unjust and hypocritical measure ... [The People] have a pretty convincing proof that the ten-pounders will

do nothing for the people whom they promised should be liberated
—they now call them 'rabble' and 'impudent disaffected rebels'—
and instead of Liberty, they offer them the Sword and Bayonet—
they have suddenly found out that these very men whom they
have been courting all their lives, and promised every good thing
to, have not sense and intellect enough to chuse a representative.

And he was a firm protectionist:

Whenever I hear a British artisan shout 'cheap foreign corn', I
always fancy I see his wife pulling his coat, and hear her crying out
'low wages', 'long labour', 'bad profits'. Is not that the case? I am
sure I am right; is it not so? And when I hear a large millowner
coaxing his workpeople with a promise of 'cheap foreign corn', I
fancy I see him shrugging his shoulders and saying, 'more work
for less money, that's all'. Very well, then, my principle of legislation is this—to encourage home growth, home labour, home
trade, and home consumption.

It was on such bases that Tory–radicalism developed.

The movement held its first conference at Bradford in January
1833. It was vital that a new parliamentary leader should be selected,
and Bull was sent to Westminster to make the choice: Viscount
Ashley, the Tory Member for Dorset, accepted the position.[17] Another great campaign developed in the North to support the young
Evangelical peer. And now reform speakers were taking a more
militant line. 'The present system', Oastler roared, at Preston,

had caused a chasm in society, and the conduct of those masters
who openly violated the law had robbed the law of its sanctity . . .
Though hope might refuse to glance across that awful chasm,
despair, maddened by hatred and revenge, would dare the leap.

Ashley introduced his Bill but the government again favoured
further investigation, this time by a Royal Commission, which was
set up in April. The Northern reformers bitterly fought an operation
which they considered would simply absolve the factory masters.
But the commissioners worked quickly and efficiently. In June their
first report observed that children's long hours promoted ill-health
and precluded education. As the most Benthamite commissioner
admitted that child workers were not 'free agents', it was recommended that labour should be prohibited under the age of nine and
restricted (by stages) to eight hours daily, with two hours' education,

for those under thirteen; inspectors should enforce the limitations. The commissioners were determined to kill the ten hours proposal (which would, in effect, as they and the reformers agreed, restrict both children and adults). An eight hours restriction would permit children to be used in relays, thus leaving adult hours unaffected. Despite bitter hostility in the textile districts, most emphatically expressed at a huge July rally on Wibsey Low Moor, the government largely accepted the report. The Act passed in August, covering most textile industries, restricted the youngest children to eight hours and 'young persons' aged between thirteen and eighteen to twelve hours, provided two hours' daily education and established the factory inspectorate. Another group now felt bitter and angry over Whig 'deception'.[18]

IV

Other working people had turned to trade unionism, sometimes to protect 'honourable' trades and traditions against unskilled inter-lopers, sometimes for rudimentary insurance purposes and sometimes to fight a class war against expanding capitalism. Occasional outbursts of violence, governmental fears of the spread of revolutionary doctrines and the rise of *laisser-faire* economics had led to less tolerant legal attitudes by the late eighteenth century, culminating with the Combination Acts of 1799 and 1800. The Acts were neither as repressive nor as effective as was once imagined—and did not apply to Scotland.[19] Nevertheless, trade unions entered the nineteenth century subject to prosecution under the common law and by statute. Prosecutions were few, but engendered considerable bitterness, which periodically affected some unionists' attitudes. The government's repeal of those sections of the Elizabethan Statute of Artificers which allowed justices to determine local wage rates and enforce artisan apprenticeships in 1813 and 1814 further offended men already engaged in defending traditional ways.

The Combination Acts never prevented trade unionism. And gradually a new race of working-class leaders started to emerge. There was John Gast, a Deptford shipwright, who attempted to unite metropolitan workers in the 'Philanthropic Hercules' of 1818. In Yorkshire John Tester (who later deserted the cause) led the Bradford wool combers in their classic dispute of 1825. And in Lancashire the energetic John Doherty built up the cotton spinners' organisation.

There was wide national agitation in support of Place and the liberal-radical Joseph Hume to repeal the Combination Acts in 1824 and to prevent a full re-enactment in 1825.[20] And an assorted range of unions emerged: desperate and ill-organised bodies of declining hand-workers; close groups of skilled men—boilermakers, steam-engine makers, carpenters and the like; district groups of textile workers and miners.

By the late twenties 'national' unionism was becoming fashionable. An Isle of Man conference in 1829 planned a Grand General Union of Operative Spinners of the United Kingdom. The grandly-named Union had a short life, but it encouraged Doherty to establish his National Association of United Trades for the Protection of Labour in 1830, with a policy of co-operation. Almost simultaneously, the Leeds (or Yorkshire) Trades Union developed from the long strike of Benjamin Gott's Leeds woollen workers in 1831. Schemes for a co-operative society, generally associated with Owen, became increasingly popular with many unionists, such as Alexander Campbell in Glasgow and Doherty in Manchester. In 1832 the National Equitable Labour Exchange for the direct exchange of goods was established in London, and thenceforth, Owen, its governor, extended his influence within the union world. The Operative Builders Union of 1831 was persuaded to establish a guild to take over the industry; the potters planned co-operative production schemes; Doherty urged on the cotton workers in his *United Trades Co-operative Journal*, *The Voice of the People* and *The Poor Man's Advocate*. By the autumn of 1833 Owen saw himself as leader of a huge proletarian movement, whose varied components would reorganise society. The National Regeneration Society would enforce a general eight-hour day; the unions would organise production; the exchanges would arrange sales. All such bodies would come together in a huge Grand National Moral Union of the Productive Classes.

The scheme was still-born. Owenite missionaries and such journals as the *Crisis*, *Pioneer* and *Herald of the Rights of Industry* were almost inevitably over-optimistic. A strike wave broke out during 1833, to be followed by masters' lockouts and anti-unionist 'documents'. 'General' unionism was never really established as each section urgently appealed for funds—which were particularly essential at the great dispute in Derby. It was not until February 1834 that the Grand National Consolidated Trades Union of Great Britain and Ireland was founded, with grandiose claims, complicated constitution and an almost entirely metropolitan membership. Blows rapidly descended upon the Grand National. George Loveless and five agricultural workers at Tolpuddle were transported for administering 'illegal oaths' to Dorset labourers. Owen and his colleagues regularly disagreed. Finances dried up. Strikes collapsed and government and employers, armed with Carleton Tufnell's new 'exposure' of unionism, stepped up resistance. Derby fell in June and the remaining handful of 'Grand National' members broke up in the summer.[21] Having brought trade unionists and factory reformers to a wide measure of organisational ruin, Owen turned to other things.

V

There were by 1834 many causes for discontent with the Whigs among their erstwhile allies. Parliamentary reform had not brought the benefits long expected by radicals. Elections remained expensive, sometimes corrupt, often violent and still subject to considerable 'influence' by patrons; for many years parliamentary guidebooks were to list the power of old landed families and some industrial dynasties, particularly over small boroughs. The Commons remained the finest club in Europe, dominated by members of the great families. Those Members who chose to call themselves radicals were a mixed bunch, with little cohesion or even interest in working together. Oldham returned 'Honest John' Fielden, a great cotton master at Todmorden, and William Cobbett. From Pontefract came John Gully, former boxing champion, racehorse owner and mine owner. Ireland contributed O'Connell's 'Tail', full of plot and counter-plot to cure Erin's assorted woes. Attwood represented Birmingham and commenced to bore the House with his views on parliamentary and currency reform. The Benthamites could claim a handful of representatives for their recently deceased master. And some others were capable of 'radical' expressions. But to a Hume or O'Connell 'radicalism' included a bourgeois hostility to trade unions; to a Burdett or Cobbett it meant a defence of old ways; to Fielden and Joseph Brotherton (another manufacturer, elected for Salford) it included protection of the new proletariat; to Richard Potter and Mark Philips (industrialists elected for Wigan and Manchester) it was more designed to protect the new bourgeoisie. What precisely 'radicalism' was supposed to mean to Benthamites may become more apparent when Bentham's writings are deciphered. What utilitarianism implied to many contemporaries, who witnessed Edwin

Chadwick's activities on the Factory and Poor Law Commissions, was scarcely reassuring for working folk. And if the Commons was disappointing to radical reformers the Lords seemed worse; warned but unreformed, it renewed its opposition to assorted reforms. While the Commons ignored radical petitions, the Lords vetoed radical causes; and the Lords, by choosing their grounds carefully, justified their claim to be at least as representative of the national will as were the Commons.

The Whigs themselves were divided. While Brougham and Durham and their followers insisted on continuing the reform programme, others became alarmed by Lord John Russell's flirtations with radicals and O'Connellites. Four conservative ministers— Stanley, Graham, Ripon and Richmond—resigned in May 1834 against Irish Church reorganisation; and gradually Stanley and Graham moved into the new Toryism of Peel. Finding it virtually impossible to hold together his disintegrating cabinet over Irish coercion, Grey himself resigned in July.

Ireland, which proved such a major stumbling-block to governments of the thirties (and later) did not arouse many English proletarian passions. Suspicions of the blacklegging and wage-cutting proclivities of Irish immigrants quite overbalanced sympathy for Ireland's multitude of alleged wrongs. But Whig hostility to trade unionism was another matter. The thousands who protested against the monstrous sentence on the 'Tolpuddle Martyrs' would have been even angrier if they had had the opportunity to read the correspondence between Whiggish magistrates and Whig ministers which determined the prosecution.[22] Talk of working-class collaboration between English and Irish workers was to cut little ice, but despite (perhaps even because of) its many failures the consciousness of class certainly grew in 1833 and 1834. It was the thoughtless egoism of the socialist Owen which did most to ruin unionism; but the Whigs were blamed. In the case of factory reform, the Whigs had gravely disappointed reformers by the Act of 1833; Owen's ludicrous 'Regeneration' scheme simply forced the Northern reformers to start anew.

Another cause for resentment was the harassment of the 'unstamped' press. Some 700 sellers of radical journals were prosecuted between 1830 and 1836, when the 'tax on knowledge' was reduced from 4d to 1d. The long battle for 'freedom', most recently fought by such journals as Henry Hetherington's *Poor Man's Guardian*, Doherty's *Advocate*, Joshua Hobson's *Voice of the West Riding*,

Richard Carlile's *Gauntlet*, James Bronterre O'Brien's *Destructive*, John Cleave's *Weekly Police Gazette* and their like was ending. Nowadays poor sellers rather than publishers and editors were prosecuted: there were 219 cases in 1835. Well-reported prosecutions left another residue of hostility to Whiggism. On the other hand, the way was now opened for that mid-Victorian slum-journalism from which crawled a later gutter-press.[23]

The most heinous of all Whig crimes in many workers' eyes was the change in English and Welsh poor laws. The Elizabethan system of poor relief certainly had some glaring errors from the point of view of contemporary social planners. It was costly; its practices varied from parish to parish; in some areas it operated the Speenhamland system of subsidising low wages; it offended the tenets of political economy, Malthusian population theories and hard pressed rate-payers' pockets and suspicions; it was often incompetently, unfairly and even corruptly administered. Such arguments counted powerfully with the Royal Commission set up in February 1832. In its first celebrated report of February 1834 the Commission recommended a thorough-going reform. The position of the recipient of relief should be made 'less eligible' than that of the 'independent labourer of the lowest class'; consequently, outdoor relief was to be abolished; the 'test' would be entry into designedly unpleasant workhouses. And administration must be centralised under a national authority controlling a network of parochial unions. Such were the provisions of the Poor Law Amendment Act hastily and almost unanimously passed in 1834.[24] Among the few who opposed the measure from the start was John Walter, owner of *The Times* and Member for Berkshire, who thought it 'pregnant with evil ... calculated to produce a revolution in the manners and habits of the British people'. Cobbett promised that 'everything that he could lawfully do, he would do' against the Act. Loathing centralisation, modern liberalism and the new attitude to poverty, Oastler told Wellington in July that[25]

> If this Poor Law Bill passes, the Constitution will be destroyed, and he will be the greatest patriot who can produce the greatest dissatisfaction—and I will strive to be that man.

3 The Foundations

In the summer of 1834, following Grey's resignation, the King hoped for a coalition ministry under the conservative Whig Melbourne. The plan failed, and Melbourne formed another Whig government. But when, in November, the premier proposed Russell as Leader of the Commons, the King dismissed the Whigs and asked Wellington and Peel to form a Tory ministry. Peel's celebrated manifesto at Tamworth enunciated a new Conservatism, involving 'a careful review of institutions, civil and ecclesiastical, undertaken in a friendly temper, combining with the firm maintenance of established rights the correction of proved abuses and the redress of real grievances'. Reformers' views varied. Some radicals hoped for a reform ministry under that wealthy radical Lord Durham; Oastler distrusted the Tamworth creed as a move towards liberalism; Cobbett maintained that Wellington was 'as good a reformer as the Whigs, and more likely to afford relief to the people'. The election of January 1835 certainly proved that Toryism was reviving, particularly in the industrial areas. But Peel did not win sufficient seats to command a majority in a Commons increasingly divided on party lines and increasingly reluctant to accept the King's choice of ministers without question. His position rapidly became untenable, and in April he resigned. Some radicals undoubtedly welcomed the humiliation of the King; but few were now likely to rejoice at the return of Melbourne and the Whigs. Furthermore, despite a Whig alliance with O'Connell by the 'Lichfield House compact', the Whigs had few further reform plans: the Municipal Corporations Act of 1835 marked the virtual end of Whiggish reforming zeal. 'The real national question', asserted Oastler, was[1]

neither the Reform of the Church, nor the Corporations, nor of the Universities, but a Reform in the great general question between Labour and Capital.

I

The Tory-radicals of Northern England increasingly turned their militant attention to the hated Poor Law. This cause again united sections of the Right and Left against Whiggism. The allies denounced centralisation and the usurpation of traditional local powers; they condemned the denial of Christian charity to the poor; and they developed a new folklore of the real and alleged sins of 'the three Bashaws' of Somerset House. Many Northern Tory journals gave support to the new and extending agitation for the repeal of the Poor Law. It was a curious alliance which was at once Tory, Anglican and traditionalist and proletarian, radical and even revolutionary. It brought together such assorted personalities as the eccentric Earl Stanhope, the contentious Bishop of Exeter, Oastler and his friends —'Parson Bull' of Bradford, the radical William Stocks of Huddersfield and the militant young Tory squire William Busfeild of Bingley —Fielden of Todmorden, the dynamic Tory ex-Methodist minister Joseph Rayner Stephens of Ashton-under-Lyne, the Salford radical bookseller R. J. Richardson, the old Tory silversmith Samuel Roberts of Sheffield and the Tory worsted master Matthew Thompson of Bradford.[2]

The new Poor Law unions had been organised with comparative ease in the South. But when the assistant commissioners turned to the North late in 1836 they arrived in the midst of a gathering industrial depression. Northern workers had already been aroused by the commissioners' plans to arrange the migration of cheap labour to the industrial districts at the request of such liberal masters as Henry Ashworth. Now the factory reformers, who had revived their network of committees to oppose Poulett Thomson's proposal to modify the 1833 Act, turned to oppose the hateful Poor Law. They ran a highly emotional and inflammatory campaign. 'Damnation! Eternal Damnation to the Fiend-Begotten "Coarser Food" New Poor Law', roared Oastler:

> The Bible being true, the Poor Law Amendment Act is false! The Bible containing the will of God, this accursed Act of Parliament embodies the will of Lucifer. It is the Sceptre of Belial, establishing

its sway in the Land of Bibles!! DAMNATION, ETERNAL DAMNATION
TO THE ACCURSED FIEND!!

To him, the Act was 'the Devil's own spawn, begotten by him when
in a very bad humour . . . the Catechism of Hell! . . . the Devil's own
Book! It must be *burnt* out and out *burnt* . . .'.[3]

A massive pamphlet campaign developed, as many Tories and
radicals again rallied to the common cause. The surgeon Matthew
Fletcher of Bury saw 'the existing Factory and pauper systems [as]
monstrous Whig engines for dealing destruction upon thousands of
our indigent and infant population'. Stanhope agreed that the Act
was 'detestable and despotic' and that 'instead of being amended,
[it] ought to be immediately and entirely repealed'. When the
assistant commissioners and guardians attempted to set up unions,
riots ensued. The movement was planned at Bradford in March and
held its first mammoth rally in May on Hartshead Moor. Now
Oastler was backed not only by such old associates as Stocks, Samuel
Bower, Lawrence Pitkeithley and Hobson and such recent friends
as the demagogic Feargus O'Connor and Stephens but also by such
metropolitan leaders as O'Brien, Hetherington and Owen. Stephens
set the standard with his assertion that 'sooner than sit down with
this Bill, they would light the tocsin of anarchy'. When further
attempts were made to establish unions, bigger and more violent
riots spread. In November Lancastrians, led by Richardson and
William Clegg, followed Yorkshire's example by founding the South
Lancashire Anti-Poor Law Association.

As the movement developed and scored its first successes in
restraining the new authorities, it faced a growing new underswell
of opinion. Radicalism was spreading again, and even the Hartshead
Moor rally ended with demands for universal suffrage. The anti-Poor
Law movement, combining Tories and radicals, Churchmen, dissenters and infidels, had an excited and wide-based support. By 1838,
however, the movement was starting to lose its impact and image.
For one thing, the commissioners had learned from their early lessons
and were now modifying the bleaker aspects of the Act in the North.
For another, despite all the talk of arming, there seemed little chance
of success. Oastler's dismissal by his employer in May 1838 severely
weakened the leadership. And gradually the North turned to a wider
radicalism. 'Keep to this one single point', Fielden insisted at a great
Lancashire rally on Kersal Moor in September; '. . . The suffrage,
and the suffrage only, should satisfy the working people of England.'

As a result, the Poor Law cause became one of many demands of a growing working-class radical movement. Oastler's influence did not die. Although they could not recognise him as a 'radical reformer' (and were mistaken in so categorising Stephens), in December, Prestwich radicals expressed 'sincere thanks to him for the invaluable service he had rendered the white factory slaves, and his strenuous opposition to the damnable New Poor Law—miscalled—Amendment Act.'[4] His final legacy to Northern radicalism was talk of physical force.

II

While the textile areas were aroused against the Poor Law, the London radicals had maintained varied activities. One group, headed by Lovett, Cleave, Hetherington and James Watson and periodically influenced by Place, had founded a succession of organisations. In 1829 they had formed the British Association for Promoting Co-operative Knowledge. They were active in the Metropolitan Trades Union and the National Union of the Working Classes of 1831. Theirs was a comprehensive radicalism initially envisaging a co-operative society on Owenite lines and the ending of that individualist system which, complained Lovett, 'enabled one man to engross for luxury what would suffice to make thousands happy'. Self-made artisans, tradesmen and journalists who had educated themselves at George Birkbeck's London Mechanics' Institute and in coffee-house debates, they were always deeply interested in extending educational opportunities. Their economic theories came from Hodgskin rather than the liberal Place and their craft background led them to prefer political activitity to orthodox trade union action. The founders of the Metropolitan Union, Place recalled,[5]

> in the first instance wished to form a trades' union for the purpose of raising wages and reducing the working day with a view to the ultimate object, the division of property among working people, but the people they called to their assistance under the circumstances of the times, and the general agitation caused by the Reform Bills, at once converted it into a Political Union, leaving the proceedings of working men's trade unions as a secondary object, the main purpose being political, the trade portion incidental . . .

The NUWC which replaced the original union was avowedly political.

Owen's communitarianism was replaced by more socialistic dreams; industrial action on traditional lines was dropped for heady talk of William Benbow's Grand National Holiday;[6] and the Union's journal, the *Poor Man's Guardian*, under the editorship of the militant O'Brien, was not reluctant to threaten violence.

Behind the militancy of the NUWC lay a bitter disappointment with the results of reform in 1832. A feeling of class antagonism consequently developed. 'The present Parliament *has* done nothing for us; it *will* do nothing for us; it never *was intended* to do anything for us!' declared the *Guardian*: 'The "Reform" Bill took care of that. That Bill originated in fraud—was carried through by conspiracy—and unless the people bestir themselves, will terminate in a military despotism.' From the Rotunda headquarters the Union sent 'missionaries' around England to establish branches and to spread Lovett's message that 'every man of the age of 21 years, of sound mind and not tainted by crime, has a right, either by himself or his representative, to a free voice in determining the nature of the laws, the necessity for public contributions, the appropriation of them, their amount, mode of assessment and duration [and] that in order to secure the unbiassed choice of proper persons for representatives, the mode of voting should be *by ballot*, that intellectual fitness and moral worth, and *not property*, should be the qualifications for representatives, and that the duration of Parliament should be but for *one year*'.[7] In the NUWC, despite its divisions and eccentricities—and its bitter split following a police raid on its rally in Coldbath Fields in May 1833—many future Chartist arguments gestated.[8]

Successive disappointments never dismayed the little coteries of London artisan radicals. Their 'National Union' gradually died, but by 1836 they were organising the Association of Working Men to procure a cheap and honest press, which supported the battle against the 'taxes on knowledge' and which was dissolved when the newspaper duty was cut in May. But for all their 'class-conscious' talk, the artisans continued to maintain many bourgeois contacts. The Association of 1836, for instance, owed much to Place and the Kentuckian Dr James Roberts Black, who had organised financial assistance for prosecuted editors from April 1835. It was such men who appear to have ensured 'the removal' (as Place put it) 'of some of the absurd notions which had been sedulously inculcated by men who ought to have known better, respecting the holding of property'.[9] Certainly, the 'socialism' of the NUWC was dropped by many of its former leaders. After early failures, Dr Black seems to have exercised increasing influence. Neither he nor his radical friends could be entirely satisfied with the reduction of the stamp duty. A further cut was, however, unlikely to be granted; and a wider political movement had traditional attractions. 'We had collected together a goodly number of active and influential working men,' recalled Lovett,

> persons who had principally done the work of our late [press] committee; and the question arose among us, whether we could form and maintain a union formed exclusively of this class and of such men.

Early Chartist writers and later historians tended to take the claims of the resulting London Working Men's Association at face value. It is, however, certain that the influence of Place and the almost forgotten Dr Black was seminal. Lovett regretted that[10]

> the working classes had not hitherto evinced that discrimination and independent spirit in the management of their political affairs which we were desirous to see . . . They were always looking up to leadership of one description or other.

Perhaps as a consequence, Dr Black's role was minimised. And ultimately the story of the foundation of Chartism was distorted: London artisans, in fact, continued to 'look up to leadership'.

The continuity of London artisan radicalism is clear. Of the twenty-eight signatories to the address of the 'Press' Association of March, 1836, nineteen—Henry Ainsworth, C. H. Baker, Charles Cole, Richard Gray, John Gast, George Glashan, Robert Hartwell, William Lovett, James Martin, D. McDonnell, Richard Moore, Anthony Morton, R. Potts, Robert Raven, John Roberts, J. Robinson, John Rogers, A. Sparks and James Sturgess—were among the thirty-three who signed the prospectus of the LWMA. The Association, formed on 16 June, also enrolled Cleave, Hetherington and Watson. Its *Address* to 'Fellow Labourers in the pursuit of knowledge and liberty' was literate, liberal and (by future standards) scarcely revolutionary. It found 'pleasing evidence of the progressive knowledge of [the] great principles of democracy' in provincial support. It 'respectfully cautioned [its] brethren . . . strictly to adhere to a judicious selection of their members—on this more than on any other of their exertions harmony and success would depend.'

The artisans' developing concern to denounce any revolutionary intent was made explicit by regular appeals for varied 'moderations':

Let us, friends, seek to make the principles of democracy as respectable in practice as they are just in theory, by excluding the drunken and immoral from our ranks, and in uniting in close compact with the honest, sober, moral, and thinking portion of our brethren . . . These few will be more efficient for the political and social emancipation of mankind than an indiscriminate union of thousands, where the veteran drunkard contaminates by his example, and the profligate railer at abuses saps by his private conduct the cause he has espoused. In forming Working Men's Associations, we seek not a mere exhibition of numbers unless, indeed, they possess the attributes and character of *men*! . . . Fellow-countrymen, *when we contend for an equality of political rights*, it is not in order to lop off an unjust tax or useless pension, or to get a transfer of wealth, power, or influence, for a party; *but to be able to probe our social evils to their source, and to apply effective remedies to prevent, instead of unjust laws to punish.* We shall meet with obstacles, disappointments, and it may be with persecutions, in our pursuit; but with our united exertions and perseverance, we must and will succeed.

Public houses would not be hired for meetings—'habits and associations were too often formed at those places which marred the domestic happiness and destroyed the political usefulness of the millions'. The sober Londoners planned a network of peaceful, respectable study groups:

Let us, then in the absence of means to hire a better place of meeting—meet at each others' houses. Let us be punctual in our attendance, as best contributing to our union and improvement; and, as an essential requisite, seek to obtain a select library of books, choosing those at first which will best inform of our political and social rights. Let us blend, as far as our means will enable us, study with recreation, and share in any rational amusement (unassociated with the means of intoxication) calculated to soothe our anxieties and alleviate our toils.

And, as our object is universal, so (consistent with justice) ought to be our means to compass it; and we know not of any means more efficient, than to enlist the sympathies and quicken the intellects of our wives and children to a knowledge of their rights and duties . . . Thus instructed your wives will spurn instead of promoting you to accept, the base election bribe—your sons will scorn to wear the livery of tyrants—and your daughters be doubly fortified against the thousand ills to which the children of poverty are exposed.

Before 'the honest, sober and reflecting portion of every town and village in the kingdom linked together as a band of brothers', the 'exclusive and demoralising influence' of 'a corrupt Government', 'a vicious aristocracy', the 'gambling influence of money', judicial corruption, politicians' 'empty-headed importance', 'money—getting hypocrisy in the pulpit' and 'debauchery, fanaticism, poverty and crime' would crumble.

The type of workers' educational association proposed by the little group of metropolitan artisans would 'draw into one band of *unity* the *intelligent* portion of the working classes in town and country'. It would 'seek by every legal means to place all classes of society in possession of their equal political and social rights'. It would campaign for 'a *cheap and honest press*', 'promote . . . the education of the rising generation' and

> collect every kind of information appertaining to the interests of the working classes in particular and society in general, especially statistics regarding the wages of labour, the habits and condition of the labourer, and all those causes that mainly contribute to the present state of things.

It would also publish its 'views and sentiments . . . to create a moral, reflecting, yet energetic public opinion; so as eventually to lead to a gradual improvement in the condition of the working classes, without violence or commotion'. All the pre-Smilesian self-help, the libraries 'of reference and useful information' and the 'rational', earnest debates would be 'actuated by one great motive—that of benefiting politically, socially, and morally, the useful classes'. But, while Chartism's founding-fathers recognised a problem which was to intrigue historians and sociologists over a century later, they evaded it. 'Though the persons forming this Association will be at all times disposed to co-operate with all those who seek to promote the happiness of the multitude,' they wrote,[11]

> yet being convinced from experience that the division of interests in the various classes, in the present state of things, is too often destructive of that union of sentiment which is essential to the prosecution of any great object, they have resolved to confine their members as far as practicable to the working classes. But as there are great differences of opinion as to where the line should

be drawn which separates the working classes from the other portions of society, they leave to the Members themselves to determine whether the candidate proposed is eligible to become a Member.

That the semantics of proletarian definition should escape precision is scarcely surprising.

The character of metropolitan Chartism was largely delineated by the founders of the LWMA. Artisans predominated—if not the top ranks of compositors, shipwrights, bookbinders and watchmakers, at least middling men like tailors, cabinet-makers, shoemakers and the like. The London poor—the labourers of all sorts and the ruined silk weavers of Spitalfields—had little contact with radicalism or with Chartism. Poverty was not a spur to political activity; rather, in London, it acted as a deterrent to men ashamed (in Richard Gray's words) of 'that want of Sufficient clothing particular [ly] those that have seen Better Days'. London was still a warren of localities with localised traditions and loyalties; its classes and groups were divided both economically and geographically.[12] The poor, in general, kept aloof from the activities of their 'betters' among the working classes of a still largely pre-factory London. Indeed, 'the silk-weavers of Spitalfields', reported the Whiggish *Morning Chronicle*,[13]

feel much indignation at being unjustly associated with the Chartists; and it is found that few, if any, of the weavers have joined them and that [the Chartists] are composed principally of shoemakers, a few tailors, and carpenters . . .

When the Spitalfields men did try to organise to improve their wretched state it was under the patronage of Oastler and the 'Young England' Tories, just as over-worked shopworkers and bakers united with Lord Ashley's support.

The LWMA remained small and select. From the 'few friends' to whom Lovett 'brought forward a rough sketch of a prospectus' on 9 June the band grew to 33 a week later, and 100 a year later; in three years only 279 members, together with about three dozen honorary members, were elected. But this 'Fabian' group quickly started its researches. One committee drew up the *Address and Rules*; Richard Gray prepared a moving report on his fellow Spitalfields silk workers; another body expressed sympathy for Belgium. Most famous of the reports was the examination of *The Rotten House of Commons*, which became a radical classic. Parliament was dominated by the old and new rich, elected by 839,519 of the country's 6,023,752 male adults—indeed, 331 MPs were elected by only 151,492 voters. Working men faced no benefit from the parliamentary clash between landowners and industrialists, or from the latter's impending victory, 'if the power and empire of the wealthy be established on the wreck of title and privilege'. Past experience showed that 'little have we to expect from any accession to that power, anymore than from the former tyrants . . .'. Under pretending reformers, the people were led 'from year to year through the political quagmire where we are daily beset by plunderers, befooled by knaves, and misled by hypocritical imposters'. The cure lay in radical reform—universal suffrage, the ballot, annual parliaments, equal representation, abolition of Members' property qualifications and a free press.[14]

As it slowly grew, the Association's organisation developed. Lovett became secretary and Hetherington treasurer. Early members included Gast, the compositors Robert Hartwell and Henry Vincent, the woodcarver Richard Moore and, as a sort of patron, Place, at whose house the Association held regular debates on economics from early 1837. Others enrolled as 'honorary members' included O'Brien, Owen, Oastler, Feargus O'Connor, Dr Black, the Unitarian minister W. J. Fox and Dr Arthur Wade (an Anglican priest from Warwick). Now the Association started to plan wider activities. As it did so, however, new rivals appeared.

In January 1837 a rival 'Left' organisation, the East London Democratic Association, issued its prospectus. Its object was

> to promote the Moral and Political conditions of the Working Classes by disseminating the principles propagated by that great philosopher and redeemer of mankind, the Immortal THOMAS PAINE . . . to discuss the principles of cheap and honest Government, and to adopt such means as may seem expedient to carry out the five grand principles of Radical Reform, viz: 'Universal Suffrage, Vote by Ballot, Annual Parliaments, No Property Qualification, and Equal Representation'.

The dominant figures in this new body were the veterans Charles Neesom and Allen Davenport, together with the wild young George Julian Harney. In aim at least, the ELDA intended to be a 'popular' movement: a weekly penny replaced the monthly shilling subscription of the LWMA. But though a more avowedly proletarian body, the ELDA never achieved any vast following.[15]

Meanwhile, a range of other radical groups had developed in various London districts, campaigning on such platforms as reform of parochial government, against Church rates and the Poor Law guardians and for press freedom. From them another succession of organisations emerged. Feargus O'Connor, after sitting as O'Connellite Member for Cork in 1833-5 and breaking with the 'Liberator', now looked for English backing. After a disastrous attempt to succeed Cobbett at Oldham—with a policy of universal suffrage, annual parliaments, the ballot, free trade, adjustment of the Debt and Church disestablishment—he moved to London.[16] After initial contacts with Lovett's artisans, in September 1835 O'Connor and a militant Irish group formed the Marylebone Radical Association. When O'Connor toured Northern England in December it was as 'delegate from the Great Radical Association', (the MRA's successor) founded by Wade, the coal merchant Thomas Murphy and Thomas Cleary in John Savage's public house, with 'true radical principles, namely annual parliaments, universal suffrage, vote by ballot, equal representation, and no property qualifications for members of parliament'.[17] After much energetic oratory and a threat to contest Glasgow, O'Connor returned to London convinced of his importance as a radical leader. But he returned to the London of the 'Honest Press Association'—and to the final break with O'Connell, the 'turncoat' and 'dictator'. From this time O'Connor saw himself as a British radical leader with a mission to unite the English proletariat with the Irish peasantry. As a reforming Irish squireen, he fancied that he could organise such an alliance.

As O'Connor mulled over the ingratitude of the LWMA, Lovett's group was approached by the Cambridgeshire Farmers' Association, under an eccentric Fellow of King's, James Bernard. The farmers voiced traditional agricultural complaints, demanding either Attwood-type currency alterations or a cut in their industry's taxation. The LWMA, opposed to any price increases, was not disposed to travel far with the Tory farmers, beyond advocating the need for political agitation. Bernard, however, sought bigger things than taking orders from a group of artisans. In 1837 he moved to London to join O'Connor and others in a new radicalism with 'Oastlerite' undertones; John Bell, who had owned the *True Sun*, now made his *London Mercury* their mouthpiece, with O'Brien as editor. Bernard's Central National Association of March undoubtedly gained support from many metropolitan slum-dwellers and ultra-radicals. Its programme combined universal suffrage and currency reform with such Northern interests as the repeal of the Poor Law, protection and reduction of working hours. The CNA's great cross, however, lay with the curious egoism of its leader.[18] It collapsed in September.

On 10 June 1836, half a dozen people claiming to be the 'central committee of the Metropolitan Radical Unions', had founded the Working Men's Universal Suffrage Club, with a subscription of £1 annually and 5s (25p) entry fee. Although these fees were reduced by half for working men, the WMUSC perpetuated the continuing tradition of allegedly working-class organisations embarrassingly short of working-class members. The Club soon disappeared, despite (or because of) a *nihil obstat* from O'Connell, the enthusiasm of the crazy Augustus Hardin Beaumont (editor of *The Radical*) and the refusal of an *imprimatur* by Place. But O'Connor made the mistake of being made treasurer.[19] Henceforth, he sought more real working-class support. Harney's Democrats appeared to be useful allies in the fight against the LWMA, those 'tools of the Whigs' as the *Mercury* described them. The attacks were often unfair and exaggerated; despite Place's long efforts to inculcate 'Malthusian' ideas among artisan leaders the extent of their liberalism is still doubtful. Furthermore the 'Paineite' ELDA proved to be of little help, and Hetherington's *London Dispatch* soon dispatched Bernard's CNA, which disappeared without trace. A London in which, despite the existence of various ultra-radical organisations (usually minute, however grandiosely titled), the LWMA was clearly most important, did not suit O'Connor; again, he turned to the North.

Meanwhile, the LWMA's own campaign had started. On 28 February an enthusiastic meeting was held in the Crown and Anchor, attended (according to O'Brien) by 'four thousand democrats, at least'. It was resolved to petition for the 'five cardinal points of Radicalism'—universal suffrage (male and female), equal representation, annual parliaments, vote by ballot and abolition of Members' property qualifications. 'The whole proceedings were originated, conducted, and concluded by working men', asserted the delighted O'Brien. Certainly, the Association's leaders—Hartwell, Lovett, Vincent, Hoare, Moore—made the most of the event. O'Brien thought that the petition would 'supply excellent material for similar petitions all over the country'. Lovett looked back on it as the 'nucleus of the far-famed *People's Charter*, which may be said to have had its origin at this meeting'.[20]

III

Birmingham was a unique town, at the centre of a vital industrial complex. Matthew Boulton and James Watt had made it an important engineering centre, as their Soho works made the world's steam engines. Its intellectuals and engineers combined to form the celebrated Lunar Society. But 'class' differences were muted in a town of generally small workshops, where small masters and aspiring journeymen worked and lived side by side. Consequently, it was possible in Birmingham to 'harmonise and unite' radical strands which were separated elsewhere; workers and masters could join to 'collect and organise the moral power of the country for the restoration of the people's rights ... and to bring all to unite in one common bond of union together', in the BPU of 1830. 'Harmony between masters and men' was the motif in dissenting, small workshop dominated Birmingham, where chapel morality, personal social aspirations, the need to acquire a 'respectable' image and the close personal relationships between master and man were traditional. The beneficiary and leader of this set of attitudes was Thomas Attwood, with his Tory background and sympathies, who gradually moved from alliance with the ultra-Tory Lord Blandford to leadership of a kind of *petit-bourgeois* radicalism.[21]

Often rather tenuous links had been maintained with the London radicals. When Hetherington carried the NUWC's message to Birmingham in October 1832 he was supported by Dr Wade, the huge Warwick clergyman, and others who distrusted Attwood and the BPU.[22] But the mammoth Union would have nothing to do with class antagonisms; from its foundation in December 1829 it had attempted to unite 'the Lower and Middle Classes of the People'. The interests of employers and workers were the same, to Attwood and his associates. 'If the masters flourish,' Attwood declared during the first reform election,

> the men are certain to flourish with them; and if the masters suffer difficulties, their difficulties must shortly affect the workmen in a threefold degree. The masters therefore ought to take their workmen by the hand and knock at the gates of government and demand the redress of their common grievances.

To the theme of class collaboration Attwood added currency reform

—that House-emptying theme which he also advanced at West-minster. Attwood's universal cure of paper money had its attractions for anti-aristocratic small masters, merchants and semi-domestic journeymen. Joshua Scholefield, Attwood's fellow-MP for Birmingham, was an early ally; and he was followed by the town's radical 'establishment'. The Attwoodites were led by John Collins, a Christian shoemaker, R. K. Douglas (editor of the *Birmingham Journal*), George Edmonds (clerk to the magistrates and a Poor Law guardian), Benjamin Hadley (alderman and churchwarden), the manufacturers George and P. H. Muntz, the lamp manufacturer T. C. Salt and their kind. Significantly, they did not enlist Attwood's own brothers, Charles (a Northumbrian Tory-radical) and Matthias (Tory MP and banker).

The original BPU was dissolved in 1834, probably (as Mark Hovell suggested) to await 'the fruits of their labours in the form of measure of social reform' and to take 'full advantage of the trade boom of 1832-6'.[23] But the Union was as disappointed with the results of the 1832 Act as any London group; and while it shared metropolitan inability to share (or even comprehend) Northern rage over the 1833 Factory Act and gave a platform to O'Connell, the enemy of trade unionism, it left a tradition of local radicalism. Birmingham radicals, accustomed to Whiggish alliances, were generally slow to co-operate with the London agitators. Through the years of comparative prosperity they were quiet. A Reform Association was founded in September 1836, but Attwood restrained demands for a revival of the BPU. 'Mr Cobbett', he declared, in November,

> used to say 'I defy you to agitate a fellow with a full stomach'.
> Nothing is more true. Men do not generally act from abstract
> principles, but from deep and unrewarded wrongs, injuries and
> sufferings.

But he forecast that the next industrial depression would make further reform 'a much quicker and easier operation'.

The depression arrived in Birmingham, as in the North, during the early months of 1837. Again masters and operatives worked together, petitioning for government help and canvassing for a re-formation of the Political Union. The time was undoubtedly ripe, and a series of district meetings culminated in the formation of a new BPU on 23 May, with 5,000 members. Within days a public address solicited support for a campaign to alleviate the consequences of the industrial recession. And on 19 June the revived Union held a great

rally on Newhall Hill to determine its policy. To Attwood's panacea
of currency reform was now added the demand for household suffrage, the ballot, triennial parliaments, payment of MPs and the
abolition of MPs property qualifications. This radical programme
appealed to Salt and many workmen but was less attractive to strict
Attwoodite currency reformers. However, the gathering depression
led even Attwood to embrace increasingly radical causes. No doubt
the alleged 50,000 crowd at the June rally had a heady influence—
and Attwood remained oblivious to the growing split between his
middle- and working-class supporters later discerned by Mark
Hovell.[24] To the eccentric reformer, every event was a victory for
his notions on the currency, which were regularly propounded to
Viscount Melbourne and the Commons. His re-election at the
General Election of August, a courteous reception by Melbourne
for a delegation of currency fanatics and the spread of BPU branches
all appeared to herald mammoth conversions to the cause. But
'adhesion' to BPU branches, Place sourly commented, 'meant sub-
mission to Mr Attwood and his absurd currency proposal, which
few understood and all who did condemned'.[25] Modern commentators are generally less condemnatory than was Place.

Perhaps Melbourne's rejection of Attwood's currency arguments
at a meeting with a disputatious Birmingham delegation on 2
November, combined with disappointment at the government's
inability to cure the nation's economic malaise, led the BPU to move
Leftwards. On 7 November, despite considerable opposition, P. H.
Muntz carried a resolution in favour of universal suffrage. Lord
John Russell's famous declaration on the 'finality' of the Reform
Act further exacerbated the situation. In July Russell had told the
electors of Stroud that 'the less frequently such a measure as the
Reform Act was discussed the better, and the more stable the law
would become ... he was not for making a change in the great
institutions of the country'. And when the Session opened in
November there was, noted the diarist Greville,[26]

an angry squabble between Lord John Russell and the Radicals, at
which the Tories greatly rejoiced. Upon the Address, Wakley and
others thought fit to introduce the topic of the Ballot and other
reforms, upon which John Russell spoke out and declared he
would never be a party to the Ballot, and would not reform the
Reform Bill. They were indignant, and attacked him in no
measured terms. The next night Charles Buller returned to the

charge with equal violence, when Lord John made (by the agreement of all parties) an incomparable speech vindicating his own consistency . . .

The fact was that Russell had made it clear that in his view the Reform Act was 'final'. Radical MPs instantly inaugurated attacks on 'Finality Jack'. Among the most angry was Attwood. But his was an individual anger. It overflowed at a meeting of the BPU council on 19 December.

Attwood considered that 'if the Queen's speech had been made by the Emperor of China it could not have had less reference to the wants of the British nation'. This was scarcely a unique observation: Peel thought that the speech 'abused the privilege of saying nothing'. But Attwood now attacked liberal radical MPs ('the bitterest enemies of the people') and the middle classes ('choked with pride, jealousy and servility'). 'The masses of the people constituted the only hope of the country' to Attwood: 'they must bring 2,000,000 of men together to stand by them and move legally at the word of command'.[27] The BPU, in fact, now urged working-class militancy. But it never entirely appreciated what passions it had helped to unleash; and when it realised what it had assisted it was dismayed.

IV

Meanwhile, the LWMA had extended its activities. In March Cleave was sent to Brighton and in May Hetherington toured Yorkshire, whither he was soon followed by Cleave and Henry Vincent. Vigorous 'missionary' activities led to the creation of a host of working men's associations modelled on the LWMA. And policy statements were drawn up by the London committees. An *Address to Reformers on the Forthcoming Elections* advocated supporting only candidates pledged to universal suffrage. The Queen was addressed on *Political and Religious Monopoly*. A plan for a secular education system, ascribing many of the woes of contemporary society to ignorance, was drawn up. And in December the *Address to the Reformers of Great Britain and Ireland* summarised the LWMA's aims.

In addition to organising propaganda tours and publications the Association sought wider contacts. Relationship was established with the BPU in June. And an alliance was forged with the sympathetic bourgeois radical group in Parliament. The radical MP's had welcomed the February rally and agreed to explore the chance of parliamentary action on universal suffrage. On 31 May the Members met representatives of the Association to discuss means of implementing the petition. The politicians generally believed, as O'Connell explained, that the Association's proposals were too optimistic and that it would be advisable to proceed by cautious instalments. The LWMA, however, stood firm. At a second meeting on 7 June a committee of six MP's and six 'working men' was set up to prepare a draft Bill for annual parliaments, universal suffrage, equal constituencies, payment of Members and the abolition of property qualifications. J. A. Roebuck was to present the measure, and his colleagues—men like O'Connell, Charles Hindley, Sharman Crawford, Hume and Sir William Molesworth—apparently pledged support.[28]

Work on the 'Bill' proceeded slowly. The radical Members seem to have contributed little—perhaps because of their innate reluctance to allow the LWMA to dominate the reform agitation. Even the principal authorship of the famous 'Outline of an Act of Parliament to provide for the Representation of Great Britain' is controversial. O'Connell, Lovett, Roebuck and Place have been suggested as the author. It is certain that the six politician committee-members—O'Connell, Roebuck, Hindley, Sharman Crawford, J. T. Leader and Colonel Perronet Thompson—were of little help. It is equally sure that few of the LWMA representatives—Lovett, Watson, Hetherington, Cleave, Vincent and Moore—had the time or ability to write the Bill unaided. Lovett certainly laid claim to the authorship:

> When I had finished my work I took it to Mr Roebuck, who, when he had read it, suggested that I should show it to Mr Francis Place of Brompton for his opinion, he having taken a great interest in our association from its commencement.

Place gave an entirely different account:

> ... not one of the six Members of Parliament had anything to do with it—nor indeed any one of the six Members of the WMA, Mr Lovett alone excepted, for whom I drew the Charter. It was my MS which he took to Mr Roebuck.

Place's explanation was that Roebuck and the LWMA had been unable to draw up the Bill, and that consequently[38]

> Mr Lovett earnestly intreated me to draw the bill. To this I consented, provided the WMA would discontinue to countenance those who at various meetings *abused* the middle classes, calling them

harsh names, imputing all manner of evil intentions to them, and thus unnecessarily making enemies where they needed friends, and provided that he, Mr Lovett, would bring me a paper stating in exact words what were the points—and how his co-adjutors thought they might be put into language the least offensive to any body, since if any among them thought that any offensive expression was necessary I would not draw the bill. Mr Lovett was, for himself, satisfied, and in a few days afterwards brought me the paper I had requested.

It is impossible to adjudicate on the issue with certainty. The most likely explanation is that Lovett and Place both played leading roles in the production of the proposal. Apportionment of their respective shares is impossible. Arguments designed to demonstrate that the ultimate programme was a purely proletarian production are sentimental time-wasters. The 'Outline' was undoubtedly the work of men of varied 'class' affiliations. Politically partisan, even polemical, assertions too often have coloured accounts of an argument over matters on which sociological investigation is scarcely possible. The 'class' definition of the authors of the 'Outline' is largely a matter of semantics. What is certain is that Place, who defended middle-class 'Malthusian' values and who hated the anti-Poor Law campaigns of Northern Tory-radicals, played a major part in drawing up the major production of the liberal élite of the London artisans, whose claim to represent the metropolitan working classes was in any case challenged by such bodies as the Democratic Association and the Surrey Radical Association.

The LWMA instantly reacted to the BPU's angry assertions of December by issuing the *Address to the Reformers*. And preparation of the 'Outline' was hastened. Lovett and Place presented their work to the twelve-man committee. Roebuck and the LWMA prepared introductory material, and on 8 May 1838 the document was finally published under the title of *The People's Charter*, 'prepared by a Committee of twelve persons, six Members of Parliament and six Members of the London Working Men's Association'. ('This was not true,' declared Place). The 'Charter' now advocated universal male suffrage from the age of twenty-one; 300 electoral districts containing 'as nearly as may be, an equal number of inhabitants'; triennially-elected returning officers; that the sole qualification for candidates' nomination should be a requisition by at least 100 local electors; annual elections every June by secret ballot; and a salary of £500 (an increase of £100 on previous proposals) for Members.[30] Unaided by the (at best) doubtful radicals, the Association now mounted its greatest propaganda campaign.

V

The new militancy of the Birmingham men continued into 1838. The Political Union envisaged a mammoth and threatening mass organisation which, while employing only peaceful methods, would threaten the government with a complete breakdown of law and order. Its principal method would be a national petition backed by thousands—or, as optimism grew, millions of signatures.[31] The rising success of the LWMA encouraged the BPU's hopes, while experience led to an apparently full-blooded radicalism. Douglas was given the task of preparing the petition and gradually contrived to amalgamate a variety of demands—universal suffrage, annual parliaments, the repeal of the Corn Laws, the ballot and currency reform. Through the early months of 1838 'missionaries' roused the Midlands, and in March it was resolved to send Collins to Glasgow as part of the 'holy and peaceful pilgrimage'. Thus by the spring both the LWMA and the BPU were planning national campaigns. Working men's associations and political unions, at least ostensibly modelled on the London and Birmingham founders, developed in many areas to propound the virtues of the Charter and the petition. Throughout the nation the greatest of British working-class movements was excitedly developing. And 'Universal Suffrage', as O'Brien insisted, 'was, after all, the grand test of Radicalism . . . your poverty is the *result*, not the *cause* of your being unrepresented'.[32]

4 *Emergence*

In the heady days of early 1838, as Birmingham reformers hopefully raised the target for signatories to the petition from two to six millions and as London 'missionaries' founded some hundred and fifty working men's associations, many regional campaigns developed. The local varieties of reform agitation continued and expanded. Working-class radicalism remained a multi-coloured thing in the early railway age, still shaped by local political, economic and social experiences and relationships and by local personalities, rather than by monolithic metropolitan pressures. Class-consciousness was undoubtedly spreading, but the chimera of proletarian unity remained as elusive as ever. For one thing, well-established localised agitations —Oastler's and Stephens's increasingly violent factory and Poor Law campaign in Yorkshire and Lancashire; the gathering religious controversy in Scotland associated with Dr Thomas Chalmers's economic liberalism and anti-'erastianism'; the currency theories of the Birmingham leaders; the educational campaigns of the London *petit-bourgeoisie*; the very different demands of, for instance, the miners of Durham and South Wales; the ancient radicalism of religiously-dissenting East Anglia—continued. For another, 'missionaries' often stamped their personalities on particular districts in ways not always intended by their employers. Little 25-year-old Henry Vincent,[1]

> with a fine mellow flexible voice, a florid complexion, and excepting in intervals of passion, a most winning expression . . . had only to present himself to win all hearts to his side. His attitude was perhaps the most easy and graceful of any popular orator of the time . . . With the fair sex his slight handsome figure, the merry twinkle of his eye, his incomparable mimicry, his passionate bursts of enthusiasm, the rich music of his voice, and above all, his

appeals for the elevation of woman, rendered him a universal favourite, and the Democrats of both sexes regarded him as the young Demosthenes of English Democracy ... [But] Vincent had every capacity for exciting the multitude; to give stability to their awakened minds was a very different thing, and this power the graceful orator did not possess. With a man of his stamp it was no difficult matter to rouse every passion into active life, but to form and mature the judgement did not lie within his power, and we must candidly acquit him of any attempt to accomplish this ... Among the Welsh his fervid declamation awakened every sympathy of the heart. His thrilling tones as he depicted the burning wrongs of the toiling class fanned the passions of that excitable people into a flame which no after prudence could allay.

The LWMA's apostle to the West scarcely represented the sober élite of London artisans. Nor did John Collins, the moderate artisan who spoke for the BPU in Scotland, entirely represent the now militant Midland radicals. Still less did some new varieties of radicalism fit easily with the initial moderation of Chartism's founding fathers, as Birmingham discussed whether to enforce its demands by Salt's plan to abstain from taxable articles or by P. H. Muntz's scheme for a delegate conference and strikes.

I

During 1837, disgruntled with the LWMA and disappointed by the failure of the Central National Association, O'Connor returned to the North. Here the Tory-radicals under Oastler, Stephens and Fielden were reaching the peak of their campaign against the New Poor Law. The tense atmosphere of the massed torch-lit rallies, the threatening bitterness of the oratory and the excitement of the mob attacks on assistant commissioners instantly appealed to the Irish demagogue. He had sampled the Northern agitation on 14 January, when he spoke in riotous Huddersfield. Oastler welcomed a new anti-O'Connellite ally in the Poor Law struggle:

I am proud to find that a Tory and a Radical can yet meet together, to advocate the Christian and natural rights of poverty and Labour ... I do feel proud to stand by that Radical Patriot who is banished from his native land by the most rapacious beggar that ever stole a potato from a starving Irish pauper.

Supported by Oastler's warm commendation, O'Connor further extended his popularity in the Northern textile districts. Finding that the dominant motif of Yorkshire and Lancashire radicalism was hostility to the Poor Law, O'Connor became an anti-Poor Law agitator. Indeed, as audiences' enthusiasm rose, O'Connor's involvement grew. By December he was insisting—entirely wrongly—at a Dewsbury rally that he had 'voted against every clause of the measure'. On 15 May he was a speaker at the huge Hartshead Moor rally, when West Riding workers first demonstrated the mammoth nature of their agitation.[2] Here was the mass following for which O'Connor hankered; but it was led by the Tory democrats. O'Connor consequently must broaden the base of his operations. In July he contested Preston at the election following William IV's death, winning the show of hands; and in November he made the almost obligatory radical trip to Scotland to 'support' the cotton spinners' leaders with some violent oratory.[3] Above all, in November, after long planning, he became a newspaper proprietor.

The idea of a new Northern radical journal seems to have been born at a meeting in Barnsley in January, when its value was stressed by William Hill, a radical Swedenborgian minister from Hull. O'Connor's biographers have suggested that the principal attraction to the demagogue was the opportunity to make himself independent of Oastler and Stephens. Hill had intended to publish the journal in his native 'Black Barnsley', a town of militant miners and weavers. But O'Connor preferred to operate from Leeds, the 'capital' of the West Riding. At the Hartshead Moor rally he approached Oastler's colleague Joshua Hobson, now a Leeds radical printer, about the publication. The problem of capital was solved by appealing for public subscriptions, and some £690 was raised, mainly from Leeds, Halifax, Bradford, Huddersfield and Hull. Shareholders were guaranteed 10 per cent interest by O'Connor but were denied any control: the proprietor was 'Feargus O'Connor, Esq., of Hammersmith, County Middlesex'. Indeed, from the start, the risk belonged to Hobson and the Yorkshire radicals and the profits to O'Connor; the work devolved on Hobson as printer and Hill as editor (at £2 a week) and the glory on O'Connor—who frankly admitted his purpose:

The power of the press is acknowledged upon all hands, and rather than oppose it, I have preferred to arm myself with it.

The weekly paper, destined to become the most popular of all radical journals, was launched on 18 November, incorporating the title of a suppressed Belfast journal with which O'Connor's republican and pro-French uncle Arthur had been associated in the 1790s. *The Northern Star and Leeds General Advertiser* cost 4½d and paid the stamp duty; its editor and printer, significantly, were both former weavers. From now onwards O'Connor gradually became a leader in his own right; and events conspired to enhance his power over the established leaders of the textile districts. *The Northern Star* became the mouthpiece of proletarian radicalism—and of its proprietor.

The West Riding communities in which O'Connor became a folk-hero had a long tradition of radicalism and agitation—a tradition best exploited since 1831 by Oastler. Since 1819 the principles of 'radical reform' had periodically been announced in the woollen centre of Leeds, often in alliance with the liberal-Whig Edward Baines of the *Leeds Mercury*. The Whig-radical alliance became increasingly strained during the controversies over the Reform and Factory Bills; and William Rider's Radical Political Union of November 1831 marked a working-class break with bourgeois reformers. The Radical Association of 1835 demanded universal suffrage, the ballot, equal constituencies, annual parliaments and abolition of property qualifications.[5] Leeds was thus fertile ground for the LWMA 'missionaries' Cleave and Vincent, who addressed a Woodhouse Moor rally in August 1837, which led to the formation of a Leeds WMA under such men as the factory reformers Rider and Hobson, the radical journalist Robert Nicoll of the *Leeds Times*, the Owenites John Francis Bray (an American-born printer) and David Green (a bookseller) and the militant Irish wool comber George White. But it was easier to establish an Association than to agree on a policy; the varied radical creeds of the founder-members mirrored the divisions among Leeds reformers and workers. As O'Connor's influence grew and the *Star* replaced the *Times* as the principal local radical journal, the 'moderate' radicals disappeared. O'Connor inevitably disapproved of the LWMA and all its works and in June 1838, at a rally on Hunslet Moor, he helped to replace the Leeds WMA with a Great Northern Union, backed by Rider, White and even Collins.[6] The GNU frankly avowed that 'physical force shall be resorted to if necessary'.

Bradford, the capital of the worsted trade, was a rougher, more militant place than a Leeds only recently 'rescued' from the genteel control of Tory merchants by a liberal manufacturing fraternity. Bradford was newer and brasher; and though its manufacturing entrepreneurs included many Anglican Tories its life was much less sedate. Here the traditions of Tester's great rearguard strike of combers and weavers in 1825 were still remembered; thousands of impoverished weavers still lived in local townships. Here the factory movement had begun and established its headquarters when Leeds proved half-hearted. And here was a centre of fierce resistance to the Poor Law, of Owenite unionism, of Political Union activity. Politically, the expanding and increasingly dirty town was dominated by a group characterised by Oastler in 1834 as

> *those Sleek, Pious, Holy and Devout Dissenters, Messrs Get-all, Keep-all, Grasp-all, Scrape-all, Whip-all, Gull-all, Cheat-all, Cant-all, Work-all, Sneak-all, Lie-Well, Swear-Well and Company, the Shareholders in the Bradford Observer.*

It was against this background that Bradford workers came to reject the remnants of Whiggish alliances. An Association of the Working Classes was established by the violent Peter Bussey—successively cabinet-maker, comber, weavers' organiser, Owenite 'Regeneration-ist' and publican—early in 1835, and a year later Bussey was a leading light in the O'Connorite Bradford Radical Association, which participated in the local fight against the Poor Law. But, despite a visit from Stephens in June 1838—with talk of resisting the Act 'even if it be at the peril of your lives'—Bradford radicalism was weakened by divided loyalties: there were agitations for the Canadian rebels, the Glasgow spinners, Owenite socialism and Bussey's attacks on soldiers as 'mere breathing automatons' of the 'ruling few'. Radical strength revived in September, when Vincent addressed some 3,000 people. The Charter and petition were adopted and the O'Connorite Bradford Northern Union was established, amid militant talk.[7] Within months a network of committees was established in the out-townships.

Halifax, Bradford's rival as a worsted centre, was largely dominated by the great liberal entrepreneurial line of Akroyds—an almost archetypal dynasty of free traders and opponents of factory legislation. Here Oastler had had less success than in most other Yorkshire textile towns, though by 1832 he had established a sizeable agitation in the huge parish. Many of his local supporters in the factory reform cause—men like Robert Wilkinson and Benjamin Rushton—became active Chartists. On 22 January 1838 a rally petitioned Parliament both for the 'five points' and against the Poor Law. 'Instead of being based upon intellect,' declared the Methodist

Abraham Hanson, 'the [electoral] qualification was based upon pounds, shillings and pence'. And Rushton, who 'had now been a common labourer 33 years', asserted that 'after having toiled 50 or 60 years, he had the consolation of knowing that he might retire into a bastille and finish his existence upon fifteen pence halfpenny a week'.[8] Halifax subsequently became a Chartist stronghold.

It was from the textile towns of the West Riding and the weaving villages between them that O'Connor's strength arose. The thousands who assembled for the great county rallies and the handfuls who gathered in Pennine hamlets alike knew that the *Northern Star* would regularly report their activities. Through the *Star* a bond of affection and loyalty grew between the Yorkshire workers and the Irish adventurer. Increasingly, the egoistic, blustering demagogue became the hero of the ever-expanding radical organisations of northern England. From now onwards the 'aristocratic' Feargus was able to command almost fanatical devotion among Yorkshire and Lancashire working people.

II

Glasgow, the metropolis of industrial Clydeside, with its coal, iron, shipbuilding and textile industries, was a growing city in the 1830s. Already the native labour force was being augmented by streams of Highlanders and Irish; and already terrible housing conditions were widely prevalent. 'I did not believe', reported J. C. Symons in 1839,

> until I visited the wynds of Glasgow, that so large an amount of filth, crime, misery, and disease existed on any one spot in any civilised country.

This view was reaffirmed by Chadwick in 1842:[9]

> The most wretched of the stationary population of which I have been able to obtain any account, or that I have ever seen, was that which I saw . . . in the wynds of Edinburgh and Glasgow.

Among an ill-housed and ill-paid population subject to cataclysmic economic and industrial cycles and regular horrifying epidemics there was inevitably a rising swell of discontent. Since the first great post-war rally at Thrushgrove in 1816 radicalism had periodically revived. In 1817, after extensive investigations by the Lord Advocate's agents Alexander Richmond and George Biggar, an abortive prosecution was inaugurated against the weavers' leaders. In 1819

Glasgow radicals produced *The Spirit of the Union* newspaper, whose editor, Gilbert McLeod, was transported. And in 1820, after the abortive 'Radical War' revolutionary activity was sternly repressed.

During the early 1830s a new radicalism evolved in Glasgow. It was moderate, liberal and temperate, devoted to the causes embraced by Joseph Hume of Montrose. Its voice was the unstamped *Herald to the Trades Advocate*, first published in September 1830. Its importance lay in its combination of bourgeois liberal interests and trade unionism. When the *Herald* was suppressed after eight months, the unions—led by Alexander Campbell, John Tait, Daniel McAulay and George Rodger—issued their *Trades Advocate*. The trades firmly supported reform at vast rallies on Glasgow Green in September 1831 and May 1832. But from 1833 disillusion set in with the Whigs —over reform, Ireland, the Corn Laws, trade unionism and local government. The *Advocate's* successor, John Tait's *Liberator*, from November 1832 mounted a militant radical-unionist campaign for a wider suffrage and factory reform, and Glasgow workers under Abram Duncan regularly demanded the vote. An uneasy alliance of reformers could be re-formed to oppose Wellington and Peel in 1834, to organise huge rallies for Lord Durham in October 1834 and O'Connell in September 1835 and (under Peter Mackenzie, editor of the bourgeois *Loyal Reformers' Gazette* of 1831) to keep alive the cause of the 'Scottish Martyrs' and 'expose' the alleged spying activities of Richmond, a former weaver who was now a parliamentary agent. Mackenzie helped to revive the Political Union early in 1834, supported repeal of the Corn Laws and condemned Owenism, unions, the *Liberator* and Richmond. He seemed to be vindicated when Richmond was non-suited in a libel action against the agents for *Tait's Edinburgh Magazine*, which had reviewed Mackenzie's 'exposure'.[10] But the Whig alliance foundered in February 1836 when Lord William Cavendish-Bentinck was elected at a by-election, despite the opposition of the GPU. O'Connor, with his friend Dr John Taylor (editor of the *Liberator* from October), encouraged the breach during his December tour. The result was the formation of the Scottish Radical Association, demanding universal suffrage, annual parliaments, the ballot and religious voluntaryism.

It was against this background that the most notable local event occurred. In January 1837 radical workers founded a trades committee largely to counter the Operative Conservatives Association of December 1836. Within months it was facing a fearful industrial depression, and by early summer sudden wage cuts provoked a series of vicious strikes. The authorities, led by Sir Archibald Alison, the redoubtable Sheriff of Lanarkshire, reacted by arresting eighteen officers of the Operative Cotton Spinners Union in July. Alison could point to a record of union violence, intimidation, vitriol-throwing, arson and possible murder. The union inevitably denied the charges and was backed by other trades and Taylor's radicals. There was a strong suspicion that Glasgow 'martyrs' were to follow those of Tolpuddle, on trumped-up charges; and O'Connell, the radical scourge of trade unions, rapidly fell from working-class favour. Through the autumn and winter a wide campaign was launched in support of the spinners' leaders—though the violence of the speeches was scarcely calculated to arouse bourgeois sympathies. In Glasgow Beaumont crazily talked of civil war 'with the aristocracy, that we might show how ready we are to shed our blood', while Stephens told workers that if the factory system were not reformed 'we shall warp in one awful sheet of devouring flame, which no arm can resist, the manufactories of the cotton tyrants'. At Leeds Dr Taylor maintained that 'the time for physical force had arrived .. It was high time to lay down the spade and take up the sword'; and at Manchester Oastler 'unfurled the royal banner of innocence—the standard of the Ten Hours Bill [against] . . . the bloody Whigs'.[11]

The trial of five spinners' leaders at Edinburgh in January 1838 did not go according to plan: the major charges were dropped, despite considerable evidence to support them. The trial itself nevertheless aroused violent hostility and the sentences of seven years' transportation were received with horror. Again, 'the base, bloody and brutal Whigs' were blamed. And again the alliance with Whigs and liberals was weakened.[12]

Through the early months of 1838 Collins reported great successes in Scotland, aided by such radicals as James Turner of Thrushgrove, James Moir of Glasgow, Bailie Hugh Craig of Kilmarnock and John Fraser of Edinburgh. Only Mackenzie sounded a sour note, attacking the violent spinners and alleging Tory influence behind the cry for universal suffrage. Eventually, after considerable planning by West of Scotland workers, Alexander Purdie, secretary of the Central Committee, was authorised in April to invite the BPU leaders to a Grand Demonstration, promising 'a larger assemblage than ever congregated on the Green of Glasgow for a similar purpose'. Attwood accepted the invitation on 5 May, in typical fashion. 'It is of high importance', he wrote,[13] that this meeting should be a day memorable in the history of Scotland and of England. We come to you with no base pride to gratify; but we come as the representatives of millions of our countrymen, determined to unite the great work of restoring the prosperity and vindicating the liberty of our country—our long oppressed, misgoverned and exasperated country. It is this great and holy cause, therefore, which we shall represent; and in our humble persons I doubt not that the men of Glasgow will take care that this glorious cause shall be gloriously vindicated.

Remember PEACE, LAW, ORDER, LOYALTY AND UNION, these are our Mottoes—under these banners we will gather the strength of the people—under these banners the people possess a giant's strength; but if they once abandon them, they become but as an infant in a giant's hand.

While Glasgow reformers publicised the great event, the Birmingham men discussed strategy. At a meeting in the town hall on 14 May Douglas's national petition was accepted by the BPU, and the delegation to visit Glasgow—Attwood, Douglas, Edmonds, Hadley, P. H. Muntz, Salt and Scholefield—was selected.

Despite a constant drizzle, the demonstration on 21 May was a great success. The two-mile procession to Glasgow Green included seventy trade unions, forty-three bands, and three hundred banners. A huge concourse—perhaps numbering 200,000—was assembled under the veteran Turner to hear a succession of speakers. Undoubtedly the man of the hour, Attwood made the most of the opportunity. He condemned the Reform Act, pledged Birmingham's support 'in the cause of peace, loyalty and order' and urged support for the petition. They would constantly petition; and if Parliament refused their demands they would finally organise a general strike. They had against them 'the whole of the aristocracy, nine-tenths of the gentry, the great body of the clergy, and all the pensioners, sinecurists and bloodsuckers that fed on the vitals of the people'. As Gammage noted, Attwood 'never seemed to contemplate the greatest obstacle of all, the newly enfranchised middle class'. Indeed, in his anti-revolutionary zeal, Attwood transferred the social structure of Birmingham to the nation at large: 'master and man must unite and compel the Government to give them justice'. Much the same message was delivered by his colleagues and by Murphy and Wade, the LWMA representatives who explained the Charter. 'We have sufficient physical power,' Wade explained, 'but that is not necessary, for we have sufficient moral power to gain all we ask.' The rally was followed by a banquet for 600 and next day Attwood visited Paisley, while his followers toured Edinburgh, Dundee and other towns.

The first great rally at which both the petition and the Charter had been presented was undoubtedly a success for the BPU; the LWMA representatives were cast in the shade. During the following weeks the petition was warmly received in many Scottish burghs by a wide range of Scottish radicals. But the Glasgow rally had set the tone for the new Scottish radicalism: with a few exceptions, the middle-class reformers kept aloof from a predominantly proletarian movement. One exception was Dr Taylor, who was, however, hostile to the moderate Birmingham-oriented leadership. His *New Liberator* had failed in May, but a month later the energetic democrat was establishing a new Republican Club on the very day of the coronation. In July he was joined by O'Connor in a Scottish tour to prevent control of the re-awakened Scottish movement from falling to Birmingham or even London. O'Connor and Taylor expressed agreement with the currently popular Attwood. They professed their anxiety to maintain radical unity. But they developed an undertone of threatened violence. They were semantically careful; but the general impression they gave was that physical force should never be ruled out, as a last resort.[1] In religious Scotland the underlying appeal to violence was not effective; Attwoodite influence for long remained dominant. The Glasgow reformers preferred the tea merchant Moir and Purdie to O'Connor as their representatives at the planned Birmingham rally of August. In the summer of 1838 there were, therefore, still many varieties of Scottish radicalism. There were men who shared Mackenzie's view that it was 'extremely unwise even to moot the question of universal suffrage' in current circumstances. There were men who considered that religious reform and temperance were the most important issues. There were those whose radical priority was free trade. And among those who adopted the universal suffrage platform there was a division between strictly 'moral force' Attwoodites, earnest advocates of London's charter and devotees of O'Connor's rumbustious all-embracing radicalism. So far, the Birmingham men were in the ascendant.

III

Radical interest and organisation varied widely in the summer of 1838. In Scotland the veteran John Fraser (once a Johnstone teacher and now an Edinburgh radical journalist) and Abram Duncan (a Glasgow trades leader) carried to the countryside the message of the petition—and of teetotalism. They uncovered a generally moderate radicalism. At Edinburgh Fraser ran *The Edinburgh Monthly and Total Abstinence Advocate*, which by October became the weekly *True Scotsman*, the mouthpiece of the radical artisans and tradesmen of the capital. In Paisley, the impoverished centre of handloom weaving, the most notable radical was the Rev. Patrick Brewster of the Abbey Church—free trader, O'Connellite and moral force advocate. At Dundee, the gaunt flax and jute capital, despite periodic discussion of arming, moral force attitudes were dominant and the liberalism of the jute barons prevailed. And at Aberdeen there was close co-operation with middle-class reformers on such issues as temperance, free trade and anti-aristocratic propaganda, under the shoemaker John Mitchell.[15] Such radicals were led by skilled workers and tradesmen—men like Fraser, an agent for Morison's pills, or the former flax-dresser Archibald McDonald of Aberdeen, who made 'chemical preparations' and ginger beer.

In the traditionally radical areas of East Anglia, Chartism had a distinct character. The handloom weavers of Norwich, the once-proud capital of the worsted industry, still provided a militant group to cheer Stephens's violent oratory. As elsewhere, the weavers were impoverished and periodically riotous. They drove out their early bourgeois leaders, preferring the heady oratory of the promiscuous and rascally publican John Dover—at least until 1841. But their 'violence' rarely amounted to more than rumoured pike-making, organised heckling at public meetings, ranter-inspired 'marches' on Anglican churches and a couple of riots in 1841. And Norwich was exceptional, being influenced by both the LWMA and the ELDA. But it was dominated always by the economic and religious attitudes of the 'constitutional' weavers' society. Ranting Primitive Methodists kept the Chartism of the Norfolk hinterland still more moderate. In Essex the early movement was dominated by self-employed, self-educated liberal nonconformist tradesmen and artisans—mild men like Robert Hall of Chelmsford—and all but disappeared when militancy mounted elsewhere. Suffolk Chartism also originally grew among liberal dissenting craftsmen in the notoriously corrupt little boroughs and among agricultural and industrial workers who continued the Anglican priest F. H. Maberley's hostility to the New Poor Law. Ipswich was the commanding and co-ordinating centre; the literate small-town liberals never made much headway in the squire-dominated countryside.[16]

The West Country also had an individualist radical tradition. In slummy and riotous Bristol a coffee-house proprietor, Robert Nicholls, formed a WMA in the summer of 1837. The first rally was addressed by Vincent in October; and in June 1838 Vincent returned, with the Welsh tinplate worker William Morgan, to explain the Charter. Economic decline led genteel Bath and Salisbury and the long-failing woollen towns of Bradford, Devizes, Frome, Trowbridge and Westbury towards radical paths. The Bath Working Men's Association of 1837, led by the shoemaking brothers Samuel and George Bartlett and the plasterer Anthony Phillips, and patronised by the radical military brothers Sir Charles and William Napier, moderately advocated universal suffrage, shorter parliaments and the ballot. The arrival of Henry Vincent in 1838 led to a wider, more enthusiastic radicalism, the adoption of the Charter and—inevitably —the recruitment of female supporters. The declining cloth towns were thereafter organised by the 'Apostle of the West', backed by such men as the radical lawyer Prowting Roberts, the hatter William Carrier of Trowbridge and R. Mealing of Bath. Some speeches were militant and angry—and certainly worried rural magistrates. Carrier, in particular, raged against 'that animal called a Government' and reverted to an older radicalism with his promises of 'plenty of roast beef, plum pudding and strong beer by working three hours a day'.[17]

Further west, Wales inevitably contributed a unique element to British radicalism. An embryonic nationalism had long been preserved in the principality. To it was added the opposition of Protestant nonconformists (particularly the Independents) to the established Anglican Church of Wales; the chapel, with its primitive, Old Testament doctrine and sometimes harshly enforced social and moral discipline, made a major contribution to the preservation of Welsh culture and the development of Welsh radicalism. Welsh workers in the expanding coal and iron industries complained of and sometimes rioted against bleak industrial conditions, wage reductions, 'truck' systems and the foul quality of life in the mining valleys. And in the agricultural counties there was growing hatred of the Poor Law, of Anglicised landlords, of turnpike charges and of conditions in the declining flannel industry.

Both the LWMA and the BPU founded branches in the principality, often incorporating established radical groups. During 1837 working men's associations were established in Carmarthen by a local solicitor, Hugh Williams, in Llanelly by the Independent minister and journalist David Rees, in Welshpool, Newtown and Llanidloes by Hetherington and a local Anglican ironmonger, Thomas Powell; in 1838 branches were established in such places as Merthyr (under the Unitarian factory owner and journalist Morgan Williams), Newport (under the Independent draper JP and mayor John Frost and the baker William Edwards), Pontypool, Narberth, Swansea, Pembroke and other places (largely through the missionary activities of William Jenkins of Carmarthen). The BPU had meanwhile organised branches in such flannel towns as Newtown and Llanidloes, under Richard Jarman and Charles Jones. Simultaneously with the rise of the two varieties of the new radicalism, the violent radical tradition of periodic riots, Dic Penderyn and the terrorist 'Scotch Cattle' was maintained by attacks on the new workhouses and the strange transvestite raids on the tollgates known as the 'Rebecca Riots'.[18] It is clear that the majority of Welsh Chartist leaders were, by any standard, middle class; and it is equally clear that they were backed by an underswell of angry proletarian feeling.

In the English West Midlands, as in mid-Wales, BPU influence was paramount. Coventry was an odd exception. Its silk industry was a domestic rather than a factory industry; it had an element of social mobility which allowed such artisans as William Andrews to become masters. Despite a long industrial decline and periodic industrial disputes, local radicalism was dominated by such Owenites as Charles Bray of the *Herald*, councillor James Whittem, the journalist J. C. Farn and the co-operative store manager William Taunton. The Political Union of January 1838 was led by Farn, Taunton, the plumber John Warden and alderman William Mayo (a watch manufacturer)—who were to support later liberal causes. The Tory-Anglican George Eld of the *Standard* voiced Northern attitudes, and the ribbon-printer Peter Hoy led local militants; but the Poor Law was sensibly administered and Chartism had no power in a town which already enjoyed a wide 'freeman' franchise and in which class antagonisms had scarcely developed. But Northampton held four WMA rallies from 1 August, 1838, under the shoemaker Joseph Wright, to hear Vincent and nonconformist ministers, and enthusiastically adopted the Charter.[14]

In the East Midlands Leicester became a notable Chartist centre, largely through the influence of Thomas Cooper, the radical journalist. The depressed framework knitters retained a potent influence in Leicester, Loughborough and the county; and the patience which they had long exhibited over their wretched condition was now declining. Low wages and hatred of the Poor Law aided the formation of the Leicester Radical WMA of August 1836 and the Loughborough Union of two years later, under the Primitive Methodists John Skevington, T. R. Smart (a teacher) and J. Culley. By October 1838 the Leicester and Leicestershire Political Union supported the Charter, lower taxation, repeal of the Corn and Poor Laws and general 'amelioration'. The Nottingham WMA of January 1838 saw political reform as 'the means by which [workers] could furnish their houses, clothe their backs and educate their children'. Local Chartists, under the hairdresser James Sweet, the lacemaker John Barratt, the framework knitter Jonathan Barber, the cordwainer James Sawter and the Rev. George Harrison, were militant champions of the low-paid knitters and spinners. Nottingham, indeed, shared the Oastlerite and Stephensite social concern of many Northern textile towns. Its hatred of the Poor Law led to another form of Tory-radical alliance which (despite periodic breaches) was still powerful in 1861.[20]

Chartism in the cotton districts was based on bitter industrial experience and above all on the glaring class divisions between masters and operatives, which so many contemporary commentators noted. The traditions of Lancastrian radicalism—of Luddism, trade unionism, meal riots, hostility to the Corn Law, political unions and 'Peterloo'—had been revived by Oastler and Stephens with their impassioned campaigns against industrial conditions and the Poor Law and by the extending unemployment and distress of 1837, particularly among the still numerous handloom weavers. The long battle against liberal economic and social theory provided the background to local Chartism. The six points were adopted at a Stockport rally in March 1837; Manchester petitioned for annual parliaments, universal suffrage and the ballot in April; the Salford Radical Association followed in December. Almost inevitably, Manchester quickly took the lead. The Manchester Universal Suffrage Association of 1838 was quickly followed by the influential Manchester Political Union. The MPU was led by such men as the chemist J. W. Hodgetts, the printer R. J. Richardson, Cobbett's solicitor son Richard and the liberal-radical journalist Archibald Prentice of the *Manchester Times*. Its first great rally was the vast Kersal Moor meeting on 24

September, with John Fielden as chairman and O'Connor and Stephens as principal speakers. Here, before 50,000 members of South Lancashire trade unions and political unions, Stephens delivered a famous speech, summing up Tory-radical attitudes towards the new radicalism:[21]

> Chartism is no political movement, where the main question is getting the ballot . . . This question of universal suffrage is a knife and fork question, after all, . . . a bread and cheese question, notwithstanding all that has been said against it; and if any man asks me what I mean by universal suffrage, I would answer: that every working man in the land has the right to have a good coat to his back, a comfortable abode in which to shelter himself and his family, a good dinner upon his table, and no more work than is necessary for keeping him in good health and as much wages for that work as would keep him in plenty and afford him the enjoyment of all the blessings of life which a reasonable man could desire.

IV

The North retained its basic social, economic and industrial interests during the developing radical campaign. Its leaders had little interest in universal suffrage *per se*. If universal suffrage 'were the law of the land next week', Oastler told C. J. Haslam of the Manchester Radical Association in 1836, 'it would in a very short time produce universal confusion and would inevitably lead to despotism'. He 'should rejoice to see the suffrage extended upon the ancient and *varied* plan, because then no *one* class would be able to rule *all* the others'. What Oastler fundamentally cared for was 'an extensive improvement in the condition of the working classes'. As a Tory Churchman, he had

> no wish to see society disorganised [and] the Government and People pitched into bloody array against each other. . . . But if the Church, Throne and Aristocracy are determined to rob the poor man of his liberty . . . then, with their bitterest foes, would I cry, *down with them, down with them all to the ground*.

But he was prepared to fight the Poor Law with every weapon. 'The inhabitants of these hills and valleys', he told Lancashire campaigners, would not 'tamely submit to be cheated against law out of their rights'. Before accepting the Act, he asserted at Rochdale, he 'would set the whole Kingdom in a blaze'. Dismissed by his employer in May 1838, Oastler briefly continued his campaign. In July he urged Halifax workers to 'have a brace of horse pistols, a good sword, a musket. . . . *They* will petition for you'. Workers should 'arm for peace, arm for justice, arm for the rights of all'.[22]

Stephens held generally similar views, though his speeches tended to be even more violent. At Leeds in November he maintained that 'there was not a mill in England that had not been built with gold coined out of the blood and bones of the operatives'. At Glasgow he threatened to 'destroy those abodes of guilt [the cotton factories], which [were] reared to violate all law and God's Book'. At Newcastle on 1 January 1838 he announced himself 'a revolutionist by fire, by blood, to the knife, to the death' against the Poor Law. Rather than accept the Act, 'Newcastle ought to be and would be one blaze of fire, with only one way to put it out, and that with the blood of all who supported this abominable measure'. If peaceful campaigning failed, then 'let the men, with a torch in one hand and a dagger in the other, put to death all who attempted to sever man and wife'. At Manchester he insisted that 'the law of devils . . . ought to be resisted to the death'; at Rochdale he maintained that 'it was right for the poor to take a dagger in one hand and a torch in the other, and do their best for themselves' against the Poor Law. Constantly, throughout the Northern counties, Stephens advised ecstatic admirers to arm—'and use their arms, if need be' against the Poor Law: 'to destroy a Poor-Law Guardian would be doing God a service'. And at Norwich in November he asserted that[23]

> England stands on a mine; a volcano is beneath her. . . . Hitherto, the people have been held in leash; they can be held back no longer; they must be slipped. . . . No Government can or shall exist that will not repeal the new Poor Law . . . Husbands and wives, brothers and sisters will war to the knife. . . .

But while Stephens regularly urged possible violent solutions to the factory and Poor Law problems, he had no faith in the universal panacea of universal suffrage. Oastler himself supported armed threats 'to roll back innovation and restore the Constitution'. And Oastler's first biographer, Stephens—to whom the 'Factory King' was 'the *beau-ideal* of the old English character'—fervently agreed. Perhaps he felt, as he declared at Saddleworth in June, that 'there was no hope of anything being done for them, unless they resorted to physical force'. But Chartism to him remained 'a knife and fork question'. He 'would not give two straws for universal suffrage, unless [it] brought peace and plenty to the cottage', he declared at Wigan in November: 'the firelock must come first and the vote afterwards'. Social reform was the vital necessity: 'universal suffrage might be a very fine thing, but as yet it was all in the moon'.[2]

Hostility to the Poor Law extended from the textile areas to the North East, where it mingled with opposition to the miners' bond and with embattled pit unionism. The local leader was the philosopher and furrier Robert Blakey, a former mayor of Morpeth. But the law was operated moderately and the expanding coal areas never experienced Lancashire's slumps. The Newcastle WMA was formed under the miners' leader Tommy Hepburn on 9 July 1837, but progress was slow, until the great rally on the Town Moor on 28 June 1838. The Quaker soap manufacturer Thomas Doubleday presided and speakers included O'Connor, the crippled South Shields tailor and newsagent Robert Lowery and such local workers as James Ayr—who wished to 'use every means—not every legal means, mark!—but every means for the attainment of universal suffrage' and the abolition of monarchy. The highlights were O'Connor's dream of Brougham being sent to a workhouse (and being separated from his wife on Malthusian grounds) and his threats to patrolling dragoons. The recently deceased Beaumont and his *Northern Liberator* had effectively stirred the North East. But local Chartism remained spasmodic; the Northern PU was founded in September and held a major rally on Christmas Day, to hear Harney, Lowery and Dr Taylor, but activity was never widespread, despite much violent talk. Durham was organised under the leadership of the printers James Williams and George Binns of the Sunderland Mechanics' Institution, who, together with Collins, secured local adoption of the petition in June. Their Sunderland Charter Association became the basis of the Durham County body.

Many cross-currents and undercurrents influenced radical meetings and radical policies in the summer of 1838. Stephens might condemn the Birmingham men as 'old women' but O'Connor was received with 'the loudest applause' by the BPU, on 6 August.[25] Talk of armed violence might make Stephens a hero in Lancashire and Taylor a leader in Ayrshire, but in large areas of Scotland and England 'moral force' was dominant. From the start of the movement there were thus many divisions. But from the late summer all sections could combine in the exciting task of preparing for a great national agitation. The giant Birmingham meeting planned the campaign. It was attended by Attwood, Salt, Edmonds, Muntz, Scholefield, Collins, Douglas and thousands of BPU supporters, Moir and Purdie of Glasgow, Fraser of Edinburgh, Dr Wade, Vincent and Hetherington of the LWMA, Richardson of Manchester and O'Connor, representing Leeds, Halifax and other Yorkshire towns, and large 'divisions' from Dudley, Halesowen, Studley, Walsall, Warwick and Wolverhampton. Attwood repeated to the vast assembly at Hollo-way Head the plan to petition twice and then to strike; and O'Connor hinted at further measures to coerce Parliament. A 'Convention of the Industrious Classes' was to be elected to organise the presentation of the petition. Birmingham would then be represented by George and Philip Muntz, Douglas, Salt, Edmonds, Alderman Benjamin Hadley, Collins and John Pearce.[26]

The LWMA, probably concerned by Birmingham's continued in-terest in currency reform and the hints of violence, decided to hold a similar meeting in London. Lovett's 400 members were deter-mined not to lose leadership to Attwoodite theory or O'Connorite violence. They could not rival the 200,000 allegedly assembled at Birmingham; but, typically, they proceeded with great formality. Their assembly in Westminster Palace Yard on 17 September was chaired by the high bailiff, Sir Francis Smedley. The claimed 30,000 attending were addressed by Leader (the local MP), Dillon Browne (Member for Mayo), Perronet Thompson, O'Connor, Wade, W. J. Fox, Lowery, Richardson, Duncan, Hugh Williams, Ebenezer Elliott (the Sheffield 'corn law rhymer'), Lovett, Hetherington, Hartwell, Cleave, Douglas and others, for over five hours. The results of the meeting can scarcely have pleased the Association. For one thing, the attack was embarrassingly wide: against coercion in Ireland, the suppression of the Canadian revolt, the Poor Law, the United States, Crown and aristocracy, the 'rich' generally, the Church in England and Ireland, the 'agricultural preponderance', the Whigs, 'the old constitution', Melbourne, Russell, Peel, 'cor-ruption', the 'armed Bourbon police' and so on. Secondly, Leader's counsels of moderation were heckled and opposed, while O'Connor, Lowery and Richardson were warmly applauded for hints of physical force. 'The men of Newcastle', according to Lowery, 'would dare to defend with their arms what they utter with their tongues'. O'Connor, typically, asserted that

He had never counselled the people to use physical force, because he felt that those who did were fools to their own cause; but, at the same time, those who decried it preserved their authority by physical force alone . . . He counselled them against all rioting, all civil war, but still, in the hearing of the House of Commons, he would say, that rather than see the constitution violated, while the people were in daily want, if no other man would do so, if the constitution was violated, he would himself lead the people to death or glory. . . . His desire was to try moral force as long as possible, even to the fullest extent, but he would always have them bear in mind, that it is better to die freemen than to live slaves. Every conquest which was called honourable had been achieved by physical force, but they did not want it, because if all hands were pulling for Universal Suffrage they would soon pull down the stronghold of corruption. He hoped and trusted that out of the exercise of that judgment which belonged exclusively to the working class, a union would arise, and from that union a moral power would be created, sufficient to establish the rights of the poor man; but if this failed, then let every man raise his arm in defence of that which his judgment told him was justice.

And Richardson 'knew' that, after their anti-Poor Law petitions had failed, Lancashire folk had armed themselves: 'he had seen the arms hanging over the mantlepieces of the poor with his own eyes'. However, at the close of the meeting, Cleave, Hartwell, Hetherington, Lovett, Moore, O'Brien, Rogers and Vincent were chosen to represent the LWMA at the Convention, Place and Roebuck having declined nomination.[27]

The LWMA thus claimed the whole metropolitan representation at the Convention and proceeded to organise collections of a 'national rent' in the capital. But O'Connor and the 'Democratic' leaders, who had been deprived of platform seats in Palace Yard, grew closer together with a more militant policy. And the message was energetically carried into the country. The Lancashire rally on Kersal Moor on 24 September was attended by twenty bands, some two hundred banners and probably 50,000 people (though the ever-optimistic *Morning Advertiser* estimated 300,000). From the chair John Fielden condemned Irish coercion, the Poor Law, low wages, the new police and the Corn Laws. The vast and excitable crowd was harangued by Stephens, O'Connor, Douglas, Collins, Pearce, Lowery and Duffy, together with several local 'Ten Hours' and anti-Poor Law veterans. At the end Dr Fletcher (Bury), Stephens

(Ashton), James Taylor (Rochdale), Bronterre O'Brien (Stockport), E. Nightingale, Richardson, James Cobbett and James Wroe (Manchester) were elected as Convention delegates. This greatest rally of the MPU gained wide trade union support, but the sentiments expressed by many speakers scarcely pleased many moderate Political Union leaders. 'Here is moral power with a vengeance', roared O'Connor,[28]

> which will be turned ere long, in spite of me, or of the most wise counsellors of the age, into physical force, because the people know that they have borne oppression too long and too tamely. . . . I have commenced the battle of the suffrage with you, and you are the forces with which I will fight that battle, even to the death, if necessary.

O'Connor was, indeed, now consolidating his position in the North, as the radical ally of Oastler and Stephens—and in other parts of the country as the ally of the East London ultra-radicals. Despite the apparent alliance, O'Connor was determined to cast the LWMA and BPU into the shade.

The next giant rally was the West Riding demonstration on Peep Green on 15 October. From Bradford, Halifax and Huddersfield thousands converged on the moor, supported by lesser contingents from Leeds and other towns: the total attendance was variously estimated at up to 250,000, amid the usual carnival atmosphere. Most of Yorkshire's radical heroes—O'Connor, the dour Rider, the experienced Pitkeithley, and others—spoke in familiar strain to an enthusiastic assembly. O'Connor was enthusiastically elected to represent the Riding at the Convention, together with James Cobbett, the stout Bradford publican Bussey, Rider of Leeds and Pitkeithley of Huddersfield.[29] There followed a plethora of (generally unanimous) elections of Convention members. On 24 October an Alloa meeting chose a mild-mannered Dunfermline worker, Alexander Halley, to represent several Scottish districts. Soon afterwards W. G. Burns, a marginally more militant Dundee shoemaker and newsagent, was elected for Forfarshire. Less proletarian but equally divided members represented other Scottish districts. Patrick Matthew (Perthshire) represented a radical strain among small Scottish lairds; W. S. Villiers Sankey (Edinburgh), a classicist and mathematician, contrived to stand for an 'intellectual' series of attitudes; Ayrshire rejected the O'Connorite Dr Taylor and the Cumnock schoolmaster John McCrae on 3 November, in favour of

Bailie Craig, a Kilmarnock draper.[30] The Scottish elections were regularly scrutinised by Abram Duncan, who, determined that Scotland should be represented by moderates, started a campaign against O'Connor's violent talk. Duncan invited Scottish radicals of all sorts to assemble in Edinburgh to insist that they would 'never appeal to physical force at any time, or upon any occasion whatever' and thus to support BPU notions. A delegate conference and a torchlight meeting on Calton Hill at Edinburgh on 5 December accepted the moderate policies of Duncan and Fraser, largely at the prompting of Brewster (the chairman), Burns of Dundee and Mitchell of Aberdeen. But by doing so they aroused the opposition not only of those Scottish Chartists who supported Oastler and Stephens (Brewster's apparent *bêtes-noires*) but also of those who sensed in Brewster's ill-informed attacks an assault on O'Connor—who bitterly opposed the Glasgow-Birmingham axis. The O'Connorite Taylor, with his 'D'hurna' plan for abstinence from taxed commodities such as tea, tobacco and alcohol, was driven to accept Carlisle's nomination. In December, however, the Scottish picture changed. Under Brewster's influence, the Renfrewshire Political Union had adopted its chairman John Henderson, a Paisley bailie and editor of the *Glasgow Saturday Post*. But Taylor soundly defeated Brewster himself at Thornhill on 1 January 1839. Next day Moir beat the brewer-publisher Alexander Hedderwick, printer of the radical *Glasgow Argus* and *Scots Times*. A stormy visit by O'Connor virtually ended Brewster's credibility. Fraser was rejected by the new Edinburgh Universal Suffrage Association; the Renfrewshire Union split up; Duncan crept to Dumfries for nomination.[31] 'Moderate' attempts to rig Scottish elections had rebounded on their authors.

Other towns and districts, with varying degrees of propriety and public interest, proceeded to elect Convention delegates. On 29 October the handloom-weaving town of Bolton returned William Carpenter, the well-known radical journalist, Joseph Wood and John Warden. Preston chose Richard Marsden, a bitter weaver apt to relive his past hardships, on 5 November. At Ashton Stephens was succeeded by the young Ramsbottom doctor Peter Murray McDouall, whose surgeon friend Matthew Fletcher was returned for Bury. Rochdale elected James Taylor, a Methodist Unitarian preacher. A militant worker, John Deegan, was chosen at Hyde and James Fenney at Wigan. Working men were also elected in Sheffield (William Gill), the Potteries ('Daddy' John Richards) and Oldham (the Oastlerite James Mills). Liverpool chose the energetic James

Whittle and Stockport Hetherington and Hartwell (both of whom also represented London). On Christmas Day at Newcastle the North East selected Harney (Northumberland) and Dr Taylor and Lowery (Newcastle); Durham chose Robert Knox. In the Midlands, Leicester and Loughborough returned the teacher Thomas Smart, whose old ally, the Primitive Methodist preacher John Skevington, 'sat' for Loughborough and Derby (which also elected Harney on 28 January). The Nottingham district was represented by Dr Wade. At Reading, Pearce, Cleave and one Benjamin Tight were elected. In the West Country Richard Mealing was returned for Bath (on 17 September) and a succession of small boroughs, including Bradford and Trowbridge (for which William Carrier was elected on the 21st). Vincent was elected at Cheltenham (together with Collins), Bristol (with the militant veterans C. H. Neesom and O'Brien) and Hull. Wales was to be represented by John Frost (Newport, Pontypool and Caerleon) and Charles Jones (Newtown, Welshpool and Llandidloes). Brighton, once famous for its co-operative ventures, originally elected one Osborne and later John Goods; Dorset returned the Tolpuddle leader George Loveless (who never took his seat); in November Norwich chose Harney, Stephens and O'Brien.

The unplanned 'electioneering' did not pass without some curious results. The 'constituencies' were meaningless and scarcely more representative of the population than was the pre-reform Commons. Partly, no doubt, because of an understanding that a membership of over forty-nine would be illegal, but equally on grounds of expense, many delegates held dual or multiple mandates. The much-condemned pluralism of the clerics was thus duplicated in the Convention: O'Brien, the militant representative of London, Leigh, Bristol, Norwich, Newport and Stockport, was the greatest pluralist, with Dr Taylor (Renfrew, Newcastle, Carlisle, Wigton, Alva and Tillicoutry), Halley (Dunfermline, Kirkcaldy, Alloa, Clackmannan, Stirling and Falkirk) and Mealing (Bath, Trowbridge, Frome, Holt, Bradford and Westbury).

London's disputes had continued. The supporters of the ELDA and the CNA, along with many others, had never reconciled themselves to the domination of the LWMA. Harney and his friends had briefly joined the Association, but only after considerable trouble. They soon provoked further trouble by attacking O'Connell's attitudes over the Glasgow spinners, and, after heated rows, in March 1838, Harney, Neesom and Ireland resigned, to form the London Democratic Association. The LDA was openly O'Connorite, popular and ultra-radical. As secretary, Harney told 'the Democrats of Great Britain and Ireland' that its aims were universal suffrage, equal constituencies, annual parliaments, abolition of property qualifications, payment of MPs, abolition of newspaper taxes, repeal of the Poor Law, an eight-hour day, prohibition of child labour and support for trade unionism. The new Association was unable to secure London representation at the Convention, but Harney and Neesom were elected in Newcastle and Bristol. However, the West London Democratic Association succeeded in returning William Cardo, a shoemaker and prominent trade unionist, for Maryleborne.[32]

One further preparation was made for the coming struggle: a Chartist press was gradually established. In Kilmarnock Hugh Craig started the weekly *Ayrshire Examiner* in July 1838, to proclaim 'moral force' objectives. At the same time John Fraser commenced *The Edinburgh Monthly and Total Abstinence Advocate*, from which developed the influential weekly *True Scotsman* of October. In Paisley John Cumming issued the *Monthly Liberator* in 1838 and *Scottish Vindicator* in 1839. In Aberdeen the WMA issued the monthly *Aberdeen Patriot*; in Paisley the well-established *Glasgow Saturday Post and Renfrewshire Reformer* gave some support; and the *Dundee Chronicle*, the *Perthshire Chronicle*, the *Scots Times* (an entrenched Glasgow journal), *The Scottish Patriot* of July 1839 and the philosophic *Scottish Chartist Circular* of September 1839 spearheaded a growing Scottish 'reform' press.[33] In north-east England *The Northern Liberator* continued to promote a literate Chartism. From Leeds *The Northern Star* created a fortune for O'Connor. *The Birmingham Journal* continued to keep a friendly eye on BPU activities. The LWMA started its weekly moderate paper *The Charter*, edited by Carpenter, in January 1839. Within a week, in February, a rival, *The Chartist*, appeared. *The Champion*, run by J. P. Cobbett since 1836, gave support to anti-O'Connorites. In April 1839 the LDA commenced *The London Democrat*, as a rival to O'Brien's and Hetherington's *London Dispatch* of 1836. Lancashire men could rely upon the radical *Manchester and Salford Advertiser* for sympathetic reporting. *The Operative*, edited by the individualist O'Brien from October 1838, gave its support. At Leicester George Bown's *Midland Counties Illuminator*, was staunchly Chartist; and other local and regional journals were to follow.

V

As the varied Chartist 'elections' proceeded, it was apparent that few of them were organised in any 'democratic' fashion. The still minute LWMA, for instance, certainly contrived to put non-'liberals' at a disadvantage. The BPU was equally reluctant to entertain anti-bourgeois sentiments. Liberal Scotland was largely determined to be Presbyterian and Temperate. In the textile counties alone there existed a viable Tory-radicalism, caring little for charters and petitions but harnessing a proletarian bitterness against industrial conditions and the Poor Law. Oastler had created this highly emotive agitation; Stephens was now its apocalyptic missionary; O'Connor was its ultimate beneficiary.

During the last months of 1838 Stephens's violence rose to extreme heights; even the *Northern Star* had to censor its report of the Norwich speech. As a consequence, the BPU men grew increasingly anxious about the activities of an elected Convention member; Douglas, in particular, was incensed. The matter was raised at the weekly union meeting on 13 November, when O'Connor stormed in to defend himself against allegations of advocating physical force. He used his usual twisted logic, withdrawing nothing, insisting that a time-limit on peaceful agitation was essential and pointing to the implicit violence of the Birmingham leadership's reliance on the threat of overwhelming numbers. O'Connor returned on the 20th to appeal to working men against such leaders as Salt, Muntz and Douglas, who alleged that Northern policies would provoke civil war. O'Connor regularly defended his recent speeches. A torch 'was worth a thousand speeches; it spoke a language so intelligible that no one could misunderstand', he had told a Rochdale crowd; and at Manchester he had proclaimed 29 September 1839 as the final date for the enactment of the Charter, as 'nature would be exhausted if it were longer protracted'. Now, however, a temporary reconciliation was patched up between the nervous, apologetic BPU leaders and the blustering and still uncompromising demagogue; O'Connor had in fact established himself in Birmingham. It remained for him to stake a claim in London. At a rowdy rally in the Hall of Science on 20 December, O'Connor and the LDA assailed the LWMA. Poor Lovett declared that 'if the people were to be called upon to arm ... he would have nothing to do with them', but O'Connor gained the day.[34]

Although O'Connor maintained the policy of 'peacefully if we may, forcibly if we must', his propaganda was modified over Christmas. Undoubtedly, one cause was the government's long-expected reaction to the mounting threats of Chartist and allied orators. On 27 December Henry Goddard, a Bow Street runner, arrested Stephens in Ashton.[35] The first Chartist martyr—who emphatically denied his Chartism—had appeared. Equally important was the Chartist denunciation of radical rivals. In December O'Connor bitterly attacked Lord Durham, 'the Household Suffrage party', H. G. Ward and the Corn Law repealers. Repeal would only be safe if carried together with universal suffrage, insisted O'Connor: 'they would then be enabled to divert the saving effected ... into the pockets of the working classes', while repeal alone would 'only lead to bloodshed, strife and civil war'—and lower wages. What Chartists wanted above all was a social policy 'to render machinery the working man's holiday instead of the working man's curse'. And always there was the denunciation of O'Connell. 'The present system of persecution', maintained John Deegan, himself a Roman Catholic, 'began when Mr O'Connell denounced Mr Stephens as an advocate of physical force'. 'His threats to put us down, on the ground of our language relative to physical force, we view with the utmost scorn,' declared the Preston Radical Association. At Bradford Bussey condemned 'the base, brutal and corrupt press' and 'that Dictator to the Whig Cabinet, the base, bloody and brutal traitor Daniel O'Connell'. On New Year's Day Halifax Chartists insisted that 'the vile apostate' did not represent the 'brave and generous hearted Irish people': he 'might be compared to Satan amongst the angels of heaven'. The Oldham 'Associated Radicals' condemned the Precursor Society's 'base and slanderous aspersions':

> Whether O'Connell enjoys the confidence of the Irish people or not, we are unable to say; but that he is unworthy of such confidence, we think, may be easily proved

—and went on to defend the three Northern heroes, O'Connor, Oastler and Stephens. And the Hull WMA resolved that portraits of 'the arch traitor of the people should be publicly burnt'.[36] Working-class radicalism was increasingly separating itself from bourgeois radicalism. The policy was ultimately to weaken Chartism itself.

5 Physical and Moral Force

In the winter of 1838-9 Chartists everywhere enjoyed the heady excitement of Convention elections and the collection of a 'national rent' to maintain the elected delegates. Great industrial cities, quiet rural towns and small villages anxiously awaiting the arrival of the *Northern Star* at the cobbler's shop shared in the gathering optimism. As the anti-Poor Law and other agitations merged into the great national campaign for the Charter and the petition, almost nation-wide enthusiasm was generated. Yet there was little unity. O'Connor now reigned supreme in the north and had demonstrated his growing popularity elsewhere; but many London and Birmingham leaders remained suspiciously hostile. In Scotland too, the moderation of Brewster's associates at Calton Hill was soon undermined by a more radical reaction, in favour of Stephens and O'Connor. The Cumnock (Ayrshire) WMA would lay down their 'own lives to save a hair of [O'Connor's] head'. O'Connor claimed to have advocated only moral force—'but by moral force he did not mean the moral power of the Scotch Philosophers nor their chippings of the Excise and their attacks upon the teapot'. And his January visit increased his Scottish following substantially.[1] In particular, the once-powerful influence of O'Connell, who had recently warned 'radical reformers' against 'miserable threats of armed violence and bloodshed', urged them to 'disown the men who thus wickedly and foolishly injured the cause of Reform' and advised them 'to allow the cause to be conducted within the bounds of law, order and commonsense', was weakened. But for all the division exemplified by the stormy meet-ings at Birmingham, London, Newcastle, Glasgow and Renfrew and bitter personal arguments, the approach of the Convention gave Chartism at least a façade of unity. Furthermore, the arrest of Stephens—and the minister's careful moderation after being released on bail—probably influenced many Chartists, especially the fearful O'Connor. On the proposal of the Oldham Political Union, preliminary meetings of Northern delegates were held at Bury and Manchester.[2]

What optimistic Chartists expected from their campaign was well expressed by Harney, in his election speech at Derby on 28 January:[3]

We demand Universal Suffrage, because we believe that universal suffrage will bring universal happiness—for universal happiness there shall be—or our tyrants shall find to their cost that *we will have universal misery*. We will have happy homes and altars free, or by the God of our sires, our oppressors shall share that misery we have too long endured. My friends, we demand universal suffrage because it is our right, and not only because it is our right, but because we believe it will bring freedom to our country and happiness to our homesteads; we believe it will give us bread and beef and beer. What is it that we want? Not to destroy property and take life, but to preserve our own lives, and to protect our own property—viz, our labour. We are for Peace, Law, Order; but if our oppressors shall break the peace—if our tyrants shall violate the law—if our despots shall trample upon order—then we will fall back upon the Constitution, and defend the few remaining of the blood bought rights left us by our fathers. The Whigs shall never violate the Constitution of this country as they have done in Canada. They charge us with being Physical Force men; I fling the charge back in the teeth of these canting liberals. Let them call to mind their own words and deeds during the humbug reform agitation. ... Again I say, we are for peace, but we must have justice—we must have our rights speedily: peaceably if we can, *forcibly if we must*. ... Time was when every Englishman had a musket in his cottage, and along with it hung a flitch of bacon; now there is no flitch of bacon for there is no musket; let the musket be restored and the flitch of bacon will soon follow. ... You will get nothing from your tyrants but what you can take, and you can take nothing unless you are properly prepared to do so. In the words of a good man, then, I say, 'Arm for peace, arm for liberty, arm for justice, arm for the rights of all, and the tyrants will no longer laugh at your petitions'. ...

O'Connor kept up the attack on O'Connell. 'You have balanced lucre against greatness', he wrote, 'and instead of laying up a store of honour for ages yet to come, you have prostituted your country and

offered her a bleeding sacrifice . . .'. Many might fear the Oastlerite–
O'Connorite appeal to arms; but Harney fairly voiced the aspirations
of the movement. The 'rent' was collected, the last elections were
held, the petition grew in size and delegate meetings were held in
Manchester, Birmingham and Bury. The most urgent militancy was
still expressed outside the movement. 'Remember, Stephens is being
persecuted because he believes the Bible to be true', Oastler told
Dewsbury radicals in January[4]

—that is, nowadays, in the eyes of the Government the unpardon-
able sin!!! . . . Once more I say, Arm! Arm! Arm! . . . Once more,
then, if you revere the Church, if you are loyal to the Throne, if
you love your wives and deserve them—once more I say, arm in
their defence.

But now all eyes and all hopes were ranged on the first meeting of
the Convention.

I

The Convention met on 4 February in the British Coffee House in
Charing Cross, moving two days later to Bolt Court off Fleet Street.
Although not all of those elected turned up, there was a sizeable
attendance: fifty-four members actually appeared. London was well
represented by Cardo, seven members of the LWMA (and two members elected elsewhere) and two LDA men elected elsewhere; as
Hovell pointed out, 'it was a matter of £.s.d. Delegates who *lived* in
London cost less than those *sent* to London.' The BPU had five
members, Scotland eight, Wales two and the industrial areas of
England most of the rest. The members were a mixed bag—prosperous Midlands businessmen, medical practitioners, proletarian dissenting preachers, an Anglican priest, ranting demagogues, publicans,
a lawyer, booksellers and a scattering of working folk from London
and the North. In general, the delegates constituted a 'respectable',
middle-aged assembly; and, to the Northerners' dismay, they met in
a still largely unsympathetic capital.

On 4 February the proceedings were opened by prayers led by Dr
Wade. Formal proceedings were presided over by Douglas, who
reported that 500,486 persons had signed the petition and that the
'National Rent' stood at £967. Lovett was appointed secretary (over
O'Brien's protests) and Bailie Craig was made the first chairman. It

was agreed that delegates' salaries should be paid by 'constituencies': in general they appear to have received (or been promised) £25 a month, sometimes supplemented by money for expenses and extra contributions.[5] Indeed, in the matter of members' payment, the Convention appears to have more closely followed Chartist prescript than in such matters as the secret vote or equal electoral districts. But the Convention certainly took itself seriously. It was flattered by receiving formal petitions from its supporters; it was delighted by the rising tide of the 'rent' organised by the Muntzes and Douglas (which eventually reached over £1,700); it was determined to maintain a respectable, serious but not deferential posture. And its image was widely reflected. 'Never did the eye of freeborn man light upon a more heavenly spectacle,' declared the *Star*, which considered the new body more important than Parliament itself. 'The eyes of the whole world were now of necessity directed to the People's Parliament. . . .'

It remained, however, a matter of importance to decide the purpose of the Convention. Undoubtedly some posturing 'MCS' were prepared to enact 'legislation'. But on the 5th, Cobbett, with inherited common sense, raised the question. The answer was postponed, but on the 14th Cobbett proposed a type of constitutional resolution: the Convention's task was to organise the petition, it should not venture into other fields and it certainly should not advocate any illegal action. This minimal role was unacceptable to excited 'MCS', to whom the Convention appeared as a valid proletarian parliament, elected (unprovably) by a majority in the country and entitled to go far beyond mere petitioning. Cobbett was defeated by 36 votes to 6 and resigned his 'seat'. What the exact claims of the Convention were remained somewhat mysterious. O'Connor, McDouall, O'Brien and their followers certainly believed that it must be prepared to go further than pleading. O'Brien even carried a resolution for a joint meeting of 'MCS' and MPS in the Crown and Anchor to sort out the differences between the two 'Houses'. The 'rivals' in the Palace of Westminster showed no sign of responding. But O'Brien also carried a motion opposing the Anti-Corn Law League and all its works, which was to be of considerable future importance.[6]

The League had grown out of the Manchester Anti-Corn Law Association of September 1838 and was formally constituted in March 1839, with headquarters in Manchester. It included both radicals and great liberal industrialists; and it took over an old radical cause. In September Place had told Lovett of growing support for repeal: 'each one argued that this was just the time to commence vigorous proceedings, the crops being short and bread dear.' But Northern Chartists largely followed Oastler's protectionism and hostility to the Mancunian capitalists. The *Star* had urged Chartists to

> make the cry of Universal Suffrage echo . . . until all have a voice in those laws which govern all. Never, never, never will the repeal of any bad law guarantee you against the re-enaction of as bad a one, until you get Universal Suffrage.

'Why do they want the Corn Laws repealed?' it asked, answering[7]

> Plainly that, by a reduction in the price of British labour, they may be enabled to beat down the price of their commodity till they can drive the foreigner from the field. . . .

After a week of deliberations, the Convention issued its *Rules and Regulations*, asserting that it had been 'elected by the Radical Reformers of Great Britain and Ireland in Public Meetings assembled, to watch over the National Petition and obtain by all legal constitutional means the Act to provide for the just representation of the People, entitled the "People's Charter" '. This declaration made the Convention appear to be a moderate, agitating body. But many members felt otherwise. From the start, the LDA had little faith in the entire exercise. 'There were too many men in the Convention', Harney had asserted at Newcastle, 'who felt no other interest in the movement than their own popularity'. On the other hand, the LWMA's organ hopefully maintained that

> The aptitude for business, the acuteness, the knowledge, the comprehensiveness of purpose, the singleness of mind, and, above all, the deep and genuine sympathy evinced for the people by the delegates who compose the Convention, would do honour to any body of men. . . .

Nevertheless, the Birmingham men were inevitably frightened by the attitudes of some of their colleagues and soon withdrew from the meetings. The petition, they thought, was now unlikely to obtain more than 600,000 signatures: it was no longer a 'National Petition' and until much more support was obtained the Convention should dissolve. Militants, naturally, took little note of the withdrawal of the BPU delegates. Certainly it was necessary to await the arrival of further signatures; consequently Convention debates were largely devoted to trivia—such as the appointment of the 'Oastlerite' Mark Crabtree of Dewsbury as doorkeeper and messenger at 30s (£1·50p) weekly. But in the evenings self-important 'MCs' tried to maintain public interest by addressing (generally small) public meetings at which more violent tones were sounded. O'Connor was an expert at rousing radical enthusiasm without committing himself. 'Suppose then', he roared at Finsbury on the 11th, 'that on the morrow the Convention, in the discharge of their sacred duty, were to be illegally arrested ... what would [the 3,000-strong audience] do?' The response was immediate: 'We'd rise', shouted the crowd. But the Convention itself was bogged down in discussion of procedural motions, O'Connor's motion of 18 February to link British workers and Irish peasants and its own legality. Inside and outside the assembly, O'Connor propounded a militant line. At Finsbury he denounced the plan for 'MCs' to convert MP's:

> all the craft, all the artifice, all the ingenuity, all the courtesy of the Convention would not gain a single Member of the House. The strongest impression the Convention could make would be by taking their petition in one hand and their ulterior measures in the other.

O'Connor, indeed, still believed that[8]

> physical force was treason only when it failed: it was glorious freedom when it was successful.

But such stuff did not appeal to Londoners, and delegates lost hope of their support.

While awaiting the arrival of further petitions, the Convention debated many subjects. An *Address to the People of Ireland* asserted that O'Connell was always

> arrayed against the principle of justice which he professed to support. The Dorchester labourers—the English infant factory children, whom he was pledged to defend—the Trade Unionists— all fell victims to his power.

Marsden of Preston, a handloom weaver, raised the problems of proletarian distress, particularly among weavers and factory operatives: 'their sufferings were no longer to be endured, and only this choice seemed to be left to them, to seize their food where they could find it, or lie down and die.' The Convention also organised an enquiry into the current state of workers in the regions. In general, the answers were moving and consolingly loyal: Leicester Chartists, for instance, talked of[9]

> a people ... devoid of every comfort, and subjected to almost every privation and want which suffering humanity is heir to; with empty bellies and ragged backs, worn down with unremitting toil, they resemble scarecrows more than Men, much less than Englishmen of yore. One consolation alone remains to them and it warms their icy hearts—it is the Convention—on that body, chosen by the People, their eyes are fixed, and their hearts set—in its virtue, in its discretion, in its perseverance they have the most unbounded confidence; they are prepared to support it to the extent of their means and ability, and if necessary to die in its defence.

But extra-mural activities also continued. At a rally of the LDA, Harney, Rider and Marsden violently demanded action: 'if the Convention did its duty, the Charter would be law in less than a month ... there should be no delay in presenting the Petition ... all acts of injustice and oppression should be met by resistance.' Outraged members, led by Whittle, condemned the attack on their timidity on 7 March and forced the offenders to apologise. But nine days later several 'MCs' enthusiastically talked of force at a rally in the Crown and Anchor. Sankey spoke of the right to use any means to obtain their ends. O'Connor returned to blustering threats; Harney demanded universal suffrage or death; and even Rogers talked of signing the petition in red. O'Brien, announcing the achievement of 1,200,000 signatures, mentioned 'an equal number of pikes'.[10]

The pattern of militancy was maintained at public meetings. Harney, with his red hat, wildly waved daggers before audiences and compared himself to Marat. And on 18 March violent talk erupted in the Convention itself, when Fletcher commended the use of 'a loaded bludgeon' against the new rural police. When the *Morning Chronicle* 'exposed' such speeches, militant delegates recalled the *Chronicle's* calls to arms during the Reform Bill troubles. But other members were appalled. Dr Wade publicly disapproved of the militant talk and resigned on 28 March. Douglas, Hadley and Salt retired to Birmingham and Fletcher (still loathing the Poor Law and police and still urging his followers 'to carry a good thick Walking Stick, for the protection of their lives and property') to Bury. And Harney excitedly proclaimed 'your country, your posterity, your God demand of you to ARM! ARM!! ARM!!!'[11]

From late February, fifteen missionaries toured areas which had hitherto given no support. They had little success and even the popular Vincent was mobbed and stoned at Devizes, together with Carrier and Prowting Roberts, on 1 April.[12] The lack of interest or actual hostility was a bitter blow to the Convention's self-esteem, and on the 22nd O'Connor carried a resolution that 'no Member . . . should, from this day forth, be sent on the business of agitating, or as a missionary, until after the presentation of the National Petition'. He went on to show other weaknesses. In addition to the 'deserters', there were members who had never or only rarely attended. The Convention must act by preparing to sit permanently following the rejection of the petition and by planning a general strike (a substitute for the threatened revolution); and its more timid bourgeois members must face the restless demands of poor supporters. The fact was that the assembly had largely wasted its time debating such matters as Richardson's curious motion of the 9th on the people's ancient right to bear arms—a subject on which wiser members preferred not to be specific; but the majority accepted Fletcher's view. As a result, the trickle of resignations continued. Joseph Wood left on 18 April, having become (to the fury of his Bolton electors) a Poor Law guardian. And the moderate Scottish delegates were increasingly uneasy. Patrick Matthew resigned on the 12th because of 'the intemperate language and ultra character of the major party of the Convention'. Alexander Halley briefly withdrew his resignation, but the once-militant Sankey left in May, after declaring that 'the people of Scotland were too calm, too prudent and too humane to peril this cause upon bloodshed'. James Moir was reluctant to leave Glasgow, and Hugh Craig and Abram Duncan both returned to Scotland. Rogers of London resigned in May, opposing any role but that of a petitioning body.

O'Connor's speech had two effects. The Convention decided to move to Birmingham, and it solved its divisions in cowardly fashion by leaving the decision on arming to mass meetings of constituents. One final task remained—the presentation of the petition which, despite its 1,280,000 signatories, was now little respected by most Convention members. At the last minute, Attwood and Fielden, the appointed parliamentary champions, professed some qualms and demanded a repudiation of violence and a pledge of loyalty to 'the principles of peace, law and order'. When the Convention refused to give such undertakings and re-asserted the right to petition, the MPS' scruples disappeared. On 7 May the 3-mile-long petition was rolled up and escorted on a decorated cart by a procession of Convention members to Fielden's London house. It was typical of Convention arrangements that Fielden was found to be absent. However, Attwood accepted the huge roll and promised to present it to the Commons. But he would not propose a Bill based on the Charter, as he could not accept the provision of 200 of the 600 proposed Commons seats for Ireland.[13] The delegates had to accept this final qualm of their champion. Next day they prepared a questionnaire to be put to a series of regional meetings. It asked whether supporters would withdraw savings, demand gold for paper money, strike for a 'sacred month', abstain from excisable alcohol, arm themselves, elect Chartists at the next election show of hands, deal only with Chartists, help any 'martyrs', refuse to accept anything less than the full Charter and obey the orders of the Convention majority. News arrived that Birmingham, now no longer controlled by the moderate middle-class Attwoodites, was enthusiastically awaiting the Convention. On the 13th, thirty-five hopeful 'MCs' set off by train for Birmingham. Ahead of them had travelled the news of their recent decisions. Lowery's moderate *Address to the People* of 6 May had been replaced by a machiavellian document produced by O'Brien, enjoining Chartists to avoid legal trouble by appearing to be law-abiding while arming and being prepared to fight any force used against them.[14]

II

Beyond the Convention, many Chartists had for months advocated recourse to physical violence. Much of the threatening oratory was as meaningless as O'Connor's heated verbiage. But up and down the country reports spread of militant groups hoarding pikes, spears and muskets for the coming revolution. Undoubtedly some of the rumours were born in the minds of apprehensive justices and their agents, determined to obtain military protection. But, after making all allowance for the exaggerations of 'physical force' propagandists and timid authorities alike, it is certain that considerable numbers of men had taken anti-Poor Law and Chartist militants at their word and had stored assorted arms. Oastler, Stephens, Fletcher, O'Connor, O'Brien, Harney, Bussey, Rider, Taylor, Richardson and their kind had had considerable influence.

O'Connor's tactics were an obvious blend of variable and

sometimes ambiguous advice. Typical was a *Northern Star* report in September 1838 headed 'The National Guards of Paris have petitioned for an Extension of the Suffrage, and they have done it with Arms in their hands'. O'Connor supported peace, he declared at Manchester, 'but if peace giveth not law, then I am for war to the knife'. Both Oastler and Stephens, in advocating the defence of ancient rights, were more open in advocating arming; and so was Harney, at the height of his republican fervour. The effect was instantaneous. Ashton men threatened violence against anyone harming Stephens— 'our pride, our boast, our glory and our Radical' to the *Star*[15]—and periodically let off firearms at excited torchlight meetings. And declining industrial conditions enhanced urban militancy in some areas. As a result, in many places Chartism took on the menacing aspect of a terrorist organisation.

Excited, worried, frightened and sometimes cowardly magistrates deluged the Home Office with reports of revolutionary plots, drilling, arming, striking (still particularly favoured by half-demented old Benbow), arson and destruction of property. Chartists who simply hoped for a bloody revolution and the larger number who hoped that physical force threats would supplement moral force policies made little attempt to hide their preparations, in order to impress local and national authorities. As Home Secretary, Lord John Russell trod a wary path. He was determined to maintain a liberal, reforming image; and although he was the 'Finality Jack' whose declaration against the possibility of further reform had incensed radical opinion, he was prepared to tolerate much militant talk—indeed, anxious JPs sometimes felt that he was too tolerant. However, Russell took some precautions. While Northern calls to arms left him unmoved and even the Poor Law commissioners' complaints provoked him to no positive action—he even boasted of his liberal attitudes at Liverpool in October—something had to be done about the torchlight rallies of late 1838. Yet exactly what could properly be done seriously exercised both Russell and Melbourne— whose parliamentary majority was now tenuous. At length, on 12 December a proclamation forbade torchlight rallies; and on the 27th the arrest of Stephens demonstrated that the government was in earnest.

Early in 1839 Russell increased his vigilance. But although in February he authorised the opening of the correspondence of Hartwell, Richardson, Vincent and Wade (a curious selection) he refused to follow magistrates' demands for a full-scale attack on

Chartists: only the Home Office would determine policy. Small measures trickled out: a cavalry regiment was transferred from Ireland to Manchester in December 1838; Frost was deposed as a JP in March 1839; Vincent and McDouall were arrested in April; three battalions were recalled from Ireland to northern England; and Major-General Sir Charles Napier, a loyal officer who was also a radical sympathiser, was appointed to command the Northern District, with over 5,000 scattered troops, from Nottingham. By May excited Chartists and excitable magistrates led the government to drop its caution. A royal proclamation forbade drilling; Lords Lieutenant were authorised to arm special constables and loyalist groups; magistrates were allowed to arrest armed Chartists. Rumours abounded of a revolution and a march on London during May, and Napier—with the highly efficient Colonel T. J. Wemyss at Manchester—carefully deployed and displayed troops in order to prevent and deter any outbreak.[16] Such professional soldiers were determined to avoid any repetition of 'Peterloo' and restrained hot-headed JPs from taking precipitate action.

III

On 6 May the government succeeded in a Commons debate on the Jamacain constitution by only 5 votes, and next day Melbourne resigned. Presentation of the petition was inevitably delayed. Dismayed by their lukewarm reception in London, flattered by Birmingham invititations, frightened by the attention of the Home Office and metropolitan police—and by the probability of a Tory government —and aware that parliamentary discussion would be postponed, the Convention delegates moved to the Midlands.

Birmingham Chartism was changing considerably. When Douglas, Hadley and Salt left the Convention their places were taken by the militant Edward Brown, Thomas Powell and A. H. Donaldson. Collins retained his seat, but Birmingham Chartism was now falling under the control of the new delegates and J. A. Fussell. Angry assemblies gathered almost daily in the Bull Ring to hear the excited Fussell and to await news of the petition. Furthermore, Birmingham was a major armaments-manufacturing town; early in May, McDouall and James Duke of Ashton were there to order sample muskets. Consequently, the town had considerable attraction for the Chartist 'physicals'.

The Convention reached Birmingham five days after the magistrates had prohibited the Bull Ring rallies. Greeted by local radicals, the delegates quickly got to work. There was a march through the town to a celebratory luncheon and a rally at Holloway Head; William Scholefield, the anxious mayor, prepared for trouble, with four thousand special constables and twenty guns. On the 14th the Convention met in the Lawrence Street Chapel and issued its manifesto to 'countrymen and fellow-bondsmen'. Its mood was now frankly militant. 'The Government of England was a Despotism and her Industrious Millions Slaves.' Parliament would undoubtedly reject the petition:

> Men and women of Britain, will you tamely submit to the insult? Will you submit to incessant toil from birth to death, to give in tax and plunder, out of every twelve hours' labour, the proceeds of hours to support your idle and insolent oppressors? Will you much longer submit to see the greatest blessings of mechanical art converted into the greatest curses of social life? . . . Will you permit the stroke of affliction, the misfortunes of poverty, or the infirmities of age to be branded and punished as crimes. . . .

Thus Northern hostility to the factory and Poor Law systems had permeated the Convention; and Northern militancy was implicit in the assertion that 'we have resolved to obtain our rights peaceably if we may, forcibly if we must'. There followed a revised list of 'ulterior measures' to be put before a succession of mass rallies: withdrawal of bank deposits; conversion of paper money; the 'sacred month'; abstinence from intoxicating drinks; refusal of rents, rates and taxes; arming; support of Chartist candidates; exclusive dealing; resistance to any rival agitations; refusal to read hostile journals; and obedience to 'all the just and constitutional requests of the majority of the Convention'. That this list marked the limit of Chartist threats reveals a certain timidity among many delegates; but it also marks a change in the attitude of the remaining moderates. Increased official action brought even Lovett to accept the manifesto.

If the support for the manifesto in the Convention was a curious alliance, the opposition was equally strange. Cleave and Halley were naturally hostile. But even O'Brien and O'Connor expressed doubts, probably from sheer funk. It was one thing to urge others to euphemistically described physical action; it was another matter to face arrest for giving such advice, especially when one was uncertain of the extent of support. 'Let no arms of any description be paraded,' advised the *Star*. 'Let even your words be carefully chosen ... .' But, typically, it added[17]

> if, as is not unlikely, the peace be broken by its professed con-servators; if the people, having given no provocation, be wantonly attacked; if British blood be shed by lawless violence, why then—then we give the people no advice at all. We merely repeat our last week's quotation: 'when it is their cue to fight, they'll know it without a prompter!'

The trip to Birmingham ended on the 16th, when Marsden and O'Connor proposed that the arrest of delegates should be answered by the 'ulterior measures'. O'Brien and O'Connor also carried re-solutions for peaceful agitation (though it was 'the sacred duty of the people to meet force with force and repel assassination by justifiable homicide'); that Chartists should attend rallies 'sober, orderly and unarmed', to avoid provocation; that officials should ensure that the meetings were legal and orderly; and that any violence should be ascribed to 'our oppressors in the middle and upper ranks'. The Convention then adjourned until 1 July.

In its cowardly way, the Convention had continued to leave the major decisions to the mass Whitsuntide meetings; now its policies were to be put to the test. Simultaneously, many authorities stepped up their precautions and 'attacks'. Powell had been arrested on 5 May and Vincent on 7 May, on account of their speeches in the West and Wales. Now arrests proceeded in Lancashire and among LDA members. Local authorities were undoubtedly alarmed by threatened and actual force. Llanidloes Chartists, for instance, had violently attacked the Trewythen Arms tavern from which London police and special constables planned to arrest local leaders, on 30 April and 7 May. When Ashton justices arrested some local Chartists on 4 May, Wemyss had to send troops to guard the prisoners. From his Nottingham headquarters Napier planned against a wide variety of Northern threats and rumours of drilling, urban insurrection, barri-cades and murder.[18] It was with the knowledge that the government was now prepared to act that the long-planned 'simultaneous' mass meetings were held.

As the Convention dispersed the rallies began. It is still difficult to determine what they represented—and even more difficult to com-pute the amount of support; early supporters, including Gammage, were inevitably inclined to accept wild guesses (though even

Gammage cavilled at the *Star*'s estimate of half a million attenders at the Kersall Moor rally). Certainly, there was much militant verbiage circulated. 'Nothing can convince tyrants of their folly but gunpowder and steel, SO PUT YOUR TRUST IN GOD, MY BOYS, KEEP YOUR POWDER DRY. . . . Now or never is your time: be sure you do not neglect your arms, and when you do strike do not let it be with sticks or stones, but LET THE BLOOD OF ALL YOU SUSPECT moisten the soil of your native land.' So ran a militant Manchester poster passed to Napier. The General wisely discounted such hyperbole.

The Army did, however, take some precautions: Wemyss attended the Kersall Moor demonstration on 25 May and Napier estimated attendance at 30,000. William Tillman, the militant Manchester leader, had threatened 'the cotton lords' with 'not only glittering banners, but a bolder front in "a wall of flesh" that should be a terror to their oppressors'. But the meeting passed quietly, despite O'Connor's attendance with Fletcher and Taylor. O'Connor had also attended the West Riding rally on Peep Green on the 21st, with O'Brien, Taylor, Pitkeithley, Mills and Bussey. O'Brien appealed for the election of Chartists at the next election show of hands:

> You support the whole tribe of landholders, fundholders, and 2,000,000 of menials and kept mistresses, together with 100,000 prostitutes in London alone. Why should you not have institutions to make these people get their living honestly? Universal suffrage would at once put the remedy within your grasp.

At Newcastle Town Moor there were more militant perorations from both local and Convention speakers. Duncan condemned police spies—'hired moral assassins, the scoundrel minions of a tyrant government'—and asserted that 'tens of thousands . . . were now in such misery that even a field of battle and a death of pain presented no terrors to them'. And Lowery 'was for peace, law and order; but he would have no peace with oppression and injustice'. Fletcher spoke at Liverpool; Taylor, Harney, Duncan and Knox at Carlisle; Duncan and Knox at Sunderland; James Watson on Kennington Common; Neesom and Mealing at Bath; Frost at Blackwood in Monmouthshire; Burns and Hartwell in Hull; Richards at Preston; Collins and Jones at Leicester (where Collins was appointed a local delegate); Bussey at Bradford; Gill at Sheffield; local orators at South Shields; Taylor and Fenney at Leigh; Harney at Penrith, Cockermouth and Wigton; Moir, Collins, Frost, Richardson, O'Brien, Taylor, Bussey and Lowery at Glasgow and around

Scotland; Stephens at London; Brown and Fussell at Birmingham.

The generally enthusiastic 'simultaneous meetings' passed peacefully, despite local authorities' fearful threats. But there was little modification of Chartist language: Richardson talked (albeit carefully) of a run on the banks; O'Brien insisted that the Commons 'represented the fellows who lived by profits . . . [and] a rascally crew of attornies, bishops and parsons, pawnbrokers and attornies . . . men who had no interest in the welfare of the country. . . . It also represented military officers, and it was a fact that about 2,000 brothel-keepers in London had votes'. To Taylor, 'exclusive dealing was one of the best plans to bring their enemies to their feet'. Bussey confirmed that 'the way to a middle class man's head was through his pockets'. And Lowery, typically, found it a 'blasphemy and mockery of religion to say that God would call men to account and yet they would be told they were too ignorant for the franchise'. Stephens, still awaiting trial, had briefly visited the London Convention and then told London crowds of his beliefs. Workmen should arm 'against the factory system . . . and the Poor Law system', rather than for political reforms. At Ashton he asserted that he

> didn't care about the Charter . . . a republic . . . the Monarchy . . .
> [or] the present order of things or any future order.

His concern was to achieve 'a full, sufficient and comfortable maintenance, according to the will and commandment of God' for the working man. His 'sermons', published as a series under the title of *The Political Pulpit*, were widely circulated.[19]

One feature of the summer campaign was a further list of Convention resignations. Rider, who thought that there were not eight honest 'MCs', led the list. He was followed by Craig (who opposed ulterior measures and was compelled to return his salary to the Ayrshire Chartists, who elected John McCrae in his place). Richardson resigned because he had never been paid; Manchester replaced him with the stonemason Christopher Dean, who seemed less 'bourgeois'. Alexander Halley, who 'was a working man but . . . not . . . a class reformer', could not accept O'Brien's call to arms, and was not replaced by his various Scottish constitutents. McDouall, who was arrested on 8 June for violent talk at Hyde in April, resigned after arguing with Ashton Chartists over diverting part of the Stephens defence fund to his own defence.[20] And arrests were proceeding in several areas.

It was against a background of moderates' withdrawal and

militants' arrests that the Convention reassembled in the Golden
Lion Hotel at Birmingham on 1 July. Inevitably, some members
were affected by the diminished audiences attending the recent rallies
and by signs of antagonism to 'physical force' methods. In Scotland
these signs had long been seen; only Taylor among delegates was in
favour of recent developments. From May, Brewster, sensing that
Scottish Chartism was in danger of breaking-up, called for a Scottish
conference to support moderation. Such a policy was supported by
Robert Malcolm's new *Scottish Patriot* (which disliked Brewster) and
many Glasgow trade unionists, notably William Pattison of the steam-
engine makers and William Thomson, the champion of the weavers
and of retail co-operatives. At last Thomas Gillespie of the Glasgow
Universal Suffrage Association invited the views of the main
Scottish groups and, on their advice, a conference was called in
Glasgow for 14 August, under John Duncan, an Edinburgh shopkeeper. Divisions were revealed by many delegations, but the consensus view (accepted by O'Connor) was that violent measures
should be avoided. The Convention was promised continued support, but a Scottish central committee—dominated by Glasgow—
was established and the message was generally moderate. Similar
regional meetings were held at Manchester on 6 May (to support
militancy) and at Rochdale on 25 June (where delegates were rightly
fearful of further arrests). And O'Connell rather haughtily told
Birmingham Chartists that their cherished claims and policies were
mistaken, proposing instead household suffrage and triennial
parliaments.[21]

On 2 July the delegates resolved to return to London on the 10th,
before Attwood raised the petition in the Commons. At the prompting of Taylor and McDouall, there followed desultory debates on
the ulterior measures. It was difficult to decide exactly what the
recent campaign had authorised. Convinced that the 'electorate' was
unprepared, Craig finally broke with the Convention. Others also
doubted the possibility of a general strike unbacked by adequate
funds. At length it was resolved to employ the less 'revolutionary'
measures against the banks, unsympathetic shopkeepers and hostile
journals. But on the 4th local events took over the centre of interest.
Mayor Scholefield arrived in the town that evening with sixty
London policemen, to find a rowdy and illegal meeting in progress
in the Bull Ring. The police were ordered to clear the partially armed
crowd and a serious riot ensued, which eventually necessitated the
use of troops. Later trouble flared up again as a mob dismantled a

churchyard wall. Taylor and McDouall were arrested, together with other Chartists. On the 5th further policemen arrived in the tense town, the justices released McDouall but held Taylor, and Lovett courageously raised the matter in the Convention. Nothing better demonstrated the brave loyalty of the 'moral force' leader, as opposed to the actual timidity of wordy 'physicals', than Lovett's behaviour at this crisis. In the Convention he carried a strong resolution against the Attwoodite magistrates, insisting that

> a wanton, flagrant and unjust outrage has been made upon the people of Birmingham, by a bloodthirsty and unconstitutional force from London, acting under the authority of men who, when out of office, sanctioned and took part in the meetings of the people, and now, when they share in the public plunder, seek to keep the people in social and political degradation.

The 'summary and despotic arrest' of Taylor

> affords another convincing proof of the absence of all justice in England and clearly shows that there is no security for life, liberty or property till the people have some control over the laws they are called upon to obey.

To save other delegates, Lovett signed the placard version of the resolution, issued on the 6th. He and Collins (the current chairman) were instantly arrested and carried to Warwick Gaol. 'In the history of the first Chartist Convention,' wrote Mark Hovell, 'there is but one cheering episode, and Lovett is its hero.'[22] Faced by the choice between Lovett's noble self-sacrifice and the general cowardice of the verbal militants, one feels bound to agree.

As delegates returned to London they faced a deteriorating situation. Taylor's advice that

> Moral force? moral fudge! 'tis mere humbug,
> For nothing persuades like a lick in the lug

had had little effect among moribund London radicals. But elsewhere similar sentiments had provoked a growing series of arrests: Stephens's seizure in December had been followed by Home Office orders for the apprehension of Vincent and McDouall in April. Four Llanidloes men were taken on 30 April and more, with Powell, on 5 May, four Ashton men on 4 May—followed by other Lancastrians and twelve London Democrats and Vincent and Edwards on the 7th. On the 6th the Westbury cobbler William Tucker, the Trowbridge cobbler Samuel Harding and a Trowbridge confectioner, John Andrews, were arrested at Trowbridge after considerable rioting; and on the 7th the militant druggist William Potts and the lawyer W. P. Roberts were added. Carrier and McDouall were netted in June. July was a busy month. On the 1st Timothy Higgins of the Ashton Radical Association was seized; as in the case of Potts, an arsenal was found in his house. Birmingham militants followed on the 4th and 5th, together with Taylor, and (on the 6th) Lovett and Collins and on the 7th O'Brien and others (for sedition at Newcastle). Later in the month the framework knitters Charles Jarratt and George Turner were taken at Loughborough (for sedition); the militant Irish wool comber and secretary of the Leeds Northern Union George White and an unemployed man named Wilson at Leeds (for extortion of money from shopkeepers); and John Crawley, a printer, and the jeweller William Young at Bath (for seditious libel).[23] It was a fearful rump of the Convention which returned to London. Chartism's principal remaining strength lay not in the militant verbosity of Convention bullies, still less in the pathetic arming of provincial workers (Napier thought that they had 'no organisation, no leaders and a strong tendency to turn rebellion into money, for pikes costing a shilling are sold for three and sixpence'), but rather in the panic of many magistrates bombarding the Home Office and the Army with impossible demands for military protection. Colonel Francis Macerone's textbook for urban guerrillas was reportedly circulated in the North. But Napier countered such stuff with an exhibition of skilled gunners at work and an explanation to Chartists of the logistic difficulties of any revolutionary army:

> armed, starving and interspersed with villains, they must commit horrid excesses; that I would never allow them to charge me with their pikes, or even march ten miles, without mauling them with cannon and musketry and charging them with cavalry, when they dispersed to seek food; finally, that the country would rise on them and they would be destroyed in three days.

At the same time, the General sympathetically pondered over the Chartist problem:

> What has made Englishmen turn assassins? The new poor law. Their resources have dried up but indirect taxes for the debt, and the poor law throws them on a phantom, which it calls their resources—robbery follows, and a robber soon becomes a murderer.

And the General came to despise many local authorities:[24]

> Alarm! Trumpets! Magistrates in a fuss! Troops! Troops! Troops!
> North, South, East, West! I *screech* at these applications like a gate,
> swinging on rusty hinges, and swear! Lord, how they make me
> swear!

IV

The magistrates were not terrorised by mere mirages. There was a
considerable volume of militant talk in the provinces, particularly in
the North. And delegates presumably could not afford to seem less
enthusiastic than their constituents. They condemned the government for using policemen to attack peaceful meetings: those attacked
were

> justified upon every principle of law and of self-preservation in
> MEETING FORCE BY FORCE, EVEN TO THE SLAYING of the persons
> guilty of such atrocious and ferocious assaults upon their rights
> and persons.

They called for the enforcement of the ulterior measures, though
playing the general strike call in low key. And, finally throwing off
Attwoodite attitudes, they condemned 'the corrupt system of Banking, speculating and defrauding the industrious, . . . [by] the fraudulent bits of paper our state tricksters dignify with the name of
money'. In the hands of local Chartist printers, these calls took on
even more militant tones when placarded around northern manufacturing towns.

On 12 July Attwood and Fielden uneasily proposed that a Committee of the Commons should consider the petition. Neither
champion was an impressive speaker: Attwood remained primarily
concerned with currency reform and was prepared to compromise
over the five points; Fielden was still basically a factory and Poor
Law reformer. The subsequent debate was generally unremarkable.
Russell chose to attack Attwood's currency theories (already rejected by the Convention). Disraeli was perceptively sympathetic,
with his attack on the post-1832 reform electorate and its assault on
'civil rights', which 'partook in some degree of an economical and in
some degree certainly of a political character'. The middle classes
had not inherited the social duties, along with the political powers,
of the *ancien régime*: Disraeli

was not ashamed to say, however much he disapproved of the Charter, he sympathised with the Chartists. They formed a great body of his countrymen: nobody could doubt they laboured under great grievances. . . .

Bourgeois radicals who had participated in Chartism's early activities were divided: Hume defended his idea of a Charter modelled on moderate, rational principles, while O'Connell assailed ultras' violence which had lost radical support. Further consideration of the petition was rejected by a bored House by 235 votes to 46.

The remaining Convention delegates now faced the final choice, which had for so long been postponed, over the ultimate sanctions which Chartism was prepared to invoke. Weakened by widespread arrests of delegates and supporters and by assorted resignations (not all of which took immediate effect), concerned by the impending trials, worried that the Convention might lose what control it still retained and still inevitably divided, the delegates had to act quickly. They appointed Lovett's wife as their secretary, but rejected Attwood's suggestion that they should organise a further petition. They proceeded to discuss the 'sacred month' and were immediately divided. Such 'militants' as O'Connor, O'Brien and Taylor initially avoided the debate, which was attended by only thirty members. Lowery and Marsden spoke strongly for striking, against opposition from Richardson, Carpenter and James Taylor. On 17 July the delegates voted for a 'sacred month' to start on 12 August, by 13 votes to 6: five members abstained and others simply stayed away. The ridiculous decision, taken at a time of gathering industrial depression, was immediately followed up with apparent seriousness. Eight members were deputed to organise Britain's major strike. But from the start there was considerable opposition. O'Connor was absent and cool; Richardson wrote pointing out that strikes would be disastrous in current conditions; Frost wrote to report that there would be little Welsh support. A Newcastle report that 'nearly all the colliers in the North . . . more than 25,000' were already on strike for 'their rights' was (to say the least) incorrect.

Disillusion grew, as the reality of Richardson's view that the 'sacred month' would receive negligible backing sank in: it would 'bring irretrievable ruin upon thousands of poor people'. On the 22nd O'Brien returned to attack the decision, withdrew his previous militant stance, praised the general strike as an ideal for the future but condemned it as too dangerous and unprepared for the present and finally proposed that the decision should be left to the people. O'Connor virtually accepted this abdication of Convention leadership and, after a confused debate full of recriminations, twelve members supported O'Brien, six opposed him and seven abstained. Burns, Carpenter, Fletcher, Lowery, O'Brien, O'Connor and Smart were authorised to solicit the localities' advice on the strike. To aid the committee's deliberations, O'Connor announced that he had always doubted the plan: it was 'a wild and visionary scheme of Attwood's, to starve the people into paper money'. Furthermore, Bussey, Pitkeithley, O'Connor, Frost, Duncan, Burns, Smart, Woodhouse, James Taylor, Richardson, Carpenter, Fletcher, O'Brien and Knox, representing industrial areas, were hostile. Seven of the thirteen original supporters represented Southwark, Bristol, Brighton, Bath, Marylebone, Lambeth and Hyde—yet 'with the exception of Bristol and Hyde, not 500 men would stop work' in such places:

> Are we thus to allow the votes of constituencies, by no means organised, to destroy the whole of the North, the Midland Counties and Scotland? ... The men of Lancashire and ... Yorkshire have been the heart and soul of this movement. By the London Delegates they have been declared the prime movers, while the same delegates have declared the preparedness of their own districts. Let us see, then: the test is easy. Let the men of Marylebone, of Southwark, of Lambeth and of Tower Hamlets prove the theory of their Delegates by the practice. Let them commence the strike. ...

The *Northern Star* now urged that 'ANY ATTEMPT TO BRING ABOUT THE SACRED MONTH BEFORE AN UNIVERSAL ARMING SHALL HAVE TAKEN PLACE, WILL RUIN ALL ... ABOVE ALL, AND BEFORE ALL THINGS, LET THE PEOPLE KEEP THE PEACE ...'. Constituents' reports generally supported this attitude, expressing loyal willingness to follow others' leads or reluctant inability to assist at the moment. On 5 August the Convention council 'implored brother Chartists to abandon the project of a sacred month, as being for the present utterly impracticable ...' and appealed for union help. Two days later it warned Chartists to avoid people 'leagued together for the purposes of firing, assassination and like diabolical objects'.[25]

The fact was that the Convention was at last cut down to size. It finally realised the futility of its own pompous and exaggerated claims to represent the working classes, particularly when cautious trade unions refused to rescue the political leaders from the results of their ill-considered decisions. But other events also undoubtedly helped to change the minds of delegates now concerned to avoid legal responsibility for any violence. As the Convention rump started its fatal deliberations, a serious riot developed in Birmingham. Starting as a demonstration to welcome Collins and Lovett, who had been bailed from Warwick Gaol, the event misfired. Missing the delegates, the mob went on a rampage in the Bull Ring until they were cleared by London constables, backed by troops. Elsewhere, supporters continued to demonstrate their divisions. On the 20th Knox announced that the middle and working classes were natural allies, depending upon each other. Next day the Northern Political Union issued a less conciliatory *Address to the Middle Classes*, asking for bourgeois help against 'the Jew swindlers and a perfumed, insolent Aristocracy' (who squandered the people's hard-earned money on 'the dancers, gamesters and prostitutes of the continental cities') but threatening that if such help were not forthcoming, 'vengeance swift and terrible will then overtake you . . . your warehouses, your homes, will be given to the flames and one black ruin overwhelm England!' The publisher (John Bell) was arrested, along with the authors. On the 22nd troops and police attacked a Newcastle meeting;[26] an almost nationwide campaign against Chartism was beginning.

Local authorities continued to arrest Chartists in August. The Manchester militants—Benbow, Christopher Doyle, the Baptist Rev. W. V. Jackson and Tillman—were seized early in the month. The Newcastle leaders followed, together with groups in many towns, including Stockport, Rochdale and Sheffield. Chartists might march to church at Manchester, Blackburn, Bolton and Stockport on the 4th—though their numbers were few—and still maintain a pretence of strength: the *Star*, for instance, warned Parliament that a refusal of justice 'would turn their appeal for the Charter into a demand for a REPUBLIC'. But from the 12th the remaining militants' attempts to organise Lancashire strikes were pathetic failures. Furthermore, the London committee gave up hope. The Convention was prorogued on the 6th, the seven committeemen called off the strike and Chartists watched the collapse of their organisation, amidst a series of trials and arrests.[27] Major trials at Chester, Lancaster, Liverpool, Welshpool, Devizes and Warwick resulted in the imprisonment of Collins, Edwards, Higgins, Lovett, McDouall, Richardson, Stephens, Vincent and scores of others.

V

As Chartism disintegrated in the summer of 1839 there were still some violent episodes. Lowery's mission to Patrick O'Higgins' little group of Dublin Chartists was ruined by O'Connellite heckling. Taylor, Harney, Bussey, O'Connor (who offered to finance a new convention from *Star* profits) and others maintained some excitement in the northern towns, and there was physical violence at Ashton, Loughborough and Newcastle. But when the Convention reassembled on 26 August it was only to indulge in futile arguments until it dissolved on 6 September—though only by Frost's casting vote in a house of twenty-three.

The post-mortems were prolonged. 'If the working classes would fight', Fletcher now believed, 'they must begin themselves, and the Convention must be not the father of the act, but the child of it.' Indeed he soon started to suspect that Chartism had been invented by London Malthusians to take over the Northern anti-Poor Law movement—a notion later to be expounded by Oastler.[28] It was widely thought that there had been 'treason' among the leaders; and it was obvious that there had been much cowardice at the Convention. The fury and disappointment led some members to start secret plots to implement the violent talk of such men as Cardo, Harney, Hartwell and Dr Taylor.

Nowhere was the angry militancy higher than in Monmouth and Glamorgan. The collapse of their hopes and the imprisonment of their hero, Vincent, further roused local workers—among whom there had long been reports of arming. Frost, the new Welsh leader, knew of rumours of a plot forcibly to rescue Vincent; and in a sense he encouraged the notion by insisting that the Army would never fire on the Chartists. Some hints (at least) of these plans were given to some Convention members. Bussey, for instance, returned to Yorkshire apparently to organise a conference at Heckmondwike on 30 September—when (according to Lovett) it was decided to organise a Yorkshire rising to support the Welsh. O'Connor allegedly appeared to approve of the plot, but then deserted. Whatever the truth of this story, O'Connor certainly crossed to Ireland on 4 October. In Lancashire also there seems to have been some sort of plan for a simultaneous rising. But, as in the case of the 'sacred month', these wild schemes were contingent upon the Welsh acting first.

With charges hanging over his head for 'violent and inflammatory language' and criminal libel, Frost modified his tactics. On 3 October at Nantyglo he tried to deter the master-collier publican Zephaniah Williams and the watchmaking publican William Jones from organising a rising; indeed, he tried to cool tempers at a secret meeting throughout the night—but unsuccessfully. Later in the month he visited Lancashire, but what he did (apart from cancelling a Bury engagement with Fielden, Oastler, J. P. Cobbett and Dr Taylor on the 14th) is unknown. Despite rumours, the Welsh secret plan was well kept: it was only on the 29th that Charles Jones (who had been on the run since the Llanidloes riots) told Hetherington of the rising. Hetherington took him to Dr Taylor, who took him to Bradford to see Bussey. It transpired that the risings were planned for 3 November. Jones was then sent urgently to Wales, to seek a postponement for ten days.

Meanwhile, the Monmouth men were regularly plotting and arguing under the tutelage of Williams and William Jones. Frost, now terrified, told Dr William Price on the 27th that the rising was to occur on 3 November. On the 1st the final plans were hatched at a secret meeting in a Blackwood tavern, when 5,000 men were promised. Next day, while buying arms in Newport, young William Davies (Frost's future son-in-law) met Charles Jones, bearing the Northern messages. But it was now too late to postpone matters. The climax to the long period of threats and plots arrived on Sunday the 3rd. During the stormy evening Frost led a march from Blackwood, Williams from Nantyglo and Jones from Pontypool to a union at Risca. Jones returned for reinforcements, and by Monday morning the drenched columns decided to act without him. The element of surprise had been lost, as the host descended on Newport. When the Chartists arrived they converged on the Westgate Hotel, demanding the release of their local supporters. And when some enthusiasts fired arms twenty-eight soldiers of the 45th Foot surreptitiously hidden in the hotel fired back. It was enough. The brave militants of the Welsh Valleys learned reality within seconds; bullying clamour would, in the last resort, be met by force. They fled, suffering fourteen dead and around fifty wounded. 'Oh! if I were twenty years younger!', exclaimed Wellington, on hearing the news.

The disaster was followed by considerable confusion. On the 5th the Dowlais ironworkers left work but were called back by Sir Josiah Guest. Many Chartists thought it wise to hide for a time; the Rhondda men briefly marched and then retreated; William David, a Baptist shopkeeper at Dinas, fled to America; the *eminence grise*, the demented Anglican surgeon Price of Pontypridd, moved to Paris; Cardiff prepared for invasion. Frost, Williams, Jones and 122 others were arrested.[29] O'Connor had an alibi in his Irish visit (from which he returned on the 6th), but other Northern leaders thought it advisable to disappear. Fat Bussey had quickly become alarmed, diplomatically became ill, hid from his followers, sent White round Yorkshire to postpone the rising and finally fled to America, where he remained for fourteen years as a farmer, publican, journalist and eventually street-hawker.

It remains difficult to determine the entire truth of the background of the first and most celebrated Chartist attempt at an actual rising. Inevitably, the affair was planned furtively. Equally inevitably, the Chartist leaders being what they were, contemporary accounts differ considerably and ascribe very varied roles to different individuals. Above all, it is virtually impossible to assess the truth of the widespread rumours that a national revolution was planned to be triggered off by the Newport outbreak. Gammage, who disliked O'Connor, adopted the account of William Ashton, a Barnsley weaver who had once been transported for trade union activities in the 1820s. According to Ashton, the Newport affair was planned by some Convention members. But Ashton found it necessary to escape to France. Before leaving, he told William Hill at Hull to make O'Connor stop the plan, which could only ruin Frost. Subsequently, O'Connor denied any knowledge of the plan; but Hill confirmed that he had passed Ashton's message to O'Connor. Gammage's conclusion was that 'what above all confirms the statement that O'Connor had a thorough knowledge of what was going on, is the fact that, at that critical period, he left the scene of danger and embarked for Ireland'. Furthermore, Gammage suspected that O'Connor sacrificed his rival Frost without compunction. He claimed some support from Lowery's assertion that

O'Connor had nothing to do with getting up that movement; but he was perfectly cognizant of it, and was the only man that could have put a stop to it, had he been so disposed.

Similar charges were made by Feargus's former acolyte John Watkins.[30]

An alternative version is the curious story told by the Tory-inclined Turcophil David Urquhart, who saw a Russian plot behind this and many other events. The chief agent was the Polish Major Beniowski, who planned an insurrection with William Cardo, John Warden, one Westrapp and a police officer. Some 120,000 men were to rise, backed by a Russian fleet, but at the last minute Urquhart persuaded the leaders not to follow a tsarist scheme—though he was too late to warn Frost. Undoubtedly, Urquhart was an eccentric russophobe; but he did have some Chartist contacts. Beniowski was a revolutionary member of the LDA, already under police observation; and he appears to have visited Newport shortly after the rising. Urquhart subsequently preached the message that Chartism was being used as a Russian tool; Charles Attwood, Cardo, Lowery, Richards and Warden accepted his arguments and several Chartists supported his anti-Palmerston campaigns in the Foreign Affairs Committees. Urquhart's account was repeated by Thomas Frost, a Croydon Chartist historian.[31]

Belief in a widespread conspiracy was widely held. Some sort of central committee, composed of regional leaders, allegedly existed in London. At Birmingham (where the non-arrival of the Newport coach was reportedly to signal the rising) Brown and Fussell certainly hatched wild plots. Lovett accepted the accounts of the plan and of O'Connor's defection. Yorkshire accounts followed Lovett, telling of Bussey's Heckmondwike conference and his subsequent desertion. At Halifax 'had not Peter Bussey been taken badly they would of commenced the same day that Frost did', and at Bradford there was undoubtedly a plan to rise. The Yorkshiremen were almost certainly in touch with Taylor and his allies in Newcastle, where Thomas Ainge Devyr was awaiting the signal.[32] But Frost's failure and local 'treason' ruined any plot. By the end of the year Napier 'did not place much belief in the truth of the report' of a 'general rising'— despite Chartist threats in many areas to rescue Frost by force of arms. The General was not entirely correct. A wide plan was concocted to avenge the Newport disaster, and information flooded into the Home Office of arming and drilling in London, Bradford, Wales, Manchester, Birmingham, Loughborough, Halifax, Newcastle, Dewsbury and elsewhere. At the suggestion of Taylor and the NPU, a new Convention met in London from 19 December, to support Frost and arrange a national rising—which was plotted in some detail by a 'secret' committee at Dewsbury. O'Connor indicated that he would join the revolt:

When did you ever hear of me, or of any one of my family, ever

deserting the cause of the people? Have they not always been
found at their post in the hour of danger?

Amid gathering excitement, the rising was planned for 12 January
1840. But O'Connor deserted the cause even before the Convention
broke up on the 8th, declaring against any hopeless violence. This
advice doubtless deterred many Chartists, but early on the 12th the
revolution began at Dewsbury, with the firing of guns and release of
signal balloons. Bradford also had a tense night. But the second
attempted rising collapsed, amidst further arrests and further flights
abroad by such men as Devyr, who had anxiously awaited news at
Newcastle. The only brief 'success' was achieved at Sheffield, where
Samuel Holberry (a former soldier) led an armed attack on the police.
One last attempt was made at Bradford on the 26th, under Robert
Peddie, an itinerant Scottish revolutionary—a man condemned by
Harney as a spy but who had more courage than his colleagues and
who was ruined by a real spy, James Harrison.[33]

The series of disasters was quickly followed by a renewed series
of arrests and trials. On 13 January, in the heavily guarded Monmouth court, Sir Nicholas Tyndal sentenced Frost, Jones, Williams
and (with a recommended commutation to life transportation)
Charles Waters, John Lovell, Richard Benfield, John Rees and Jacob
Morgan to death for high treason and others to imprisonment. On
appeal to the Court of Exchequer on 1 February the death sentences
were commuted to transportation for life. On 29 February O'Brien,
Devyr, William Thomason, John Mason and James Ayr were found
not guilty and only John Bell was sentenced (to six months' imprisonment, for seditious libel). Thereafter the prosecutions were
successful. In March the Yorkshire rioters were sentenced at York
assizes. Of the Sheffield men Holberry received four years' imprisonment, Thomas Booker and James Duffy three, William Booker, John
Marshall, Thomas Penthorpe and Joseph Bennison two and William
Wells and William Martin one. From Bradford, Peddie, William
Brooke and Paul Holdsworth were sentenced for three years, John
Walker, Joseph Naylor, John Rhyding and Rishworth for two years
and Thomas Drake and two others for eighteen months. The Barnsley leaders Peter Hoey, John Crabtree and William Ashton were
imprisoned for two years. At Liverpool the sentences included two
years for W. V. Jackson, eighteen months for William Barker,
Daniel Ball and O'Brien, one year for Charles Morris, nine months
for Richardson, Doyle and William Butterworth, eight months for

Samuel Scott and six months for John Kaye, Frederick Davidson, James Luck and Peter Murdin. At Chester Benbow was imprisoned for sixteen months, Isaac Johnson, James Duke and John Livesey for a year and others for shorter terms. At Monmouth Vincent received an extra year and Edwards fourteen months. At Devizes Roberts, Carrier and Potts were sentenced for two years, at Taunton three Somerset men received from three to nine months, at Durham Williams and Binns were imprisoned for six months and others for shorter periods, and at York on 11 May O'Connor was sentenced for eighteen months for seditious libel in the *Star*.[34] Almost everywhere, Chartism was in ruins, with its campaigning reduced to unsuccessful petitions for its gaoled leaders.

VI

As the Chartist petitioning for the Newport 'martyrs' developed early in 1840, it was organised by 'conventions' at Manchester in March and at Nottingham in April. Some delegates were still disposed to support violence, but the majority now favoured appealing for their heroes' release: Frost and his colleagues had set the pattern in December 1839 by declaring that they had

> never entertained any feeling or spirit of hostility against your Majesty's sacred person, rights, or immunities, nor against the Constitution of your Majesty's realms as by law established.

And from this campaign developed a healthy re-thinking of Chartist principles and strategy. Chartism, after all, had received a measure of sympathy from some surprising sources. Frost's defence counsel, Sir Frederick Pollock, had declared to the Newport jury that

> However differing in opinion from those who are called Chartists, I must do them the justice to say that Chartism so far is not treason, nor the assertion of public conviction of it rebellion.

And Northern Chartists were fortunate in the choice of Napier as military commander. At a private meeting with the leaders, he had promised to keep troops and policemen away from the Kersall Moor rally:

> But meet peaceably, for if there is the least disturbance I shall be amongst you and at the sacrifice of my life, if necessary, do my duty. Now go and do yours!

Behind the General's tolerance lay a deep personal concern. 'There is among the manufacturing poor', he noted at Nottingham,

> a stern look of discontent, of hatred to all who are rich, a total absence of merry faces: a sallow tinge and dirty skins tell of suffering and brooding over change . . . poor fellows!

Stephens was to express a similar attitude in 1848, when he asserted that

> The people at large know little and care still less about the Charter . . . [but] their social condition . . . is truly appalling.

But when the wild men of Chartism threatened real violence they harmed their own cause. When, on 10 March, J. T. Leader proposed a Commons Address to the Queen soliciting a pardon for Frost, Jones and Williams, he had only six supporters.[35] The new Chartism gave the movement the chance of repairing the tarnished image in a society which knew that, in the last resort, revolution could be repelled with comparative ease.

The search for the new form was not easy. Most of the Chartist journals had collapsed, most Chartist leaders were interned or had emigrated, many rank-and-file members were frightened, disorganised or disillusioned. But an important dialogue gradually developed. At Leeds a Radical Universal Suffrage Association founded in April, aimed at 'the attainment of Universal Suffrage and the other main points of the Charter by the use of every moral and lawful means'. The LRUSA was organised by a Methodist-style 'class' system, and a similar system was advocated by R. K. Philp in Wiltshire. In April also the Metropolitan Charter Union, led by Hetherington, proposed to 'keep the principles of the People's Charter prominently before the public, by . . . any . . . . legal means'. Almost simultaneously, the Newcastle NPU was revived to gain 'Universal Suffrage by every moral and lawful means . . .'.[36] Thus the reviving English organisations tended to echo the moderate sentiments of the increasingly independent Universal Suffrage Central Committee for Scotland, backed by the weekly *Scottish Chartist Circular* (edited by William Thomson, the weavers' champion).

Individual Chartists made a wide variety of suggestions for the future of the organisation. The militant Harney, who had temporarily dropped his revolutionary fervour to become a Scottish lecturer, recommended assorted remedies which illustrated his personal schizophrenia. Now he commended the moral force policies of the

Scots. But he did so in ways which scarcely represented the views of
the Scottish leadership. He soundly condemned the free trade notions
of the Anti-Corn Law League, with which many Scottish Chartists
had some sympathy (partly because of their determination to avoid
any taint of 'Toryism'). And he scarcely enhanced Scottish Chartism's moderate image with his address to democrats:

> The men of Scotland have recommended petitioning. Shall we
> join them in that? My answer is—Yes! Not because I imagine
> petitioning will get the Charter. . . . Neither do the men of Scot-
> land, but they adopt it as a means of furthering their organisation,
> and of annoyance to their oppressors.

He 'still believed that it was physical force, or the fear of it, to which
in the end they should be compelled to resort'. Scottish Chartists
actually seem to have veered between the entirely 'moral force' arguments of Brewster and the belief that the ultimate sanction of violence should be retained; their most impressive historian has demonstrated that 'physical force' men, determined to inaugurate violence,
were few. The Scots, in other words, were generally determined
never to indulge in revolutionary action but were reluctant entirely
to lose the possibility of threatening such action.

Many Scottish Chartists were influenced by the 'Christian Chartist' message of Arthur O'Neill of Maryhill, Glasgow, a young
freelance preacher. Through 1840 Chartist churches were widely
established, and by 1841 'a Chartist place of worship was . . . to be
found on the Lord's Day in almost every town of note from Aberdeen to Ayr'. Others practised a variety of self-help schemes, organising popular concerts and discussions, dancing classes for female
supporters, lecture courses, temperance propaganda (through the
columns of the *True Scotsman*, the *Scottish Patriot* and the *Chartist
Circular*) and Chartist co-operative stores. Lowery, generally agreeing with such moderate courses, proposed to drop Conventions and
to fight parliamentary elections. An anonymous 'Republican' also
proposed to abolish the Convention—but on the grounds that it was
weak and 'puerile'. He envisaged a secretive, insurrectionary network
of cells tightly controlled by a seven-strong 'Great Central and Secret
Directory'.[37]

Some Chartists made their proposals for the movement's future
from prison. O'Connor, who had grown rich from the profits of the
Northern Star, now saw the establishment of a daily *Morning Star* as

a prime necessity. Capital of £20,000 would be raised from sympathisers, readers and himself; and the profits would finance a twenty-strong Convention and a platoon of lecturers. R. J. Richardson proposed a complicated new constitution which owed something to the United States, which was still widely admired by some Chartists. Vincent, whose *Western Vindicator* had ceased publication in December 1839, now expressed a temperate 'Christian' attitude. Above all, Lovett and Collins, unfairly and (initially) harshly imprisoned at Warwick, dreamed of a revitalised organisation.

In a remarkable pamphlet Lovett and Collins announced that the aim of Chartism was

> the regeneration of all, the subjugation of none; its objects . . . are to place our institutions on the basis of justice, to secure labour its reward and merit its fruits, and to purify the heart and rectify the conduct of all, by knowledge, morality and love of freedom.

Although 'discord and folly had to some extent unhappily prevailed, for want of sufficient investigation', Chartism was 'yet destined to become a great and efficient instrument of moral and intellectual improvement'. To forward this aim the authors proposed a 'National Association of the United Kingdom for promoting the Political and Social Improvement of the People', to

> unite, in one general body, persons of all CREEDS, CLASSES, and OPINIONS, who are desirous to promote the political and social improvement of the people.

The Association would peacefully support the Charter, erect public halls to be used for children's schools and adults' evening classes, establish teachers' training colleges, agricultural and industrial schools for orphans and public libraries, publish tracts, present prizes to supporters, organise missionaries and raise funds. Lovett and Collins prepared detailed rules for the Association, libraries and schools, down to specimens of lesson cards. The pamphlet ended typically:[38]

> Ignorance and selfishness may lead men to neglect . . . important *duties*, but they cannot long remain neglectful of them, *without suffering in some way the penalty of such neglect.*

Vincent soon adopted the plan for halls where Chartists could acquire 'Political, Moral and Scientific Information' and Lowery found the scheme 'one of the most comprehensive and practical . . .

ever ... yet offered to the public'. But O'Connor bitingly condemned it in the *Star*.

Behind the ferment of ideas Chartism was reorganising itself surprisingly quickly. The climax came on 20 July, when twenty-three delegates assembled in the Griffin tavern at Manchester. Most members were 'new' men; only Deegan, Smart and James Taylor among old 'MCS' attended. The assembly proceeded to assess the plethora of plans for Chartism's future. It resolved to form a National Charter Association of Great Britain, to federate local 'classes' 'wards' and 'councils'. A weekly subscription of 1d was to be levied. It was decided to move Chartist motions at political meetings, to enjoin temperance and to support Chartist candidates at election shows of hands. William Tillman (formerly secretary of the Manchester Political Union) and James Leach (an energetic protectionist operative, also from Manchester) led a provisional executive. But the NCA started slowly. For one thing, there was considerable concern that the new constitution might be illegal under the Corresponding Societies Act of 1799; Lovett refused to join on this ground. Place was convinced (as he told Collins) that

> The Association is to all intents and purposes an illegal assembly and every member thereof ... may be transported for seven years. ... Any one who thus commits himself must be a very silly fellow. ... If these men should go on, as I suppose they will, and in time be prosecuted, what sympathy will they deserve? What sympathy will they receive? None. How will they have promoted the good cause? Not at all. ...

As a result of such views, the original NCA constitution was gradually modified; local election of local officials was replaced by election of delegates to a general council which would select local and executive officers and thus avoid the provisions of current Acts against corresponding societies and conspiracy. But many Chartist groups long remained undecided about affiliation to an apparently O'Connorite organisation. Their doubts were not removed by the NCA's manifesto, which condemned government attitudes on the Newport men and the Poor Law, invited advocates of rival Chartisms to reunite, attacked free trade, urged the collection of subscriptions, advocated the backing of election candidates and suggested the establishment of a London convention of adopted candidates.[39] Despite a bad start and a seeming hostility to trade unionism, however, the NCA was to become a vital organisation in Chartist history.

6 The New Chartism

The National Charter Association faced many early difficulties. Its original plan to register all members' names made it look like 'the attorney-general's registration office for political offenders' to one Chartist, while doubts over its legality deterred other associations. By February 1841 only 80 local branches had joined; but thereafter the revised constitution took effect and in October there were 204, in November 263 and by December 282 localities.[1] However, the NCA was far from representing the totality of Chartism. The Scottish movement was now self-contained, devoting itself to a variety of 'good' causes. And in England new schemes were taking shape.

Lovett and Collins were released on 25 July 1840, when Lovett went on a recuperative holiday while Collins addressed the Warwick Chartists and a great Birmingham rally on the 27th. The Birmingham men and their guests from many districts now supported the NCA plan, which Leach explained to them. But Lovett had other plans. After a public dinner with Wakley and Duncombe in London on 4 August, he refused Samuel Smiles's offer of a post with the *Leeds Times*, started a bookshop and worked on his National Association scheme. Further releases of old leaders provoked a crop of demonstrations. McDouall was greeted at Manchester on 22 August and subsequently toured the North and (with Collins and White) Scotland. Lesser leaders also received warm welcomes from old supporters. But the celebrations scarcely hid the divided state of Chartism. The *Northern Liberator* was now the voice of Urquhart's anti-Palmerston campaign, backed by Charles Attwood, Ayr, Cardo, Cargill, Doubleday, Lowery, Mason, Richards and Warden, operating from Newcastle. In London, Lovett gained support for his National Association from Hetherington, Vincent, Cleave, W. J. Linton, Mitchell, Moore, Neesom, the barrister J. H. Parry, Spurr and Watson, backed by *The National Association Gazette*. And the Chartist church movement spread beyond Scotland, notably to Birmingham (where Collins and O'Neill presided) and Bath (under Vincent, after his release in January 1841). Leicester, Loughborough and Nottingham men supported the NCA through the Chartist Association of the Midland Counties, backed by *The Midland Counties Illuminator* (edited from 1841 by Thomas Cooper). But Cooper soon led a secession of the 'Shakespearean Association of Leicester Chartists', bitterly denouncing John Markham's orthodox NCA branch. At Leeds the Radical Universal Suffrage Association yielded to an NCA branch, but there were also a Total Abstinence Charter Association, a Charter Debating Society and a Chartist church group. And in the Black Country, Chartists under such figures as the barber John Jones and Joseph Linney of Bilston gained colliers' support. Aided by the Dudley draper Samuel Cook, the Wednesbury tube manufacturer Benjamin Danks and D. A. Aulton of Walsall, they periodically channelled assorted demands.[2]

Against such splintering of effort O'Connor regularly fulminated in the *Star*. He approved only of the Manchester plan and soundly berated 'Knowledge Chartism, Teetotal Chartism and Christian Chartism'. In particular, he wrote,

> I object to knowledge Chartism, because it impliedly acknowledges a standard of some sort of learning, education or information as a necessary qualification to entitle man to his political rights.

O'Connor was primarily concerned to prevent Chartism from being taken over by 'middle-class' interests. From prison he egoistically sought to control the new novement, stressing his claimed aristocratic descent, his proletarian sympathies and his alleged expenditure on the cause. Most NCA men, together with the Leicester Shakespearians (soon to become a uniformed para-military body, under 'General' Cooper) agreed with O'Connor; the Lovettites, most Scots (especially after Dr Taylor's illness and death in December 1842) and other 'moderates' emphatically disagreed. O'Connor's former mentor, Oastler, had been imprisoned for debt in December 1840.

As the movement in all its aspects slowly gathered force, the Chartist press again grew. O'Brien and Carpenter ran the *Southern Star* from late 1839; Philp and Vincent issued *The National Vindicator* from Bath in 1841; Cleave founded an *English Chartist Circular* in 1841; from Leicester Cooper ran his *Illuminator*; O'Connor's *Star* continued to dominate the North. But NCA progress was sluggish. In June 1841 eighty-three branches participated in the election of an executive to replace the provisional committee appointed at Manchester. The voting resulted in the election of Dr McDouall (3,795 votes), Leach (3,664), John Campbell (secretary: 2,219), Morgan Williams (2,045), George Binns (1,879) and Philp (1,130); Abel Heywood, a Manchester bookseller, acted as treasurer. The vitality of Chartism was amply demonstrated by the number of ventures; but only the NCA appeared to be pursuing Chartism pure and simple. Julius West fairly commented that the voting figures 'suggest that the total membership of the eighty-three branches in question did not exceed five thousand'. Mark Hovell, however, thought that 'with new men and new methods, Chartism made great progress during 1840 and 1841. The new organisation tended towards much greater efficiency' —for instance, by gaining over 2,000,000 signatures to a petition for the release of Frost, presented by T. S. Duncombe in May 1841.[3] The next traumatic event was the release of O'Connor on 30 August.

I

From York Castle, O'Connor had sent a constant stream of advice to the Chartists. In particular, he maintained his efforts to recruit proletarian Irish support. This inevitably involved detaching immigrants from the spell of his old enemy, O'Connell, 'the dictator to the Whig Cabinet, the base, bloody and brutal traitor'. Progress was slow: most Irishmen stood by 'the Liberator', except in the militant linen-weaving town of Barnsley. O'Connell's advice to avoid 'the insane or dishonest Radicals of England, who instead of appealing to common sense, declared their reliance on arms' was thus followed. While O'Connor and his friends saw O'Connell as a Whig tool, the latter professed to see Chartists as 'torch-and-dagger Tory-Radicals . . . the base hirelings and partisans of the Tory faction'. O'Connell claimed in January 1839 that

> the attempts of the Tory Radicals to produce confusion and civil strife have always failed among the Irish resident in England . . . With few exceptions, the Irishmen who live in England have totally avoided any communication with that body; and they have acted in a similar way in Scotland. They show that they are convinced that the only sure path to justice and prosperity is that of peace and good order.

Certainly, many more Irishmen rallied to the repeal movement than to Chartism. The Roman Catholic priesthood was heavily involved and there was clerical talk of refusing the sacraments to Chartists. Hostility between repealers and Chartists rapidly developed in the North. When O'Connell proposed to link the bourgeois and working-class radicals of Leeds in January 1841, O'Connor urged Chartists to devote 'but *one*, one, ONE, *only* ONE *day* . . . to your own cause and [the] defence [of] . . . The Tyrants' captive, The oppressor's dread, The poor man's friend, and the people's accepted present'—himself. Chartists were roused to break the rally. In the event O'Connell dared not attend (he believed that the O'Connorites would kill him), Hume's household suffrage proposals were rejected and O'Connor was cheered.[4]

O'Connor's victory at Leeds may have encouraged some Irish participation in Yorkshire Chartism, but it also encouraged the more numerous Lancashire Irish to employ similar tactics against the Chartists. 'We have completely defeated the Chartists', John Kelly reported from Manchester in May:

> they called a meeting . . . for the express purpose of passing a vote of censure on Mr O'Connell, but the Repealers attended, and had a chairman appointed and a vote of thanks and confidence passed to Mr O'Connell.

The O'Connellite Lancastrian mob was to prove a valuable ally for the Anti-Corn Law League against the Chartists. And in Ireland itself Patrick O'Higgins's Irish Universal Suffrage Association of August never made much headway against the Loyal National Repeal Association. In December the Roman Catholic workman Corbett told the IUSA at Dublin that the Association was 'not now afraid of any opposition'—indeed, 'he courted it':

> He was a Catholic and a Munsterman, and he repudiated the unchristian threat of bringing over 500,000 Munstermen to cut down their English Protestant brethren for no other reason than that of having formed a Chartist Association, the object of which he knew to be that of obtaining the rights of the working classes, in the benefits of which his countrymen would be equal participators.

But he carried little weight against the entrenched O'Connellites, and it was in vain that O'Higgins urged O'Connell to drop Whiggism and support the Charter.

The differences were widened by O'Connor's advice that, after supporting their own candidates at the summer election shows of hands, Chartists should aid the Tories. To Whig and liberal radical horror, this counsel was widely followed in the North. 'The Radical and Chartist votes were courted wherever there was a contest by the Tories', observed Henry Cockburn, 'to whom these votes were almost invariably given'. And Oastler delightedly quoted the Whig *Morning Chronicle's* view that 'the Chartists, such as are voters, have almost to a man supported the Tories'. 'Of the conduct of those persons calling themselves Chartists, who had lent themselves to the Tories', Glasgow liberals could 'neither think nor speak but with feelings of unmitigated disgust'. Nowhere, they complained, 'did the Chartists . . . contest the election with, or oppose the return of, any Tory'.[5] The result was a Conservative victory, backed by some surprising successes in the industrial areas.

Throughout his imprisonment O'Connor had published a stream of self-pitying and bombastically egotistical proclamations. A series of complaints about alleged sufferings and regular assertions in the *Star* established the myth of a martyred and brilliant leader. 'I found you a weak and unconnected party,' O'Connor insisted, on entering prison. '. . . I am leaving you strong as the oak that stands the raging storms.' He 'desired that no horse should draw him to his resting-place, but that he should be carried upon the shoulders of working-men from the prison-house to the house of death . . .'. In weekly homilies 'to the fustian jackets, blistered hands and unshorn chins of England, Scotland and Wales and to the ragged-backed, bare-footed Irish' he preached an uncomplicated Chartism, led by himself. He warned against involvement in side-issues: 'if every abuse of which they now complained was abolished tomorrow, their order would not derive a fraction of benefit from the change'. His 'plan for carrying the Charter [was] . . . two short words—DAILY PAPER'. He 'gloried in the rich and consoling reflection [of] not one drop of blood shed through five years and a half.' And, in praising himself for founding 'the first paper ever published in England exclusively for the people', he claimed that 'from September 1835 to February 1839 I led you single-handed and alone'. As his release approached, he invited readers to

judge whether oppression has broken O'Connor's heart, or O'Connor has broken oppression's head. . . . O! Monday will be a great and glorious day for Chartism and right.

A climax of self-praise was reached in a prison poem:[6]

> O'Connor is our chosen chief,
> He's champion of the Charter:
> Our Saviour suffered like a thief
> Because he preached the Charter.

Such stuff might disgust Lovettites and Christian Chartists, but it had a wide popularity. Place sourly commented that 'O'Connor obtained supremacy by means of his volubility, his recklessness of truth, his newspaper, his unparalleled impudence and by means of a body of mischievous people whom he attached to himself by mercenary bonds'. But to humble folk, looking forward to the weekly spelling-out of the *Star*, the message was magnetic, moving and mercurial. 'The immense majority of Chartists in Leicester, as well as in many other towns', recalled Cooper, 'regarded him as the only really disinterested and incorruptible leader.' When, at O'Connor's suggestion, a ten-man Convention was elected to supervise petitioning, only Collins represented a non-O'Connorite faction. And when O'Connor presented a list of eighty-seven personal followers as the élite of the movement his selection was widely accepted.

O'Connorism thus became the dominant motif of Northern Chartism. The self-styled 'unpaid, untiring, unpurchasable, unflinching friend' of the people was ecstatically received by the fustian-jacket brigade when he was released (two months early) on 30 August. Fifty delegates hastened to make obeisance at York and then O'Connor set off on a triumphant tour of Ashton, Bolton, Bradford, Dewsbury, Halifax, Heywood, Holmfirth, Huddersfield, London, Oldham, Rochdale and Stockport and of Glasgow, Larkhall, Paisley, Dunfermline, Aberdeen, Montrose, Alloa, Stirling, Perth and other Scottish towns (where he was continually attacked by Brewster). Many of the crowds greeted the tall, energetic champion with the new Chartist hymn (composed by Thomas Cooper):

> The lion of freedom comes from his den,
> We'll rally around him again and again,
> We'll crown him with laurels our champion to be,
> O'Connor, the patriot of sweet liberty.
>
> The pride of the nation, he's noble and brave,
> He's the terror of tyrants, the friend of the slave,
> The bright star of freedom, the noblest of men,
> We'll rally around him again and again. . . .

O'Connor's dynamism gave a new boost to the NCA, already controlled by his fervent apostles. Already encouraged by the nation-wide support for its spring petitions on Chartist prisoners, the Association now started a steady growth. Now began the dual tasks of organising a new Convention and petition and of weeding-out any men of doubtful loyalty to 'the great I AM'.[7] Hopes started to rise for success during 1842.

II

The elimination of O'Connor's rivals was carried through with great energy and by a variety of methods (including O'Connor's financial hold over *Star* agents). The intellectualism of Lovett was a prime target. The National Association for Promoting the Improvement of the People had attracted many moderate men, but before its London branch was established O'Connor denounced it. He distrusted the 'superior' men who claimed to represent London workers; indeed, 'London was rotten'. National Association supporters faced three possibilities. They could stand by the Association's *Address* of March 1841, with its assertion of the 'great truth' that 'you must become your own social and political regenerators or you will never enjoy freedom. For true liberty cannot be conferred by Acts of Parliament or by decrees of princes, but must spring from the knowledge, morality and public virtue of our population'. If they did so, they risked incurring O'Connor's displeasure and sanctions. So, while Lovett and his immediate followers left the mainstream of Chartism, other supporters like John McCrae of Kilbarchan and George Rogers of London—penitently confessed their error. Secondly, they could resign office—like William Pattison in Lanarkshire—to the O'Connorites. Or they could try to retain offices in both the NAPIP and NCA, like Vincent. All faced the heated attacks of the *Star*, to which Lovett's scheme seemed to be a bourgeois conspiracy to divide Chartists. Indeed, Hill invited 'an appropriate dialogue' between a Lovettite architect of a 'Temple of Liberty' and 'a handloom weaver with nine children awaiting its completion as a means of relief'. The 'new move' was bitterly and sometimes unfairly denounced at O'Connorite rallies and was quickly reduced to insignificance. O'Connorite suspicions of middle-class involvement were justified: NAPIP subscribers included such MPS as Charles Buller, Richard Cave, Slingsby Duncombe, Wynn Ellis, Howard

Elphinstone, Milner Gibson, Hume, General William Johnson, the Hon. C. P. Villiers, Thomas Wakley, Henry Warburton, Peter Wason, P. W. Williams, Benjamin Wood and Sir Matthew Wood, together with Dr John Epps, Lords Brougham and Radnor, Sir John Easthope and George Grote. O'Connorite denunciation reached a climax in John Watkins's sermons justifying the murder of Lovett.[8] And the result was inevitable. The NAPIP, with its library, coffee house, Sunday school, dancing lessons, classes in phrenology and high subscription (8d monthly, to the NCA's annual 8d) flickered briefly in the hall at Holborn. But elsewhere the 'new move' was still-born, clutching as a last hope at the political straw of female enfranchisement.

The next O'Connorite row was with O'Brien. Bronterre had been a friend of O'Connor and, through his development of a Chartist philosophy in the *Star*, had become 'the Chartist Schoolmaster'. In a long succession of journals—*The True Sun* (1832), *The Midland Representative* (1831-2), *The Poor Man's Guardian* (1832-5), *The Destructive* (1833-4), *The London Dispatch* and *Twopenny Dispatch* (1836-9) the *National Reformer* (1836-7), the *London Mercury* (1837), *The Operative* (1838-9) and the *Southern Star* (1840)—he had predicted revolution to ensure the application of the labour theory of value. Class cooperation to such a bitter, temperamental man had been an impossibility. His prison sentence appears to have cleared his head considerably. For one thing, his theories took on a more positively socialist tinge and yet allowed him to think of collaborating with bourgeois liberals. As the 1841 election approached both he and O'Connor recommended Chartists to contest the shows of hands. But when O'Connor added advice to support the Tories, O'Brien 'dissented *in toto*':

What! Vote for a Tory merely keep out a Whig! Vote for a villain who wants to put down me and my principles and my party by brute force, merely to get rid of another villain who has tried the same game and failed! No! damn me! if I do. . . .

O'Connor must be 'mad' to adopt 'such a gross lump of Cobbettism': an alliance with Toryism would 'annihilate [Chartism] *morally* as a political party'. When O'Connor claimed some curious consistency (mainly by attacking O'Connell) O'Brien replied firmly. Clearly, most Chartists followed O'Connor. O'Brien stood at Newcastle as a 'Conservative Radical Reformer'—by which he seemed to mean an anti-Corn Law, anti-aristocratic liberal. His Chartism was evaporating, and after his release in October he became editor of the free-trade radical *British Statesman* (1842).

The NCA issued a strangely composite post-election manifesto. Chartism, it claimed, had defeated the hated Whigs; but 'the terror of Chartism had ended in the triumph of Toryism' and 'the cry of Tory and Chartist coalition' should not be repeated, 'when the truth was well known that the people turned the tide of public opinion against the Whigs, but never in favour of the Tories'.[9] Oastlerite hostility to free trade remained, however, a policy of the NCA. Some liberals had already preferred the Anti-Corn Law League to Chartism. At Sheffield Ebenezer Elliott, the 'Corn Law rhymer', had long favoured free trade and broke with the Chartists in January 1839, over their insistence on the priority of the Charter and support for physical force. He was 'for the Charter, but not for being starved to death first'. At Leeds Samuel Smiles favoured a similar middle-class alliance. But firmer Northern Chartists remained hostile to the claims of their traditional opponents among the great factory masters who dominated the League. When Leaguers reported back to Manchester on 28 February 1839 after their first London conference their meeting was invaded by Chartists. An 'honest Pat Murphy' (a potato-wheeler who, according to Prentice, 'whatever his honesty might be, was not very cleanly, and very far from being sober') was called to the chair, and pandemonium broke loose: the League was humbled in its capital, amidst cheers for Stephens and Oastler.[10] From this time hostility between Leaguers and Chartists had rapidly mounted.

For all its apparent energy, however, the NCA was not very strong. The growth of branches did not invariably represent any extensive membership. In October 1841 nearly 200 branches had only 16,000 paid-up members. By February 1842 membership had reached 40,060, but contributions were irregular. Not only was it necessary to cease publication of the *Executive Journal of the NCA* after four numbers but by the spring of 1842 Campbell was in debt. The fact was that 'in every hamlet where two or three Chartists could be gathered together an Association had been formed'. Yet this struggling little organisation readily challenged other bodies. At Leeds it fought the middle-class radicalism of the *Leeds Times*, whose description of Chartism as 'a Knowledge Agitation' and whose support of a Chartist-radical alliance offended such militants as Rider. Under Smiles's editorship the *Times* had changed its attitudes, supporting the Leeds Parliamentary Reform Association (a body led by the local liberal bourgeoisie) and the League: household suffrage and free trade replaced universal suffrage and factory reform in its columns. Backed by the *Star*, Chartists fought through 1841 against the 'Fox and Goose Club' proposed by advocates of middle- and working-class unity.[11] At Birmingham the former Leeds leader George White, now a *Star* reporter, opposed O'Neill's Christian Chartism, Salt's 'Birmingham Association for Promoting the General Welfare' and O'Connellite activities: he reportedly provoked 'great wavering' among local Repealers. Assorted other middle-class attempts to take over Chartism were widely repulsed. Chartists who succumbed to the attractions of paid League employment were sarcastically attacked, along with the subsidised Operative Anti-Corn Law Associations. At Sunderland the Leaguers were repelled by 'violent opposition'. At Leicester League rallies were invaded by a Chartist host. Everywhere the message was given that repeal without the Charter would be disastrous for workers.[12]

Chartist methods against the League are well documented and initially were very successful. At Huddersfield in March 1839, complained one free-trader, Chartist behaviour

> was such as to excite the unmitigated disgust of every well-regulated mind, and to us it is a matter of perfect astonishment how a body of Englishmen can be found so utterly lost to all sense of decency, and so determinedly opposed to candour, honesty and fair dealing. Everything in the shape of argument or appeal to facts was denounced as lies—the most ribald abuse of the speakers was indulged in, and they were clamoured down by hooting, hissing, stamping on the floor, and every other species of unmanly annoyance. . . .

Gammage considered that

> The outraged feelings of the operative classes enabled the Chartist leaders to thwart the corn law repealers in nearly every effort that they made. . . . The reasons given by various men . . . for not going with the League widely differed. With a very large number it was a detestation of the social tyranny exercised by manufacturers, which led them to believe that anything coming from such a quarter was not likely to be very favourable to their interests.

The WMA stream believed that Corn Law repeal could only be

achieved by a reformed Parliament, while 'by far the largest' body of Chartists (including O'Brien) contended, in Gammage's words,

> that Free Trade under the existing arrangements of society, so far from being beneficial, would rather prove injurious to the producing class.

Gammage believed that 'the result of the Chartist opposition to the Free Traders drove those agitators into holes and corners'. This view received confirmation from League writers. 'We were afraid to hold public meetings', John Buckley remembered,

> because they would come down in strength and move resolutions in favour of the Charter, protesting that they were as good re-pealers as we were but the repeal of the Corn Laws was more of a manufacturer's question than a working man's, and taking this view a few Chartists unconsciously became protectionists.

O'Connell confirmed in 1839 that radicals were 'so checked and thwarted by the Chartists that it was very unlikely that [they] would do much during that year to give support to the popular cause'.[13]

Northern Chartists, schooled in Oastler's traditionalist protection-ism, inevitably saw a movement headed by such old enemies of factory reform as the Ashworths of Bolton, Bright of Rochdale, the Gregs of Styal, Hume, O'Connell, Mark Philips and Thomas Potter of Manchester, the Marshalls of Leeds and the Akroyds of Halifax as another manifestation of liberal hostility to working-class interests. But Chartists were not all hostile to free trade for such reasons. London democrats rejoiced that 'the middle classes were foiled in their favourite question . . . [because] had they succeeded they only would have had the advantage'. Rider expressed Yorkshire senti-ments in the *Star*:

> Who are that blustering, canting crew,
> Who keep the cheap loaf in our view,
> And would from us more profit screw?
> > The League.

> Who cry 'Repeal the curs'd Corn Law',
> And would their workmen feed with straw,
> That they may filthy lucre paw?
> > The League.

> Who wish to gull the working man,
> And *burk* the Charter, *if they can*,
> With their self-aggrandising plan?
>
> The League.

Some Chartists went further and became staunch protectionists. Campbell's pamphlet on the matter 'served as a text-book for the local leaders'. Leach insisted that repeal would simply reduce wages. His view was widely preached by protectionist orators, and his pamphlet on the factory system was published at the expense of W. B. Ferrand's Tory brother-in-law, William Rashleigh. At Macclesfield West typically argued that 'until the Charter became the law of the land, it was worse than useless to agitate for the repeal of either the Corn Laws or any other bad laws'.[14]

Rebuffed by most Chartists in its pleas for an alliance, the League quickly changed its tactics. Its considerable funds allowed it to employ a corps of travelling lecturers. And its alliance with O'Connell allowed it to protect its meetings with such ruffianly 'lambs' from the ranks of the Roman Catholic Mancunian Irish as 'Big Mick' Donohoe, J. J. Finnigan and John Kelly. Paid by the League, Irish toughs now routed Chartist hecklers at Manchester and broke up the rallies of the itinerant protectionist lecturer Dr W. W. Sleigh. This reversal of roles began in May 1841, when one Duggan and the League organiser Edward Watkin set loose the 'boys' on the Chartists, 'who were driven out of the hall four times ... [and] regularly thrashed ...'. On 8 June, at a League rally in Stevenson Square, the Irishmen 'laid about them to such good effect as to drive the Chartists out of the square'. By September the outnumbered O'Connorites thought it necessary to protect their own rally by soliciting police assistance. In winter encounters they were regularly worsted. On New Year's Day of 1842 the Chartists were shouted down by Irish bludgeon men—'their bounty being a good swig of whisky and a few shillings'. The *Star* maintained that

> The League, in order to ensure a triumph and carry their point, selected Irishmen for speakers, who endeavoured to work upon the prejudices of their countrymen, who understood nothing about the question at issue and thus made it dangerous for any but their own party to be in the room.

In July Con Murray complained that, as a Chartist, he was ejected from the Roman Catholic chapel at Campsie by one Fr. Green. 'I ask you', wrote W. H. Clifton, 'To the People of Ireland', is it not more honourable to stand up boldly, as the Chartists do, than to truckle to such a contemptible faction as the Whigs, whom you have so long supported and whom you are now, with your 'Liberator' at your head, helping into office. ... Only ask yourselves calmly what have the Whigs done for you, and you will have no answer that will show their friendship.

But even denunciations of Orange hostility to 'our poor, oppressed and unoffending Catholic brethren' and Clifton's bitter attack on the Anglican Church of Ireland had no effect. In March an O'Connellite riot violently ruined O'Connor's speech in the Manchester Hall of Science.[15] In addition to employing such physical force tactics (soon to be deplored by the Temperance leader Fr. Hearne and by O'Connell), the League—wearing a moral force cap—recruited such workers as Heyworth Hargreaves of Halifax and John Murray of Liverpool to its pool of speakers. And it effectively employed the description of 'Tory-Chartists' for O'Connorites, while apparently permitting its missionaries to pledge sympathy for suffrage extension.

Against the capitalist finance and skilled organisation of the League, Chartists had little chance. Their shifting attitudes on free trade (as on so many subjects) could not stand up to the consistent single-mindedness of the League, any more than Leach's Manchester men could withstand the physical assault of 'Big Mick's' hired bullies: the local Irish, observed Leon Faucher, 'were so strictly organised that in the twinkling of an eye one or two thousand could be collected at any given spot'. As a result of their divisions, the Chartists' 'intellectual' case against the League was inevitably weakened. O'Connor for long challenged Cobden to debate the free trade issue, being typically confident of the issue. When, at last, Cobden took up the gauntlet and the two men met in public debate at Northampton on 5 August 1844, Feargus was undoubtedly the loser—with Bright delivering the final blow. O'Connor, thought the disappointed Gammage, thus gave 'the League the greatest victory they ever obtained'.[16]

III

Despite O'Connor's assorted rows, Chartism was growing again. The NCA had some 300 branches by the end of 1841 and around 350 by April 1842. But the numbers were constantly inflated by

O'Connor: 'never lose sight of the fact that we are 4,000,000 and more', he wrote. Optimism rose with the collection of signatures for the second petition. Indeed, hope and honest belief remained Chartism's only real strength. Perhaps 176 of the claimed 401 branches paid nothing to central funds in the second quarter of 1842. Perhaps (as Hill alleged) the executive was incompetent and even venal. Yet brave and often impoverished lecturers and writers continued to propound their cause. The most impressive and moving aspect of Chartist history was that, despite all its charlatans, cowards and crooks, the movement retained the devoted loyalty of so many working men. At the heart of this support lay Chartism's social concern for Northern workers. 'Hundreds of times' the *Star* claimed to have shown that 'machinery, when rightfully applied, was one of the greatest blessings', which 'might be made into MAN'S HOLIDAY . . .', with great effects on workers' lives:

> Often and again have we declared ourselves to be in favour of as much and as perfect machinery as can by possibility be introduced, *provided it is rightfully used* and . . . shown that the wrongs and miseries entailed upon the working people by the present extensive use of it arises from the fact that *it is not rightfully applied* . . . . By the *abuse* of machinery, we mean such an application of its powers as enabled JOHN MARSHALL of Leeds to accumulate to *himself* upwards of TWO MILLIONS of money!, while it consigned those who *worked* the machinery, which was called his, to penury and want, to long hours, short wages, and by consequence, dear food!

In an April letter 'To the Working People of England', O'Connor asked, in Oastlerite style,

> have your masters as great an interest in your health, your lives, your comforts and your entire condition as the black slave-owner has in the well-being of his stock of human flesh? Has he an interest in your sobriety, your morality, your freedom or your independence? No; he has a clear and direct interest in the destruction of your every comfort and in the annihilation of every trace of character and nationality.

Northern Chartism never entirely lost its Tory-radical character. In one respect organisation had improved. Instead of the *ad hoc* plan of 1839, the second national Convention was to be elected by ballot in twenty-four English and a maximum of twenty-five Scottish and Welsh constituencies; members would be paid for up to four weeks. Northern influence was underlined in the new petition, which assailed the National Debt, royal incomes, low wages, long hours, the Poor Law and the Church before reciting the six points. But Northern dominance had its dangers, and the Convention had to be postponed from February to April. The Scots in particular, at a Glasgow convention on 3 January, had condemned references to repeal of the Irish Union and the English Poor Law. Only a sustained campaign by O'Connor brought the Scots into line. Irish Chartists simultaneously investigated O'Connellite attacks on rare priestly supporters and on the movement generally, reporting that many clergy were misled by O'Connell's endeavours 'to confound Chartism with infidelity' and to label Chartists as 'midnight assassins, torch-and-dagger men'. They knew that the only chance of realising O'Connor's dream of an Anglo-Irish proletarian union was to recruit some of the ham-fisted O'Connellite clerical dictators. They generally failed.

Eventually the national Convention met in Dr Johnson's Tavern on 12 April. It wasted much time on bickerings between O'Connorites and O'Brienites. But on the 19th Duncombe gave the Commons notice of his intention to present the petition. And on 2 May 'MCs' and many London supporters proudly escorted the petition—allegedly bearing 3,317,752 signatures—to Parliament. Next day Duncombe proposed that the Chartists should be heard, claiming that nearly 100,000 workers, organised in over 600 associations, had subscribed hard-earned pence for the cause. Seconded by Leader, he was supported in the Commons, in various ways, by such men as Bowring, Fielden, Hume, Wakley, O'Connell (who 'did not wish to identify himself with the petition at all' but remained 'a decided advocate of universal suffrage') and Roebuck (who condemned the 'malignant and cowardly' O'Connor). But notable opposition came from Graham, Macaulay, Peel and Russell, and the resolution was rejected by 287 votes to 49.

In reporting the event, O'Connor condemned the 'vile speeches of Roebuck and Macaulay', and Chartist rallies soon attacked parliamentary opponents. The Commons had 'once more declared its hatred of liberty [and] spurned the voice of an indignant people', asserted the Convention. It was impossible again to petition 'the *present* House without degrading their cause'. Now Chartists would memorialise the Queen, remonstrate with Parliament, continue national agitations, expand their organisation, commence electoral campaigns and plan a representative legislature. Behind such policies there remained Chartism's concern with factory legislation and Ashley's Mines Bill. Watkins added the claim that 'no man could be a Christian unless he were a Chartist,' explaining that 'we are doing the work of GOD upon earth—we are instruments in His hand, and think ye not that the afflictions from others will not be rewarded hereafter?'[17]

Chartists thus again faced the old problem of what to do after being rejected by Parliament. And they continued to face difficulties over schemes for class collaboration. A new body had been gestating since the winter of 1841, under the Birmingham alderman Joseph Sturge, a Quaker merchant and free trader. The aim was to unite such Chartists as Lovett with such bourgeois radicals as Prentice and Bright—an aim first announced in Edward Miall's virulent *Nonconformist* journal in 1841. There should be a 'Reconciliation between the Middle and Lower Classes', on the basis of 'a full, fair and free representation' and the removal of 'the enormous evil of class legislation'. Some Leaguers regretted this division of middle-class radical activities, while others followed Sturge, whose views were warmly welcomed at a League conference at Manchester on 17 November. Sturge and Sharman Crawford then prepared the 'Sturge Declaration', which was widely circulated in December, with its celebrated protest that

> a large majority of the people of this country are unjustly excluded from that full, fair and free exercise of the elective franchise to which they are entitled by the great principle of Christian equity and also by the British Constitution.

The next stage was the organisation of the Birmingham Complete Suffrage Union in January 1842.

Following another League conference in February the CSU quickly grew among middle-class dissenters, who disliked the religious and political Establishment but feared the militant talk of the O'Connorites. Complete Suffrage Associations, merging a form of Chartism with free trade sympathies, were widely established: by April there were over fifty. Supporters varied considerably. In Scotland they included the Rev. Dr John Ritchie, the Rev. Patrick Brewster, the Rev. William Marshall, Councillor James Taylor of Glasgow, provost John Henderson of Paisley, the Temperance leader John Dunlop of Brockloch and the trade unionist William Pattison. In Suffolk, under the influence of Vincent, the Ipswich tailor William Fraser and R. G. Gammage, the CSU gained considerable popularity.

At Leicester, the Baptist minister J. P. Mursell, the bookseller J. F. Winks and the hosiers William and John Biggs, in the West, Vincent, Thomas Spencer (curate of Hinton Charterhouse), Philp, Prowting Roberts, Charles Clarke of Bath and the Unitarian ministers Henry Solly of Yeovil and William Leash of Chapmanslade gave support. And this patently anti-O'Connorite group was soon joined by such men as Cobden's brother Charles, Collins, Lovett, Lowery, Mills, O'Neill, Place, Richardson, Wade and James Williams.

O'Connor inevitably reacted against a League 'plot'. Sturgeism was denounced as 'complete humbug'. NCA officials who 'deserted' —like Philp and Williams—were violently attacked. And the whole CSU philosophy was assailed:

> . . . Complete Suffrage would merely tantalise you with the possession of a thing you could not use, and would entirely prostrate labour to capital and speculation . . . . Repeal of the Corn Laws without the Charter would make one great hell of England. . . .

When the expanding CSU called a conference at Birmingham for 5 April, O'Connor urgently summoned a rival NCA rally. The Complete Suffrage meeting (which lasted for four days in the Waterloo Rooms) with 105 delegates, was much more impressive. In addition to a distinguished bourgeois attendance, it was supported by Collins, Lovett, Lowery, Mills, Neesom, O'Brien, Richardson and Vincent; known O'Connorites were ejected. To Sturge's concern, the points of the Charter were carried; but Lovett eventually agreed that adoption of the Charter *in toto* should be decided at a second conference. After these semantic troubles—under which Chartism was taken up in all but name, while Northern social demands were dropped and liberal sympathy for free trade was implicitly adopted —a CSU petition was prepared. The alarmed NCA Convention later unsuccessfully asked Crawford to postpone his parliamentary motion on the subject: he refused and on 21 April was defeated by 226 votes to 67.

Both CSU and NCA petitions having been rejected at Westminster, the battle between rival 'Chartisms' grew. To O'Connor 'the true position for the people, and the only safe one' was to oppose any alliance with free traders as (in the words of the Merthyr men) 'a direct step towards a betrayal of the Chartist cause'. In May he warned against 'the secret machinations of their enemy', noting that O'Connell had joined the Union council. And in June O'Higgins's Irishmen praised English Chartists for their aid, notwithstanding

O'Connell's reported threat to lead 500,000 armed men against them. But co-operation with middle-class reformers continued to develop. In London, Place extended co-operation by forming the Metropolitan Parliamentary Reform Association on 20 May, backed by the Leaguer Taylor (as chairman), Dr Black (the secretary), Hetherington and Westerton. He also adopted the six principles without referring to the Charter. In the end, however, O'Connor himself prevaricated over class antagonisms. If some collaboration was essential to the success of Chartism (and to the maintenance of his own leadership) then O'Connor was prepared to collaborate. 'Such a union was what he had been long wishing for', he maintained in late July.[18]

The *Star*'s credulous readership apparently accepted the *volte-face* almost without question. To coat the pill, O'Connor singled out one group, 'the industrious portion of the middling classes', as sharing the workers' difficulties and interests. He urged such people to support universal suffrage, as a means of protecting property—and to support it under the Chartist banner. And to underline his new sympathies O'Connor even joined Vincent, McDouall and Cooper in urging Nottingham Chartists to support Sturge in an August by-election. Other old leaders, notably Stephens and Doherty, stood by the anti-Poor Law champion John Walter. The tough local 'lambs' were hired by the Tories to protect Stephens and Walter, but the O'Connorites, led by Feargus himself, routed them after a violent battle. At the poll Walter succeeded by 84 votes, though he was subsequently unseated for bribery. It seemed that O'Connor had finally broken with the old Tory-radical alliance which had first provided him with a mass audience, and had joined the advancing middle-class radicalism of his old enemies. 'O'Connor's great mistake was uniting with Sturge', mourned Oastler from his cell.[19]

VI

In the industrial areas 1842 was a year of depression, widespread unemployment and wage reductions. The choice for many operatives, as Factory Inspector Horner reported, was 'employment on any terms, or starvation'. Inevitably, tempers in many districts ran high. There were riots at Blackburn in May, and on 5 June Marsden told a large crowd on Enfield Moor that they should march under arms to London to demand the Charter from the Queen.[20] Emotions were heightened by the case of Samuel Holberry, the young Sheffield

Chartist imprisoned for conspiracy and riot in March 1840. Holberry, like other West Riding Chartists, was imprisoned at Northallerton but after the death of his associate John Clayton was removed to York Castle, following the appeals of his friends. But the young revolutionary's health could not stand prison conditions, and the Home Office agreed to his release, subject to sureties for his future behaviour. However, Holberry died on 21 June and was thereafter celebrated in Sheffield as 'a martyr to the cause of Democracy'. His funeral on the 27th provoked an immense rally and a new folklore. Harney delivered a graveside oration:

> Our task is not to weep; we must leave tears to women. Our task is to act; to labour with heart and soul for the destruction of the horrible system under which Holberry has perished. ... Compared with the honest, virtuous fame of this son of toil, how poor, how contemptible appear the so-called glories that emblazon the name of an Alexander or a Napoleon! ... Come weal, come woe, we swear ... to have retribution for the death of Holberry, swear to have our Charter law and to annihilate for ever the blood-stained depotism which has slain its thousands of martyrs, and tens of thousands of patriots and immolated at its shrine the lovers of liberty and truth.

The Leicester stockinger John Bramwich produced a poem for the occasion:

> Great God! is this the patriot's doom!
> Shall they who dare defend the slave
> Be hurled within a prison's gloom,
> To fit them for an early grave? ...
> Oh! may his fate cement the bond
> That binds us to our glorious cause!
> Raise, raise the cry, let all respond,
> Justice, and pure and equal laws.

And in 1844 J. M'Owen, answered the query 'Father! Who are the Chartists?':

> Millions who labour with skill, my child,
> On the land—at the loom—in the mill, my child.
>   Whom bigots and knaves
>   Would keep as their slaves;
> Whom tyrants would punish and kill, my child. ...
> And they've sworn at a Holberry's grave, my child,

(That martyr so noble and brave, my child)
   That come weal or come woe,
   Still *onward* they'll go
Till Freedom be won for the slave, my child!

Holberry scarcely deserved his eulogies; but Chartism needed its martyrs after the rejection of the second petition.

Chartists were not alone in talking of possible violence. The League's determination to embarrass the Conservative government had led some of its supporters to make equally threatening gestures, and Oastler cautioned his Northern supporters against falling into the 'trap': 'if the Leaguers urge you to violence, leave that work to them!' As the 205 remaining NCA localities elected a new executive (McDouall, Leach, Campbell, Williams and Bairstow) in June rumours were spreading that the League planned to provoke major strikes by extensive wage-cuts or lockouts. Indeed, reductions in the West Midlands had already provoked some strikes.[21]

In early August the strike enthusiasm spread to the North. Here, Chartists had certainly discussed striking, but were scarcely in a position to organise it. Workers were provoked by threatened 25 per cent reductions at Ashton cotton mills in July and started a wave of strikes on 5 August. A rally on Mottram Moor combined the demand for the Charter with the Oastlerite call for 'a fair day's wage for a fair day's work'. Thereafter touring mobs of 'turn-outs' travelled through the Lancashire mill districts, forcibly drawing the boiler plugs in order to create a general strike. As the 'Plug Plot' spread, Chartists naturally sought to use it, by carrying resolutions to 'stay out' until the Charter was accepted. Chartist leaders assembling at Manchester were astonished at the scene. 'Not a single mill at work! Something must come out of this, and something serious too', Campbell declared on the first sight of Manchester, to Cooper who had narrowly escaped arrest in the rioting Potteries. The sixty delegates honestly confessed that they 'did not originate the present cessation from labour' but 'strongly approved of the extension and continuance of the present struggle till the PEOPLE'S CHARTER became a legislative enactment'. But though, for once, the Chartist leadership was near the scene of action, its chronic divisions prevented it from assuming command; McDouall raged about 'leaving the decision to the God of justice and of battle'. The rioters took little notice of philosophies, as they engaged in the sort of spontaneous outburst which Oastler had long predicted and which the NCA was unable to organise. Working people closed the mills in Ashton, Bacup, Blackburn, Bolton, Burnley, Bury, Chorley, Crompton, Droylsden, Dukinfield, Heywood, Hyde, Manchester, Newton, Oldham, Preston, Rochdale, Stalybridge and Stockport. The ragged hordes who swept over the Pennines to close Yorkshire mills in Batley, Bingley, Birstall, Bradford, Bramley, Calverley, Cleckheaton, Dewsbury, Gomersal, Halifax, Hebden Bridge, Heckmondwike, Holmfirth, Honley, Horbury, Horton, Huddersfield, Keighley, Leeds, Littletown, Marsden, Millbridge, Mytholmroyd, Ossett, Pudsey, Skipton, Stanningley, Thornhill and Todmorden cared little for Chartism. Their protest was against foul industrial conditions. As they arrived at Horton near Bradford they were greeted by local radical weavers singing the union hymn:[22]

> Oh, worthy is the glorious cause,
>   Ye patriots of the Union;
> Our fathers' rights, our fathers' laws
>   Demand a faithful union.
> A crouching dastard sure is he
>   Who would not strive for liberty
> And die to make old England free
>   From all her load of tyranny:
> Up, brave men of the Union!

And up the brave men of the 'Union' briefly went. But they 'went' without much Chartist support. The *Star* attacked McDouall's 'wild strain of recklessness', and O'Connor desperately tried to prove his own moderation. McDouall's bravery immediately evaporated, as he fled abroad.

Unrest spread via Carlisle to Scotland, where conditions were desperate in several areas. The weaving town of Paisley faced near starvation; the Lanarkshire miners struck in protest against wage cuts; rallies of the unemployed on Glasgow Green demanded instant relief; Dunfermline weavers burnt down local factories; in several burghs it was resolved to strike until the adoption of the Charter. Yet in general the moderation of the Scottish radical press and Chartist leadership restrained Scottish Chartists. The principal scene of activity was the flax and jute town of Dundee, where the shoemaker-preacher John Duncan and the Democratic Society organised a strike at a series of excited meetings on Magdalen Green in August. But the affair ended with the tragi-comic march of a ragged group of Chartists to Forfar, the arrest of the leaders and the real tragedy of Duncan's death in a lunatic asylum in 1845.[23]

The strike wave soon ended. By late August many workers were returning on the employers' terms; by late September all was over. And it soon became apparent that the Chartists had made another strategic error. They could never have organised the strikes; they had only sought to take advantage of disputes caused by industrial troubles; but they were widely blamed for the events. The over-worked Graham at the Home Office and the Tory publicist Croker continued to suspect that the League might be at the root of the trouble, but were never able to gain proof. Graham was 'by no means prepared to use Military force to compel a reduction of wages . . .'. He regarded the government's role as being 'to preserve peace, to put down plunder and to prevent . . . intimidation'. But although he accepted that workers had 'just cause of complaint against their masters' and was sickened by the panic of cowardly justices, he considered that 'a social insurrection of a very formidable character' could only be met by force. And it was the Chartists who were arrested. By late September John Mowbray was complaining of the 'languid state' of the cause in the North East.[24]

In the autumn of 1842 Chartism was once again rent by bitter re-criminations. McDouall, Cooper and others had undoubtedly been excited enough by the opportunity offered by the strikes to advocate violence in some form. But O'Connor had opposed such talk, and the NCA had limited itself to asserting that 'all the evils which affected society . . . arose solely from class legislation' and urging workers to stay out until 'the only remedy for the present alarming distress and widespread destitution'—the Charter—was adopted. Lovett added his voice, urging workers to 'avoid *violence* . . . [and] restrain outrage'. But Chartists were widely arrested and sentenced. From October 274 cases were tried in Staffordshire, resulting in 54 sentences of transportation and 154 of imprisonment; Cooper, initially released, was later sent to Stafford Gaol for two years, during which he wrote his celebrated *Purgatory of Suicides* (1845). Fewer cases were tried in Lancashire, culminating with the trial of O'Connor and fifty-eight others in March 1843. Chartists again raised defence funds.

O'Connor, as usual, had temporised. While Hill had condemned the strikes entirely as a League plot, O'Connor had seized the main chance. Both men had opposed McDouall's fatal motion, but O'Connor had agreed to its being publicised by the NCA executive (of which he was not a member). Feargus was therefore surprised to be arrested in late September, and henceforth blamed McDouall for the disaster—even opposing the collection of funds to support him in exile. McDouall returned to Britain in 1844, blaming O'Connor for his flight and subsequent poverty. It is difficult to decide between two such convincing liars. Another whipping boy was the executive, which appears to have been neither efficient nor altogether honest. Cooper consequently proposed its replacement, and a December investigation of its activities and accounts led to its disappearance. The League itself remained highly suspect in many Chartist (and Tory) minds. O'Connor therefore turned another policy somersault, condemning 'the leaning of the Complete Suffragists to the Free Trade party': now the CSU must be destroyed as a 'League Job'. The opportunity was soon at hand. The CSU-Chartist alliance was to be cemented at a Birmingham conference on 27 December, which was to be elected (on Lovett's plan) half by electors and half by non-voters. O'Connor denounced this scheme and urged Chartists to secure election wherever possible. After some bitter arguments, the result was a Chartist victory: to Sturge's mortification, O'Connor was returned for Birmingham. The CSU and others were aware of the danger; as O'Brien wrote,

> A conference composed of such materials as Mr Feargus O'Connor would pack into it would soon find itself utterly powerless and without influence for any purposes but those of mischief. . . .

But the CSU could do nothing against O'Connorite packing. 'The Chartists were anxious to get their men elected if possible at the Complete Suffrage meetings,' recalled Gammage, 'in order to avoid the expense falling on themselves alone, and in many cases they succeeded in so doing.'[25]

The conference, attended by 374 delegates, assembled in the Birmingham Mechanics' Institute. The arrogance of a section of the CSU, in rejecting the Chartist name and presenting a secretly prepared 96-clause 'New Bill of Rights' in place of the Charter, achieved the almost impossible by uniting the Chartists. Lovett proposed and O'Connor seconded a motion to substitute the Charter for the Bill— although Lovett (whose 'lip . . . was curled in scorn' as O'Connor spoke, according to Gammage) scarcely enjoyed the alliance. Middle-class CSU men were dismayed by Lovett's opposition; his known hostility to O'Connor and sympathy with a class-collaboration policy had seemed to guarantee his support. But honest Lovett could not accept the dropping of that document which had advocated

> just and equal representation ... in plain and definite language, capable of being understood and appreciated by the great mass of the people ... [and for which] vast numbers had suffered imprisonment, transportation and death. ...

It was in vain that Lawrence Heyworth maintained that 'it is not your principles that we dislike, but your leaders'. To Chartists there was something sacred about the old cause and the old styles; and there was a blasphemy, a sacrilege in the proposed change. 'Give up the Charter! The Charter for which O'Connor and hundreds of brave men were dungeoned in felons' cells, the Charter for which John Frost was doomed to a life of heart-withering woe!' roared Harney. He would not give way,

> to suit the whim, to please the caprice or to serve the selfish ends of mouthing priests, political traffickers, sugar-weighting, tape-measuring shopocrats. Never! By the memories of the illustrious dead, by the sufferings of widows and the tears of orphans, he would adjure them to stand by the Charter.

Chartists were simply not prepared to be patronised by tactless and supercilious Complete Suffragists. To Cooper it seemed that

> there was no attempt to bring about a union, no effort for conciliation, no generous offer of the right hand of fellowship. We soon found that it was determined to keep the poor Chartists at arm's length.

The varied Chartists carried Lovett's motion by 193 votes to 94 on 28 December. Sturge thereupon led a secession of the majority of CSU delegates to the local temperance hall, to prepare a Bill for presentation by Crawford. The breach was accompanied by expressions of hope for future collaboration. But the fact was that O'Connor had broken another danger to his controlling position.

O'Connor's constant purges inevitably cut down conference membership. Having done his duty, Lovett departed. By 31 December only thirty-seven delegates remained in the NCA-dominated section. And even now the NCA men (who were joined by a few CSU delegates, including Solly, while Vincent threw in his lot with the CSU) were divided. Cooper wanted an annual convention, from which a five-man executive should be elected annually, with only the secretary being paid a regular salary. His plan was (for the moment) generally accepted. But White bitterly opposed Parry's proposal for continued co-operation with the CSU, and O'Connor, while professing to calm matters, provoked further divisions. Many Chartists left the conference to face their trials, often with great courage: White, while conducting his defence, insisted on the provision of sandwiches and wine and William Jones maintained a running fight with Baron Gurney. The sheer guts of men about to go to prison deserved a worthier cause than the highly personalised, self-centred O'Connorite dream. Place might protest; Lovett might be sickened; Oastler was inevitably almost unheard. What was left of organised English Chartism was now controlled by the megalomaniac Irishman. Place's rival Metropolitan Parliamentary Reform Association soon disappeared.

The triumph was almost complete. Real or potential rivals to the despot were either running ineffective evening classes (like Lovett) or about to be imprisoned (like the now doubting Cooper). The CSU was cut down to its appropriate size. Its Bill, proposed by Crawford, was rejected by 101 votes to 32 on 18 May 1843. And when, on 31 January 1844, it dared to hold a rally under Crawford at the traditional venue of the Crown and Anchor tavern, O'Connor and his supporters contrived virtually to destroy it. But O'Connor was now the monarch of a declining kingdom. By fair means and foul, he had converted the Chartist remnant into a personal following. He was now to try to mould it to new purposes. A sign of coming attitudes was given in the *Star* in January 1843:[26]

> Chartism is superior to Christianity in this respect, that it takes its name from no man. . . . There should be no sectarianism in it. Chartism is no invention of one man, any more than truth is. Our cause has no father but the First Great Cause. . . . What greater honour can a man have than to be a Chartist? . . . We worship Truth—we worship God.

This was not the first or the last appearance of such arrogance. And it was sadly unfounded. 1842 marked a Chartist peak never to be reached again.[27]

7 New Directions

For many years O'Connor had toyed with new schemes for relieving proletarian distress. The idea of a small-farm society of peasant proprietors had long held a fascination for him. In a sense, the attraction was almost hereditary: his revolutionary uncle Arthur had advocated small farms in his paper on the *State of Ireland* (published in 1789 and re-issued by O'Connor in 1843). Equally important, no doubt, was Cobbett's advocacy of spade husbandry as a means of spreading employment: O'Connor himself joined the growing number of paternalist promoters of allotments in the 1830s in Cork. What started as a means of raising the standards of the Irish peasants developed in O'Connor's mind into a method of rescuing English operatives from the harsh life enforced by the mill and the machine and the capitalist. Inevitably, the perennial attraction of a 'back to the land' dream—which, in different ways, had drawn such diverse characters as Marie Antoinette, Owen and Cobbett—exercised its usual charm.

The gestation of the Land Plan was a long process. O'Connor was hinting at the scheme as early as July 1840. He had vaguely raised the issue at the 1842 Convention, and it continued to exercise his fertile mind.[1] But early in 1843 he faced other problems. Above all, his trial was approaching. Graham had hoped to charge O'Connor and Hill with high treason for their part in the Plug Plot, but the Attorney-General, Sir Frederick Pollock, resolved to prosecute O'Connor and fifty-eight Northern Chartists and strike leaders together for seditious conspiracy. O'Connor was to be treated as 'a general conspirator' and would be proceeded against not 'for Libel merely, or for acting as a Delegate, or taking part at the Meeting of Delegates'. Pollock's plan was

to try him in the same indictment with the worst of the

defendants who headed mobs, made seditious speeches and stopped mills and factories. I shall blend in one accusation the head and the hands—the bludgeon and the pen . . . .

Chief Baron Abinger's special commission led to radical protests in Parliament, but the trial opened at Lancaster before Baron Rolfe on 1 March, and O'Connor almost brilliantly defended himself. After eight days Rolfe's summing-up was surprisingly sympathetic—indeed, it was annoyingly so to Pollock, who (as the energetic defender of the Newport men) knew something about Chartism. The result was disappointing to the authorities: sixteen men were found guilty of threatening language, while fifteen (including O'Connor) were guilty of encouraging a strike. And an error in the indictment led to the release of the prisoners. O'Connor was thus free to pursue his ends. And the quality of his supporters had been movingly described by poor, victimised Richard Pilling, a Stockport cotton worker:

> I was twenty years among the hand-loom weavers, and ten years in a factory and I unhesitatingly say that during the whole course of that time I worked 12 hours a day with the exception of 12 months that the masters of Stockport would not employ me; and the longer and harder I have worked the poorer and poorer I have become every year, until, at last, I am nearly exhausted. If the masters had taken off another 25 *per cent* I would put an end to my existence sooner than kill myself working 12 hours a day in a cotton factory and eating potatoes and salt.

It was appropriate that in his introduction to a report of the trial O'Connor should write of 'a means of insuring a fair day's wages for a fair day's work, which, after all, is the aim and end of the People's Charter'.[2]

With his rivals imprisoned, exiled or simply disgusted, O'Connor was now free to organise Chartism to his taste.

I

Chartism, in fact, was entering a period of decline. It had been permanently weakened by O'Connor's regular arguments and bullying tactics. After the cyclical trough of 1842 it was further weakened by a slow but general economic improvement. The angry desperation of an impoverished Pilling in 1842, willing to fight for any cause which would guarantee food for his starving children, could quickly give way to the optimistic, apolitical operative of a period of comparatively general employment. The six points, and even the social and economic reforms which seemed more important to 'Oastlerite' Northerners, could easily be forgotten by men enjoying unaccustomed levels of prosperity. Chartism therefore needed new attractions—and something more than the 'young patriots' christened as John Frost or Feargus O'Connor.

A middle-class alliance having failed, O'Connor reverted to his old notion, hitherto held in reserve. He had periodically publicised land schemes for some time and—without committing himself—had encouraged others to develop the subject. O'Brien had suggested a small-farm system in November 1841, and Hill had provided sympathetic space in the *Star* for the discussion of the possibility of mitigating urban misery by settlement on the land. John West, a Halifax speaker, suggested establishing Chartist communities on waste lands, and O'Connor took up the issue. To Feargus, a return to the land would increase agricultural productivity and extend workers' personal independence. But, perhaps above all, it would counter the dominance of the machine. The reclamation of 15,000,000 waste acres would be both profitable and socially effective; machinery hitherto had had the same effect on operatives as the railways had had on horses 'sold to the knackers for their flesh'. O'Connor's argument was that agricultural settlement would benefit both the settlers and the remaining industrial workers, whose conditions would inevitably improve with the removal of 'surplus' labour. As a result, machinery would become 'man's holiday instead of man's curse'.[3]

Hitherto, the land question had been rather vaguely discussed. Chartists generally agreed with Leaguers in condemning what later radicals were to call the 'land monopoly' of the great entailed estates protected by primogeniture and 'privilege'; but they could not publicly agree with such liberals, on principle. In 1843 O'Connor started to publicise his (as yet) largely unplanned theories. 'You are, in a word, a poor, beggarly, lousy set of devils!' he told the operatives '. . . Now mark what you might be! Just what you have made others comfortable, independent and happy! Thanking no man for the means of subsistence!' Settlement on the land would liberate workers from the tyranny of the industrialist and landlord. In a series of letters 'To the Producers of Wealth' O'Connor explained his 'plan'

Five thousand industrial workers should be placed on around forty estates. Each family should have four acres and each estate should have a school, library, hospital and social centre. As every small farmer would personally own his land, he would qualify for a vote: so land settlement would aid the achievement of Chartist aims. Furthermore, the scheme would make thousands self-supporting and would be followed by government patronage of further schemes, which would lead to universal suffrage.

Everywhere and by every means, O'Connor painted his glowing alternative to the bleakness of industrial life. He even posed as an expert on spade husbandry, producing in the summer *A Practical Work on the Management of Small Farms*. To many a resident of Hunslet, Ancoats, the Gorbals or Stepney the dream of a rural life had enormous attraction, while to other Chartists the Land Plan was a divisive scheme which would divert the movement from its real aims. It was now essential for O'Connor to convert a revitalised NCA to his panacea. But NCA activity, together with *Northern Star* circulation, was declining during 1843. A convention initially planned for April finally met in Birmingham on 5 September. The *Star* and many supporters devoted themselves to attacking the opposition to Graham's Factory Bill, with its proposals for working-class education. Such old enemies as 'Neddy' Baines, 'his pal of *The Nonconformist*' and 'sleek-haired Dissenting Parsons' came under bitter attack. Other Chartists, led by Harney, Doyle, West and others, continued to attempt to link Chartism with the Irish movement for repeal of the Union. Wide Roman Catholic hostility to Graham's Bill (which was withdrawn in the summer) made it difficult to link the two Chartist interests. But O'Connor still favoured 'the incorporation with us of my brother Irishmen'.

The 1843 Convention of thirty members met for four days to reconstruct the NCA and, as advance notices put it,

> to consider and devise a PLAN for the organisation of a society to enforce upon public attention the principles of a People's Charter and to devise means for their practical accomplishment.

O'Connor dominated the proceedings, and the future of the NCA was planned as he had suggested. The Association would use only moral force; members should pay 1d weekly; branches would be arranged into districts; there should be an annual convention. The governing body would be an executive committee of twenty-eight members, elected by the Convention. O'Connor's influence was proved when the first executive was chosen. He yielded over his scheme to balance Cooper's proposed five-man executive by a council of thirteen men elected in the regions, but replaced it with a more centralised executive. Now the executive included Bairstow, Thomas Clark, Doyle, Harney, Hobson, Philip McGrath, Marsden, David Morrison of Swindon and Wheeler, who were closely connected with O'Connor. Wheeler, a *Star* agent, became secretary. And O'Connor graciously accepted the treasurership, as a

> reacknowledgement of a Solemn League and Covenant with the working classes . . . which nothing but their own good conduct would have induced me to undertake.

Control was almost complete—and was accomplished with regal condescension.

The reorganised NCA accepted O'Connor's other policy: it would 'provide for the unemployed, and means of support for those who were desirous to locate upon the land'. Gammage, who had already condemned O'Connor's original 'dual' plan of control, was strongly opposed to the new plans in their entirety, as 'one of the best schemes for dividing and breaking up the Chartist movement that could possibly have been invented by the genius or folly of man'; the NCA, as a political association with branches, was patently illegal. And 'the adoption of the Land Plan, illegal in its very foundation and therefore destitute of that one essential where large funds are employed, security—was the next great folly which was to contribute to the disgrace of the Chartist movement.' But, despite warnings, the new NCA went ahead, with its leaders largely paid by O'Connor because of the chronic shortage of funds. 'The Charter and The Land' were to be its mottoes.

To present a better image of the Association, it was resolved to approach Lovett. Consequently, Mason and A. H. Donaldson wrote to him offering the post of NCA general secretary, to unite the Chartist factions. But Lovett bluntly declined. 'Whatever may be the merits of the Plan you are met to discuss,' he wrote,

> I cannot overlook O'Connor's connexion with it, which enables me at once to form my opinion as to any good likely to be affected by it, and which at once determines my course of action. You may, or may not, be aware that I regard Feargus O'Connor as the chief marplot in our movement in favour of the Charter; a man who, by his personal conduct, joined to his malignant influence

in the *Northern Star*, has been the blight of democracy from the first moment he opened his lips as its *professed* advocate. Previous to his notorious career there was something pure and intellectual in our agitation. . . .

The predominantly O'Connorite Association was thus left on its own.[4] And in the autumn of 1843 neither it nor its slightly planned land scheme achieved much popularity.

II

After the Convention O'Connor and the dandified radical MP Thomas Slingsby Duncombe toured the Northern and Scottish industrial areas, to revive Chartist enthusiasm. It was an uphill task. The Scottish organisation, as Harney and Hill had noted in the summer, was disintegrating; some influence was retained by some of the Chartist churches, but many old supporters were now devoting themselves to other causes—education, temperance, improved sanitation, factory reform, poor relief and even proletarian drama. Furthermore, there were periodical middle-class attempts to wean the remaining Chartists away from their Tory-protectionist sympathies and into an alliance with the CSU and Anti-Corn Law League. O'Connor brought to this situation a hope of Chartist unity centred on the NCA and the land scheme, and Scottish enthusiasm flickered again. There was a colourful procession of the trades at Aberdeen (where, thought Gammage, 'Duncombe must have looked with a pitying smile upon men who could waste so much upon those gaudy trappings. . .'). There were soirées at Edinburgh with both CSU and Chartist leaders. And there was a banquet at Glasgow on 30 October, when O'Connor launched into a wide attack on his enemies—the bourgeoisie, liberals, Complete Suffragists, Leaguers and the Church of Scotland—and proposed to carry the Charter by relying on men like Duncombe to block other legislation in the Commons. But despite O'Connor's claims, the permanent results of his visit were meagre. At Dumfries the strong WMA joined the NCA; but Moir held the Glasgow Charter Association aloof, until 1844. Elsewhere, the latest historian of Scottish Chartism finds interest in the national Association alive only at Paisley, Govan, Aberdeen, Alva and Lochee.[5]

Improving conditions and continued secessions left Chartism in the doldrums during 1844. There were occasional cheering events. From January the trial of O'Connell provided considerable pleasure: O'Connellites, wrote Feargus, were

> *boastful in profession,* TYRANNICAL IN POWER . . . the most vicious, the most contemptible, the most servile, the most crouching, the the most insolent and jobbing . . . the most unblushing, the most unscrupulous, the most unprincipled supporters of the Whig administration.

In March O'Connor told the ultimately exonerated O'Connell

> You hate Chartism, not because it opposes principles for the accomplishment of which you contend, but because it prevents you from converting principle to class and personal purposes.

O'Connell's later sympathy with federalism seemed to be treason; in October Feargus optimistically thought that 'the abandonment of the "Repeal of the Union" by Mr O'Connell must of necessity cause a vast accession to the Chartist ranks. . .'. In January London Chartists rallied to greet the released prisoner George White, who

> solemnly declared Mr O'Connor to be in his opinion an honest man and an indomitable patriot. He believed if Mr O'Connor had the wealth of a Rothschild that he would apply it to the happiness of the human family.

In March White organised a Leicester petition for the release of the local hero, Cooper. In the West Charles Bolwell, McGrath and Thomas Clark held a series of successful meetings. When Crawford announced a scheme for a filibustering radical party in the Commons O'Connor was able to defeat it, principally on the ground that Duncombe should lead the group. In the summer 'a handsome piece of plate, worth about £700' was presented to Duncombe for his work on behalf of the working classes. And at a convention at Manchester under O'Higgins in April the final form of the National Charter Association of Great Britain was agreed. Fees were fixed at 3d on entrance and 1d weekly. An annual convention would elect the executive (to which O'Connor, Clark, McGrath, Doyle and Wheeler were reappointed) and the executive would nominate a general council.[6]

The 'credit' side of 1844 was, however, overbalanced by the debits. In Lancashire, Yorkshire and Scotland, following Oastler's release from prison in February, a new 'Ten Hours' agitation had attracted such Chartists as Leach, Jackson, Doyle and Scholefield in Lanca-shire, Allan MacFadyen in Glasgow, Robert Cochran at Paisley and Oastler's many old allies in the West Riding. These men did not desert Chartism but preferred to seek immediate ends—and Ashley was soon to show how close to achieving their Bill they actually were. As Leach put it, 'he would stand second to no man in the advo-cacy of the Charter, [but] he did not think this a proper time for its introduction'. Other Chartists returned or turned to other alter-natives. In East Anglia the agricultural labourers protested against rural conditions with a wave of incendiarism; many Scots favoured their now traditional temperance bodies; in Wales there was a revival of Rebecca-style rioting. Everywhere, the revival of trade union activity attracted Chartists. In Lancashire hostility to the 1834 Poor Law and anger over Graham's failure substantially to amend it remained strong: Fielden and James Taylor led the agitation.

At Leeds 'municipal Chartism' was developing. In 1840 the Chart-ists returned John Jackson, a Holbeck miller, to the Improvement Commission, and in 1842 the tobacconist William Brook and the *Star* reporter William Hick secured the victory of the full Chartist list of nineteen, including Hobson. In the same year the Chartists, led by Benjamin Knowles, secured all seven elected positions as church-wardens for the redoubtable Tory and factory reform sympathiser Dr Walter Hook, vicar of Leeds—and they continued to win these contests for several years. When the Improvement Commission ended in 1842 the Chartists turned their attention to the town coun-cil, with a committee led by Hobson, Brook and the tailor William Barron. They were not immediately successful, but in 1843 Hobson and Jackson were returned in Holbeck, and in 1844 were joined by the butcher George Robson and Brook and in 1845 by Thomas White. Leeds Chartists' involvement in municipal elections was to last until 1853. It was an impressive story in its way, graced by such men as Hobson, the preacher-editor Joseph Barker of Wortley, the Temperance Chartist Dr F. R. Lees and the co-operator, merchant and future Liberal MP R. M. Carter.[7] But it inevitably weakened the involvement of Leeds Chartists in the national movement.

Other Chartists also were involved in local government. But Chartists were not invariably successful at elections. For instance, in May 1844 Vincent fought a parliamentary election at Kilmarnock (on a largely CSU policy) with high hopes, but secured only 98 votes. And divisions continued to extend. The Convention refused to ratify the Land Plan, most members advocating a separation between the scheme and the NCA. O'Connor's wandering speech on protection and free trade was patently inferior to Cobden's at the Northampton debate on 5 August, and rumours spread that Feargus had been bribed. And O'Connor felt bound to move the ailing *Star* to London. He had already dismissed Hill in July 1843, and control passed to Hobson (sacked in October 1845) and Harney. Meanwhile, another Chartist writer had appeared in Scotland. McDouall, newly returned from France, spoke at winter meetings ostensibly on behalf of the NCA: but it soon transpired that he planned to establish a Glasgow Chartist journal and to re-establish a separate Scottish organisation, and he was disowned by the executive. In the circumstances O'Connor's belief that '1843 was the year of slumber, 1844 the year of waking and thought' was optimistic.[8]

III

All else having failed, O'Connor retained two great hopes in 1845. One was a determination to press on with the land scheme. The other concerned a possible alliance with the trade unions. Unionists had provided many early Chartists. But their involvement had long evaporated. Graham's fear in 1842 that the Manchester 'Delegates were the directing body; they form the link between the Trade Unions and the Chartists' was mistaken: the operatives' strike-wave was, in a sense, a rejection of Chartist methods. Periodic Chartist attempts, like McDouall's of 1842, to recruit a meaningful number of unionists regularly failed from that time—partly because other Chartists, like Leach, offered Chartism as an alternative to unionism. O'Connor himself had never had much faith in the unions who had so regularly rejected his leadership. He could recall that when Sheffield Chartists called for local participation in the 'general strike' of August 1842 seven union secretaries disclaimed all interest; and there were many other examples of haughty apathy. Yet allies were desperately needed. Perhaps his connection with William Prowting Roberts, 'the Miners' Attorney-General', the great legal defender of trade unions and a staunch Chartist, led O'Connor to change his mind. Already, he rejoiced, in June 1842, that the 'once aristocratic' Manchester mechanics, had 'come out bodly for the principles of democracy'.

The changed attitude was underlined by the new title of O'Connor's journal—*The Northern Star and National Trades Journal* (though scarcely by the price increase from 4½d to 5d). From its new venue in London, hoped O'Connor, the journal would (under McGowan's direction)

> be the means of rallying the proper machinery for conducting the Registration Movement, the Land Movement, the National Trades' Movement, the Labour Movement and the Charter Movement.

More fervently, he invited Chartists to

> keep your eye fixed upon the great Trades' Movement now manifesting itself throughout the country, and I would implore you to act by all other trades as you have acted by the Colliers. Attend their meetings, swell their numbers and give them your sympathy; but upon no account interpose the Charter as an obstacle to their proceedings. All labour and labourers must unite; and they will speedily discover that the Charter is the only standard under which they can successfully rally. . . . A combination of the Trades of England under [Roberts's] management and direction would be the greatest move ever witnessed within the last century. It would be practical Chartism; and therefore it is our duty to aid and assist it, and not to mar it by imprudent interference.

But the results were scarcely reassuring, despite the loyalty of some miners' groups (supported in their major disputes by the *Star*) and the appointment of O'Connor's friend Duncombe (who had recently led Commons opposition to Miles's Bill to enlarge justices' powers in industrial disputes) as president of the National Association of United Trades for the Protection of Labour, of which the *Star* was the official organ, in 1845.[9]

The *Star* enthusiastically greeted 'Labour's Parliament', on the formation of the NAUT in March 1845. 'Wales is absent; Scotland is absent; Ireland is absent; many parts of England are absent,' it confessed: 'still, it is *the most perfect* representation of the working classes that has yet been seen.' Nevertheless, trade unions by and large refused to have anything to do with Chartism—at least in its O'Connorite form. O'Connor consequently reverted to his old attitude towards unionism. The ideal of a united working-class phalanx was, as ever, a mere chimera. 'The pompous trades and proud mechanics', asserted the *Star* in November 1845, 'were now willing forgers of their own fetters'. O'Connor returned to his old reliance on support from 'the fustian jackets, blistered hands and unshorn chins'. Union lack of interest in the fate of the Monmouth leaders enraged him:

> never was there more criminal apathy than that manifested by the trades of Great Britain to the sufferings of these men . . . if one half that was done for the Dorchester labourers or the Glasgow cotton-spinners had been done for Frost, Williams and Jones they would long since have been restored.

The building up to the mid-century 'respectable' moderation of 'New Model' unionism among craftsmen already prevented wide unionist participation in Chartism.

Irish support also remained minimal. In January 1845 the *Star* condemned Papal interference in Irish politics. In May O'Higgins urged Irish repealers in Britain to form

> a cordial union with the people of England, amongst whom you reside, to the end that your interests which are mutual and identical should be promoted, that differences hitherto existing between Repealers and Chartists should cease. . . .

> The Corn Law League tried their hand at dividing the Chartists. The old Orange party put forth their strength for a similar purpose. The Whigs sent their spies to burn Birmingham and to raise a rebellion amongst the isolated miners in Wales. Religious fanatics were not idle either. They charged all Chartists with infidelity. 'Infidels', 'Socialists', 'miscreants' and 'Chartists' were used as synonyms. In Ireland the Chartists were denounced as Orangemen. Every means that human ingenuity could invent were employed to deter the Irish, but particularly the Catholics, from joining the CHARTIST RANKS, just as if there was infidelity in UNIVERSAL SUFFRAGE, VOTE BY BALLOT, ANNUAL PARLIAMENTS, EQUAL REPRESENTATION, NO PROPERTY QUALIFICATIONS and PAYMENT OF MEMBERS.

> . . . Bear in mind that all Chartists are Repealers; that the Charter includes domestic legislation; but that the Repeal of the Union does not include universal suffrage, or any other proposition in which the non-electors are directly interested.

The *Star* repeated that 'the Repeal that is to give Ireland to [the Irish] must be preceded by the Charter' and hopefully predicted that ' "YOUNG IRELAND" would, in the long run, be compelled to come out for the People's Charter'.

It was widely believed that, despite organisational and financial weaknesses, a huge number of workers remained resolutely Chartist in sympathies. What was needed to arouse them was a policy relevant to their present condition and a postponement of the impractical proposal to implement the Charter forthwith. The Land Plan met both criteria, and O'Connor finally determined to promote it as his principal policy. 'I have been much thwarted and harassed on this subject', he recalled:[10]

> When the Birmingham Conference unanimously and wisely adopted the Land Plan in 1843, the acrimony of the knavish for a season triumphed over the judgment of the prudent, and I, among others, was compelled to 'bide my time' till common sense had resumed its place.

Having 'bided his time', O'Connor now resolved to carry the Land Plan at the annual convention.

Only fourteen delegates assembled at the London Parthenium on 21 April 1845. But when, next day, O'Connor's long-planned scheme was finally unveiled, the members were enthusiastic. It was resolved to set up the Chartist Land Society—which was founded on 19 May. Shareholders were invited to purchase shares of £2.10s (£2·50p) by weekly subscriptions of 3d or more. It was argued that 'good arable land might be rented in some of the most fertile parts of the country at the rate of 15s [75p] per acre', and might be bought at 25 years' purchase—that was, at £18.15s. per acre'. Two thousand paid-up shareholders could therefore buy 120 acres (on which sixty families could settle) for £2,250. A further £1,800 would be expended on building cottages, £425 on stock and implements and £425 on early subsistence. The allotments would be perpetually leased at £5 p.a. If sold cheaply at 20 years' purchase the £300 rent would produce £6,000, which could be expended on the purchase of 144 acres for 72 allotments. Within four years the capital would have reached £10,317 3s 4d— enough to settle 123 people on 246 acres: by the tenth year 372½ allotments would be purchased by £37,324. O'Connor, Wheeler, Clark and Doyle were appointed directors. The Society would 'show the working classes the value of land as a means of making them independent of the grinding capitalist . . . [and] the necessity of securing the speedy enactment of the People's Charter, which would be for them nationally what [the] society proposed to do for them sectionally'.

It was easy to pick holes in the scheme, not least because the four-acre farm had become a two-acre allotment. But O'Connor threw his whole energy into the scheme. He rejected socialistic variations—from the communitarian Owenite experiment of Queenwood Hall near Tytherly to O'Brien's scheme for nationalisation of the land—in favour of peasant proprietorship. 'His plan had no more to do with socialism than it had with the comet', and he thought nothing of O'Brien's claim that a supporter of a land society 'was practically enlisting himself on the side of the government against his own order'. Socialist theories never influenced O'Connor—or most of his followers. But Feargus travelled widely in Britain and on the Continent to test his beliefs against practical experience of small farming schemes. He fought off rival plans, such as Carpenter's land scheme;[11] Like Oastler, he opposed emigration (advocated by some CSU men and, increasingly, by craft unions) as a solution for 'surplus' labour; he met but apparently ignored Engels and Marx. But he was prepared further to change his own plan.

By August his costings had been amended. Fifty households might be settled for £1,875, with cottages costing £1,500 and capital of £750. Of the predicated £5,000 invested, £875 would remain and the rental would be £250. A mortgage for £4,000, subsidised by £125 from the surplus, would permit the settlement of another fifty persons, and this process would be repeated for seven years, until the original capital in hand was used up. By that time there would be eight estates, and the first seven would be mortgaged for £28,000 and have a rental of £2,000. The improved land would command much greater values: O'Connor thought that the first property would bring 20 years' purchase (£5,000) at once, or 30 years' purchase (£7,500) after two years. Within four years the properties might be sold for £60,000, which would produce a profit to the Society of £27,000. The miracles to be achieved with a capital of £5,000 were seemingly endless. But they still did not appeal to all Chartists. When Cooper emerged from Stafford Gaol in May O'Connor instantly sought his support and even offered to print his prison saga, *The Purgatory of Suicides*. O'Connor 'invariably expounded his Land Scheme to me', Cooper later claimed,[12]

> and wished me to become one of its advocates. But I told him that I could not, and I begged him to give the scheme up, for I felt sure it would bring ruin and disappointment upon himself and all who entered into it.

O'Connor thus lost another friend.

In December a convention was called at Manchester, according to

McGrath's later reminiscences, 'exclusively for the consideration of the land scheme'. A small group assembled in the Carpenters' Hall to be regaled by O'Connor's statistical diatribes. Income now amounted to £3,266, according to Wheeler, while expenses totalled only £184. But the sum for buying land approached merely £2,700. Seven trustees—Titus Brooke of Dewsbury, J. G. Dron, William Dixon of Manchester, Duncombe, Leach, John Sewell and Duncan Skerrington of Glasgow—were appointed, and Roberts returned to the treasurership. As chairman of the conference, Skerrington stressed the need for a legal status for the company, either by registration as a friendly society or by incorporation as a joint-stock company. But there were difficulties in either course, and it was not for some time that an application was made for registration, after long consideration by Roberts's London agent, George Chinnery.

Backed by such enthusiasts for the rural life as the Manchester weaver Doyle, the dyer McGrath, the London protectionist Martin Wheeler (the secretary), the Chartist organiser Thomas Clark, the Chelsea plasterer William Dixon and two East End tailors James Knight and William Cuffey (auditors), O'Connor turned the major Chartist body into one—albeit the largest—of several land schemes. The vision had a wide appeal, when explained by O'Connor:[13]

> The first use the land would be to them was to ease the labour market of its surplus; the second was to create a certainty of work for the people; and the third was to create a natural rate of wages in the artificial market; for so long as there was a surplus to fall back on, or a workhouse from which to produce labour, so long would work be uncertain and wages low.

As support rose, further organisation became necessary. Thomas Allsop, a London broker, gave financial advice, and a Land Plan Office was opened in Dean Street, Soho. Week by week the *Star* reported the receipt of substantial subscriptions and the formation of many sections of the 'Company'. The Lancashire cotton towns witnessed the greatest enthusiasm. Support in Yorkshire, London, the North-East and the Midlands was slower but growing. Wales and Scotland proved difficult to arouse, but many country districts were surprisingly energetic. The plain intent to

> purchase land, erect dwellings and allot them to its members upon such terms as shall enable them to become small freeholders and to live in comparative comfort and independence

held attractions for many conditions of men.

The rising flood of subscriptions made a decision on the legal form of the organisation more urgent. The Land Society was part and parcel of the NCA, yet it obviously had an increasingly independent life of its own. In order to operate legally, it required legal status through any means from obtaining a Royal Charter to registration as a friendly society. Chinnery's rules were designed to secure friendly society status, the cheapest option. But Tidd Pratt, the Registrar of Friendly Societies, would not accept a society with such ill-defined purposes, whose receipts were paid by McGrath and McGowan into O'Connor's account and whose proceedings would rest upon lotteries. No hint of such troubles reached the owners of 'fustian jackets, blistered hands and unshorn chins', to whom O'Connor addressed himself from 11 January 1846. Such men were regularly regaled with accounts of the joys of rural life—and sometimes with patently absurd predictions of the economic benefits of allotment cultivation. The historian, conditioned by erudite contemporary attacks on the scheme, by other historians' largely anti-O'Connorite views and by simple hindsight, has often been tempted to write off the Land Plan as at most a silly venture and at worst another nail in the Chartist coffin. In a sense, it was both; but it was something more. To many men for whom Lovettite 'intellectualism' meant as little as the 'revolutionary' calls of cowardly, quickly emigrating demagogues, the Land Plan offered hope of a new life. Those who subscribed their often meagre donations towards Chartist land settlement were not utopian dreamers or bourgeois experimenters with sociological theory. They were people making a last attempt to escape from the increasingly 'capitalist'-dominated working ethos and even from urban industry itself. Perhaps they were misled; inevitably they were largely ill-informed. But the hard-earned little subscriptions of operatives, spelling out *Star* propaganda in their down-town slum rooms, or of village folk hearing the message from the literate schoolmaster or cobbler, have a moving and noble quality. Perhaps the dominant motive was hostility to the ever-widening power of machinery. Not that, as O'Connor put it,

we wish to destroy it if it could be made MAN'S HOLIDAY instead of MAN'S CURSE; but it must be destroyed, or its injustice and inequality must be curbed by the possession of THE LAND.

Despite widespread hostility, such a philosophy had a great appeal.

In March 1846 O'Connor bought the 103-acre Herringsgate estate near Watford for £1,860, and this sign of the reality of the scheme led to increased support. By April 1,487 people were full shareholders and on 19 May, as O'Connor prepared to pay for the land, there was a balance of £8,081. But continued uncertainty over the scheme's legal status prevented the group from owning land, which technically became O'Connor's personal property. Then began an exciting period of further planning, the investigation of other properties, the designing of estates and buildings. O'Connor, Doyle and their astute building foreman Henry Cullingham threw themselves into the work of creating the first Chartist township, organising everything from publicity to supervising and participating in the building jobs. Another Hertfordshire property, 130 acres at Carpender's Park, was bought and quickly sold at a profit.

An important new figure now entered the movement. Ernest Jones was a 27-year-old poet and lawyer who had been brought up in affluence in Germany. By 1845 he had lost a considerable fortune, become secretary to a railway and joined the Chartists. 'Perhaps', he confessed,

> it was a novelty to have a connection of aristocracy mix with [Chartists], but he did not see why, because his forefathers held Conservative opinions, he was not to hold, and hold sincerely, democratic principles.

Jones quickly became a leading Chartist poet, representing a variety of attitudes and moods.[14] There was the summons to the working man:

> Up! Labourers in the vineyard!
> Prepare ye for your toil!
> For the sun shines on the furrows,
> And the seed is in the soil.

There was the assertion to the 'cotton lords and corn lords' that

> Our lives are not your sheaves to glean—
> Our rights your bales to barter:
> Give all their own—from cot to throne
> But ours shall be THE CHARTER!

There were stirring lines on the Chartist destiny:

> Labour! labour! labour! toil! toil! toil!
> With the wearing of the bone and the drowning of the mind;
> Sink like shrivelled parchment in the flesh—devouring soil;

And die, when you have shouted it till centuries shall hear!
Pass away unheeded like the waving of the wind! . . .

No! No! we cry united by our suffering's mighty length:
Ye—ye have ruled for ages—now we will rule as well!
No! no! we cry triumphant in our right's resistless strength;
We—we will share your heaven—or ye shall share our hell!

And there was a Chartist warning to the establishment:

We seek to injure no man;
We ask but for our right;
We hold out to the foeman
The hand that he would smite!

And, if ye mean it truly,
The storm may yet be laid,
And we will aid you duly,
As brothers brothers aid;—

But, *if ye falsely play us*,
And if ye but possess
The poor daring to betray us,
Not the courage to redress;

Then your armies shall be scattered,—
If at us their steel be thrust,—
And your fortresses be battered,
Like atoms in the dust.

And the anger of the nation
Across the land shall sweep,
Like a mighty Devastation
Of the winds upon the deep!

Always, Jones presented an optimistic, cheering message:[15]

My countrymen! why languish
Like outcasts of the earth,
And drown in tears of anguish
The glory of your birth?
Ye were a free-born people
And heroes were your race:

The dead, they are our freemen,
The living—our disgrace!

The romantic enthusiast soon supported the land scheme, in typical fashion:

Courage, poor slave! deliverance is near.
Oh! she has breathed a summons sweeter still:
Come! take your guerdon at O'Connorville!

IV

As his agricultural interest grew, O'Connor changed his mind on another matter. Many Chartists had originally inherited traditional radical hostility to the Corn Laws. But from about 1840 Chartists generally had been opposed to the League, composed as it was of many of their old enemies. O'Connor had constantly attacked the 'mountebank cosmopolites', who sought a panacea for everything in free trade; 'the League was ONE ENORMOUS LIE'. As late as May 1844 O'Connor told 'the grown-up men of England' that

The Free-Traders have been foremost in their opposition to the Ten-Hours' Bill. They have subscribed hundreds of thousands of pounds to carry a repeal of the Corn Laws. . . . [They] would not accept a repeal of the Corn Laws at so great an expense as the loss of two hours' labour of women and young persons.

But his chastening confrontation with Cobden in August presumably started a new line of thought; within days he announced that Cobden was 'decidedly a man of genius, of reflection, of talent, and of tact'. By 1845 O'Connor's attitude was changing towards Peel; the *Star* was praising his 'progressive' policies and preferring him to its ancient enemies among the Whigs. Over the increased Maynooth College grant of April, the *Star* felt that 'while we denounce the measure, we are justified in praising its proposer'. And the December Conference dropped Chartist hostility to repeal of the Corn Laws. Both contemporaries and later writers suspiciously 'explained' Chartist attitudes.[16]

Leaguers regularly explained the Chartist alliance with protection with the formula that

The itinerant lecturers of Chartism want money, the Monopolists want support from the masses; each hopes to gain by a profitable exchange, but each dreads the power of the other to supply the pressing want.

Their most bitter invective was poured on protectionist lecturers and their Chartist supporters. Dr Sleigh's lecture at Saddleworth in October 1843 was reported to consist of 'tirades of abuse against masters, Free Trade and the Anti-Corn League'. After some heckling,

> The redoubtable Joshua Hobson, the publisher or editor of the *Northern Star*, then came to the rescue of the doctor, and spoke about two hours in the true *Ferrand* style, abusing masters and employers, the Free Traders and the Anti-Corn Law League, his speech being a mixture of Chartism and Toryism, and a compound of heterogeneous absurdities. A resolution was moved in favour of the Buckingham doctor's panacea for all our social ills . . . : it was declared to be carried. There were but few Free Traders present, as the distribution of tickets had been quite exclusive, and confined to the Tories and their workmen and friends.

League journalists maintained this level of reporting, Hobson rivalling the Oastlerite Tory squire Ferrand as the principal villain:

> Mr Hobson is a fellow-labourer with the editor of the *Standard*; he is the publisher of the *Northern Star*, and as bitter an enemy to the League as any other trader on passion and prejudice, on ignorance and vanity, on false pretences and shameless assertions.

They rejoiced when Ferrand was heckled at Rochdale in December:

> Mr Ferrand's career of personal slander has received a wholesome check. . . . The Chartists and working people of Rochdale have set an example, not only to their own classes, but to the landed aristocracy, in disclaiming help that could only disgrace their cause. It would be something for the decency of Monopoly to do the same. . . .

But they wrote too soon. At Ferrand's Manchester meeting, they fumed,

> There was the Rev. Mr Stephens of Ashton notoriety, side by side with the editor of the High Church organ; there were ex-Chartist leaders, the worn-out tools of O'Connor, cheek and jowl with Tories of the ancient Jacobite school; there were, in a word, Eldonites, Cobbettites, O'Connorites, Stephensites, Oastlerites,

in fact, there were men of every kind, excepting the rational men of free trade.

And their real attitudes appeared when they furiously attacked protectionists for supporting Ashley's Ten Hours amendment to Graham's Factory Bill in March 1844:

> A large section of Monopolists have supported Lord Ashley's amendment . . . they have made an attack on the manufacturing interest in the hope of injuring the League. . . . The operatives, mulcted of a portion of their wages, and having had bitter experience of what 'short time' really means in the summer and autumn of 1841, will be animated by a firmer determination than ever to obtain the enfranchisement of industry, and adequate remuneration for labour. Deceived by the tales of self-elected delegates, the misrepresentations of discharged cotton spinners, and the visionary dreams of itinerant and mendicant Socialists, the Monopolists have taken a step which it will be exceedingly difficult, if not quite impossible, to retrace. They have established the principle of interference between the employers and the employed. . . . For the first time in the annals of commerce, a British Parliament has asserted its right to restrict the profits of capital and the wages of labour. . . .

In June 1846, when the Ten Hours Bill almost succeeded, Leaguers pointed out that Ten Hours leaders, like Sadler, Oastler and (until recently) Ashley had always been protectionists. Indeed,[17]

> the most ardent champions of the Ten Hours Bill in the present House of Commons are Mr Bankes, Mr Colquhoun, Mr Ferrand, Lord George Bentinck and the rest of the 'gentlemen below the gangway'. Among the manufacturing capitalists, we do not know of one advocate of the Ten Hours Bill who has not been a supporter of the Corn Law. Mr Feilden, it is true, has voted for Free Trade, but in public and private he has spoken against it.

Bourgeois radicals inevitably disliked any connection with Tories and strongly opposed the continuing Oastlerite sentiments of many northern Chartists. 'Though a Chartist myself and always acting with the party,' wrote Holyoake (whose Chartist involvement was actually minimal and whose 'memory' on many points was at least doubtful),

> I never joined in their war upon the Whigs. . . . The Whigs were

the traditional friends of liberty. The Tories were always against it. The Chartists suffered indignities at the hands of the Whigs and allowed their resentment to shape their policy. To spite the Whigs the Chartists gave their support to the Tories—their here-ditory and unchanging enemies. The Whigs were the only polit-ical party standing between the people and the aggressive master-fulness of the Tories. It was upon Chartist resentment towards the Whigs that Lord Beaconsfield traded—and supplied the Char-tist leaders with money to enable them to express it. I knew many who took money for that purpose. Francis Place showed me cheques paid to them to break up Anti-Corn Law meetings, because that cause was defended by Whigs. I saw the cheques which were sent to Place by Sir John Easthope and other bankers, who had cashed them.

Holyoake's general untrustworthiness and lack of chronological sense makes one doubt his assertions. Disraeli was in no position to subsidise Chartist protectionists on any meaningful scale in the 1840s. And Holyoake's principal connection with the Northern reformers was a poor biography of Stephens, published in 1881.

An equally late and hotly anti-O'Connorite writer, R. G. Gammage, suspected an entirely different financial transaction. In his view, 'O'Connor was true to his character, consistent in inconsistency', as repeal drew near—but so, it should be added, were many other partisans. To Gammage, Peel—'a statesman of the ex-pediency school'—mesmerised the 'expedient' O'Connor. The fact was that Peel apparently mesmerised Britain. Chartists were not the only group to accept the 'spirit of the age', in late 1845; politics was in a state of flux, as Whigs and radicals sniffed a chance of party vic-tory and long-yoked Tory back-benchers yearned to leap at the throats of Peelite traitors. But a change in O'Connorite policy was condemned by the first Chartist historian:

> When the League was in bad odour, nothing but ruin was pre-dicted by O'Connor in case of its success. Now it would make the Land Plan triumphant, by bringing down the price of land, and thus enable the people more freely to purchase. In short, his laudation of Peel's measure was the very antithesis of the amend-ment which he proposed at the Northampton meeting. We ask, was not his whole opposition to the League a mere sham? And was there not a good understanding between himself and that body?

Gammage wrote of 'our natural inclination to believe the best of all men, until their acts furnish proofs of their culpability'—an arrogantly phrased assertion instantly followed by character assassinating notes on the fact that O'Connor and Cobden travelled together on the same train to the 1844 Northampton confrontation. 'It is also worthy of notice that O'Connor and Cobden met and conversed at Blisworth after the meeting,' commented Gammage, obviously a pioneer of the 'sinister' smear technique:

> Certain it is, that no speech was better calculated to give the victory to Cobden than that of O'Connor at Northampton. A portion of the parties protested against the shifting policy of O'Connor: others were dissatisfied, and thought his conduct strange; but he had so moulded the majority to his will that they yielded him a blind obedience, and charged the men who remained consistent with being in the pay of the Protectionists; but as all candid men will at once see, if there were any pay in the case, it was more likely to be on the side of those who had turned apostates to their former professions, than on the side of those in whom no change had taken place.

For a variety of reasons, O'Connor joined the winning side in the spring of 1846. And in July he won the show of hands at a Nottingham by-election against Hobhouse.[18]

V

Despite the dominance of the Land Plan, Chartists maintained an interest in other problems. Some supporters became so convinced of the merits of economic liberalism that they deserted the movement altogether. In the citadel of *laisser-faire*, the *Manchester Guardian* welcomed workers' realisation that

> their interests and those of their employers are identical, and that the doctrines taught by Feargus O'Connor, Richard Oastler and other firebrands of the same school were only ministering to their evil passions and prejudices.

Other men who had once been connected with Chartism returned to the revived factory movement. In 1846 Oastler and Fielden were again leading such reformers as Mills of Oldham, Leach of Manchester, Pilling of Stockport, Fletcher of Bury, Mark Crabtree of

Dewsbury, Leech and Pitkeithley of Huddersfield and Cochran of Paisley in the last great Ten Hours campaign. The proposed re-organisation of the militia provoked some Chartists into forming a National Anti-Militia Association, with the cry of 'No vote, no musket!'[19] And in Scotland the usual assortment of campaigns con-tinued, though generally in diminishing key. In Dublin the arrest of O'Higgins for 'sedition' roused O'Connorites to further attacks on O'Connell. In London the NAUT pressed ahead with its own plans to settle unemployed workers on the land. And O'Connor finally associated Chartism with Peel's 'almighty measure' to repeal the Corn Laws: it was 'an instalment of those concessions which sooner or later must and would be made to the democratic mind of the country'. Although Chartism was not mentioned by Peel, O'Connor urged followers to

> derive consolation from the fact that in every word uttered by [Peel] and in every clause of the measure proposed you will re-cognise an apprehension, if not a dread—a knowledge, if not an aversion, of our progress.

The change of attitude on the Corn Laws required considerable explanation, which strained even O'Connor's powers. Peel, he told 'the imperial Chartists' had

> purposely proclaimed a falsehood when he said that the demand for free trade was one in which the working classes had almost un-animously joined the League. This sophistry was necessary, not more for the purpose of parading our gigantic strength to frighten the aristocracy, than to withhold a knowledge of it from foreign powers, who are one and all haunted by the rapid progress of our principles. But this is an insult that we can afford to bear and to forgive, the more especially as the measures, emanate from what influence they may, are preeminently calculated to advance our principles.

Peel's measure was not 'anything like a final settlement between labour and capital', but 'the Ministerial boon . . . must inevitably help labour to its fair share of representation' and then labour would 'see but one enemy—an enemy, however, which might be conver-ted into a bosom friend—THE LAND AND MACHINERY'. The benefits of the Bill were that

> It would invite the foreigner to furnish those articles of food

which require but little labour in the production, while, to contend against foreign competition, it would compel the landlords and the farmers to apply a larger amount of native industry to the cultivation of their lands.

And, after all the battles with Leaguers, another matter had to be explained:

Now, had free trade been proposed in the Whig style—had it been granted as a boon to the increasing power of the League and a sop to the monied interest, unaccompanied with those wise, salutary and statesmanlike adjustments proposed by SIR ROBERT PEEL, not all the power at the disposal of the government could have averted the horrors of a revolution.

Putting on a brave face, the *Star* maintained that 'PEEL had earned for himself a glorious immortality' and 'warned' 'little JOHN and his Whiglings' against any attempt to oust him.[20]

Despite his other interests and his concern at continuing signs of English workers' hostility to the employment of undercutting blackleg Irish labour, O'Connor and his phalanx continued to concentrate on the land scheme. In July Pratt again refused registration as a friendly society, as the plan remained a lottery providing no benefits for the generality of members. But subscriptions to the first section of the company now totalled £10,998 and to the second division £811, and in October the re-named Chartist Co-operative Land Company was provisionally registered under the Joint Stock Companies Act. Excited interest grew after an open day at Herringsgate (now re-named O'Connorville) on 17 August, when O'Connor proudly demonstrated his newly developed smallholdings and his famous 'Chartist cow', Rebecca, to admiring thousands.

A convention at Leeds in August mainly concerned itself with the Irish situation, the new Coercion Act and whether any form of Anglo-Irish co-operation remained possible. O'Connor now dreamed of a land bank, in which members could save towards their shares and earn 4 per cent on their money. This invitation to legal troubles frightened other directors, but was apparently welcomed by the throng of prospective participants. Further ballots were announced and further prospectuses issued. By the winter 6,000 members had paid £13,000 towards 10,000 shares at £2 10s in section 1 and 4,000 people had paid £2,000 in section 2. Ballot winners would receive perpetual leases, with rents computed at 5 per cent on the capital spent and the opportunity to buy the lease. Each allottee would receive a house, plus two, three, or four acres (with £15, £22 10s or £30 in cash), depending on the ownership of one, one and a half or two shares. In October 170 acres were bought at Lowbands near Gloucester for £8,560, the purchase being completed in December. At the 'annual conference of the Chartist Land Company' at Birmingham in December, further decisions were taken. The title would be changed to the National Co-operative Land Society, with Duncombe, John Sewell and Ernest Jones as trustees; cottage sizes were fixed; directors were to be paid 35s (£1·75p) weekly; and the Land and Labour Bank was to be established. Receipts now totalled £22,799 and the highest hopes were entertained of the bank. A third set of rules was prepared.

Press criticism, never long stilled, now rapidly grew. Alexander Somerville was particularly virulent in the *Manchester Examiner,* and the new Liberal *Daily News* was to be equally hostile. There were many doubts about both the legality and the practicability of the scheme. But supporters sensed a new purpose and excitement: as Jones wrote on O'Connorville.[21]

> See there the cottage, labour's own abode,
> The pleasant doorway on the cheerful road,
> The airy floor, the roof from storms secure,
> The merry fireside and the shelter sure,
> And, dearest charm of all, the grateful soil,
> That bears its produce for the hands that toil.

And O'Connor's toil and energy were undoubted: he acted, as he claimed, as 'the Land Company's bailiff, contractor, architect, engineer, surveyor, farmer, dungmaker, cow and pig jobber, milkman, horse jobber, etc.' And his publicity was effective. A team of speakers, including Clark, Jones, McDouall, McGrath, West and the young Arbroath shoemaker Samuel Kydd, spread the message widely. O'Connor and Jones started the monthly *Labourer* to back the campaign. Constantly, O'Connor talked and wrote of inspecting further splendid properties and of the delights of the rural life, while Jones 'poured the tide of his songs over England, forming the tone of the mighty mind of the people'. In all this, old-style Chartism appeared to have little part; indeed in March 1846 O'Connor apparently dropped the ballot, as it would 'put a mask on an honest face', and in March 1847 his 'plan' became simply the 'National Land

Company'. But Feargus saw the company as the saviour of Chartism. Its 'great advantage . . . is this,' he maintained,

> that it supplies food for sensible agitation in good times and in bad times. Good times have always been destructive of Chartism, but now assist it, because it is then that the working classes have the best opportunity of subscribing to the Land Plan, while bad times compel them to think about the land as the only means of escape.

Furthermore, details of three or four roomed cottages and of agricultural techniques helped to maintain interest.[27] Legal and economic doubts did not affect Northern operatives or land-hungry labourers. During 1847 some 600 branches were established and subscriptions rapidly rose.

1847 was, indeed, a year of success. Fielden at last gained the passage of the Ten Hours Bill in May. O'Connor bought 297 acres at Minster Lovell for £10,878 and 268 at Snig's End for £12,200 in June and started to buy 500 Worcestershire acres at Mathon for £15,350 in July. On May Day the first delighted settlers—chosen by lot at Manchester—arrived to take up possession of O'Connorville and were joined by Wheeler, who passed his secretarial duties to McGrath and in October resigned his directorship to Dixon. Legal advice led to further constitutional changes: bank and company were divided, and at a conference at Lowbands in August 'company' rules were changed. Fifty delegates accepted the separation, abolished the 'sections', appointed O'Connor as owner of the bank and resolved to pay company directors Clark, Doyle, McGrath and Wheeler £2 weekly. As half-shares were unknown to joint-stock companies, it was provided that shares should cost £1 6s (£1·30p) and that two shares should be the qualification for two acres, three for three acres and four for four acres. The success of the scheme, as well as legal considerations, made these changes desirable. Between December 1846 and August 1847 £49,520 had been received, and by November 42,000 members had subscribed some £80,000. O'Connor could fairly claim that much of this success was due to him. Careless (though not, as often alleged, dishonest) over complicated accounts and legalistic details he might be; arrogant and intolerant towards rivals and changeable in courses he certainly was; but he honestly believed in and sincerely worked for his Land Plan, his own personal contribution to the rescuing of British workers. Lowbands was opened in August, after long toil by O'Connor, Doyle and the faithfully productive Rebecca. And O'Connor received some reward.

At the July elections Chartist candidates appeared on several hustings, generally to disappear after the show of hands. Continuing Chartist interest was demonstrated by the candidatures of such men as Harney (who frightened Palmerston at Tiverton), Roberts (Blackburn), Vincent (Ipswich), McGrath (Derby), Kydd (Greenwich), West (Stockport), Thomas Dickenson (South Shields), Clark (Sheffield), J. H. Parry (Norwich), George Thompson (Tower Hamlets) and others. Middle-class radicals who proceeded to the poll fared almost as variably as did 'true' Chartists: Fielden, Miall and Sturge were defeated, while Duncombe, Wakley, W. J. Fox, Crawford, Perronet Thompson, Muntz, Scholefield and Bowring were successful. For the Chartists, Jones did badly, Parry well and O'Connor superbly. At Nottingham Feargus, allied with John Walter, the Tory son of his 'enemy' of 1842 (who had just died), resoundingly defeated Gisburne and Hobhouse. The result, reported Walter's *Times*, was 'about as surprising an occurrence as could possibly arise from the mere movements of human opinion and feeling'. At this peak of his career O'Connor announced his plenary indulgence to 'all the dissevered elements of Chartism—the O'Briens, Lovetts, Vincents, Coopers, and all'. He invited them 'to return to the popular embrace and join in a national jubilee'. If the 'Old Guards' joined him, he would

> cheerfully shake hands with every man who had honestly differed from him and ... zealously struggle with him, a good soldier in the good fight.

As a Member of Parliament he proposed (more privately) to follow the leadership of Duncombe. But he reserved his freedom on Irish questions. O'Connell was now dead and the ideal of an Anglo-Irish proletarian-peasant union was thus encouraged. 'Young Ireland', which in some ways assumed the mantle of Irish leadership, had, however, announced that it[23]

> desired no fraternisation between the Irish people and the Chartists, not on account of the bugbear of physical force, but simply because some of their five points are to us an abomination. . . . Between us and them there is a gulf fixed, and we desire not to bridge it over but to make it wider and deeper.

O'Connor undoubtedly still hoped to change such attitudes, now that he was the voice of the people in Parliament, still a potential Irish leader and already a considerable British businessman.

VI

The new MP inevitably had to reduce the time devoted to bucolic labours; Doyle was deputed to superintend the transformation of Minster Lovell into Charterville, while O'Connor attended to his parliamentary duties. McGrath continued to organise the collection of weekly sums, but the central accounts were kept—or, more strictly, not kept—by O'Connor. The land schemes remained illegal and, despite considerable activity on the part of Chinnery, plans to obtain registration were botched. But sufficient money continued to flow in to overwhelm the minute secretariat. O'Connor ignored such problems. He lashed out at doubting editors—generically 'ruffians' and, in the case of the *Weekly Dispatch* editor, an 'unmitigated ass . . . sainted fowl . . . canonised ape [and] nincompoop!' He addressed crowded rallies on the pleasures of rural life, with flattering reactions. He talked of asking Parliament for a Bill to legalise the company. The acclaim, the loyalty, the cash flow, the heady personal publicity continued: an O'Connor tartan design was put on sale in the autumn. But the long journalistic campaign against the scheme was starting to have its effect; by October things were starting to go wrong. Receipts began to decline, from £5,099 a week in July to £3,063 on 28 October and £893 on 18 November, as the race eased to join the company which closed in December. O'Connor remained oblivious to such mundane matters, to the suspicions of the new company to be formed in 1848, or to the complaints of fellow-directors facing 100 letters daily and overwhelming administrative problems in coping with some 60,000 subscribers. He was, however, aware of the cost of registration as a joint-stock company and on 19 February 1848, as the *Star* announced a new company (with shares at £5, £7 10s (£7.50p) and £10 for two, three or four acres) he raised his plan to amend the Friendly Societies Acts in Parliament. Some petitions were collected to back the extension of friendly society status to the Land Company. O'Connor apparently still felt optimistic: in January he was buying 280 acres at Dodford near Bromsgrove for £10,350 and organised a further ballot in Soho.

In Parliament O'Connor had never been effective. The preparation of a short Bill on the Land Company took months; even the leadership was divided over future plans, as Jones showed with his surprising pledge at Middleton that any shareholder could buy an unballoted plot at cost price. In any case, Feargus remained passionately interested in Irish politics. He regularly denounced the Irish Coercion Bill and John O'Connell—that 'lickspittle spaniel only fit to be kicked'—who followed his father's policy of allying with the Whigs.[24] To O'Connor, the 'land system' had been destroyed by the horrors of the famine; now, he hoped for both land reform (particularly on tenure) and repeal of the Union. In December 1847 he still hoped to liberate both Britain and Ireland:

> '*Ireland for the Irish*!' and '*England for the English*!' is the mutual cry. Let it be shouted, side by side . . . it will be the knell of oppression—it will be the birth-peal of freedom—for the solitary fortresses of tyranny must sink before the confluence of our united nations.

Early in 1848 he made common cause with Smith O'Brien's Irish Confederation of January 1847, even sharing platforms with such 'militants' as John Mitchel (who, in February 1848, broke with the Confederates to announce a republican, democratic policy in the *United Irishman*). When the Confederates quickly reunited on hearing of the Paris revolution and generally agreed on threatened violence (by an embryonic National Guard), though still divided on social policies, O'Connor's 'agreement' with them had some importance. At last he had allied with a militant Irish group—and one which shared his hostility to the O'Connellites. The alliance was formalised on St Patrick's Day, 17 March, in Manchester Free Trade Hall, when Leach, J. J. Finnigan, O'Connor (who hoped the audience had come 'to receive absolution from me' for opposing previous alliances), Peter Feeney and F. T. Meagher were present. Now liberated from 'The Liberator's' influence, Confederate Irishmen in Manchester, Barnsley and elsewhere unwisely announced their 'military' preparations and congratualted the French on their latest revolution. They were soon to be protesting at the arrests and trials of Mitchel, Meagher and O'Brien. Their blustering threats came to nothing and their promises to the Chartists were worthless.[25]

In addition to these affairs, O'Connor was inevitably heavily involved in the business of the general Chartist body. The economic crisis and industrial slump of the winter of 1847–8, which helped to reduce Land Plan subscriptions, also revived interest in Chartist panaceas for working-class distress.[26] 'Plenteous boards there will be,' the

Star asserted on Christmas Day 1847,'—but not for the poor.' Even in February the *Manchester Guardian* had prepared its Liberal readers for the passing of the Factory Act with the forecast that

> There certainly never was a time ... when a limitation to ten hours would interfere less with the engagements of the masters, or the earnings of the workpeople, than the period now before us. ...

The fact was that proletarian Chartism grew once more during an extending depression. Another petition was prepared and another convention was elected, to meet on 4 April in Tottenham Court Road. And, like the Irish Confederates, many Chartists were excited by the news of the February revolution in Paris against King Louis Philippe's 'bourgeois monarchy'—which sparked off risings throughout Europe. As the news of each revolt in each monarchical capital arrived, Chartist hopes rose once more.[27]

VII

Chartists' previous interest in international affairs was not particularly impressive. Certainly, Lovett's National Association had followed established radical precedent in condemning Czar Nicholas I when he visited Britain in 1844 and was thus led to express sympathy with Polish aspirations—though subsequent Polish stories of Chartist involvement are surely exaggerated. Some Chartists also shared radical sympathy with varied European nationalist movements—particularly with the Italian and Hungarian agitations. So Lovett and Hetherington helped Duncombe to condemn Graham for authorising the opening of Mazzini's correspondence in March 1844. At an anniversary dinner of the Democratic Association in August 1845 Harney, Rider, Cooper and Beniowski waxed eloquent over republicanism and Mazzini; and in celebrating Hunt's birthday in November O'Connor was joined by such men as the French revolutionary Michelot, the German tailor-socialist Weitling and Harney in condemning the *ancien régime*. The Fraternal Democrats of 1845 attracted Harney and Jones to an often class-conscious internationalism; but the association was minute, 'meeting monthly at a dingy public-house in Drury Lane', recalled Thomas Frost:

> It was composed of democratic refugees from most parts of Europe, but chiefly of Frenchmen, Germans and Poles, with a sprinkling

of such advanced reformers of this country as, like Julian Harney and Ernest Jones, were 'Chartists and something more'.

Harney and Jones long continued to participate in the activities of the international radical freemasonry, periodically associating with the exiled Marx and his succession of militant but tiny bodies. Others participated in the more liberal 'Mazzinian' People's International League founded at the Crown and Anchor on 28 April 1847 to support self-government and nationality: Bowring, Duncombe, Epps, Fox, Linton, Moore, Carpenter, Cooper, Vincent and Watson were among its leading supporters. But though Dr Marx of Brussels and Citizen Engels of Paris were rapturously received by the Fraternal Democrats on 27 November 1847 as actual representatives of a proletarian internationalism, Communist Leagues and the like had little attraction for most Chartists. The *Star* rejoiced at the difference between Parisian 'national workshops' and English 'bastilles'. The lesson which it drew from events in France was that[28]

> as France had secured for herself her beloved republic, so Ireland must have her parliament restored and England her idolised Charter.

In the country, Chartists and others demonstrated that the French events had had considerable effect, particularly against a bitter industrial background. Early in March there were riots in Aberdeen, Edinburgh, Glasgow, London, Manchester (where, however, even Leach accepted that the trouble was the work of 'mischievous imps and lads') and elsewhere. Jones assured the Fraternal Democrats that 'the Book of Kings was fast closing in the Bible of Humanity' and joined Harney and McGrath in telling much the same message to Parisian revolutionaries. O'Connor, however, was determined that

> as long as he lived the Charter and the Land should never be lost sight of, nor placed in abeyance by any foreign excitement or movement, however they might use events for the furtherance of those great objects. . . .

His principal aim was still to 'insure happy homes, and protection for all—the release of women from slave labour, and the release of little children from the abodes of pestilence, disease, immorality and death'—but he 'would not be found backward in moulding passing events to future advantage'.[29] There now opened a dramatic period in Chartist history.

8 *Finale*

In the winter of 1847–8 Chartist enthusiasm reached new heights. The third petition was progressing so well that O'Connor now thought in terms of five million signatories. Crowded meetings greeted the Land Company lecturers, McDouall, West and Kydd. Leach and others were making hopeful contacts with the new and energetic Irish agitation. Harney was forging some links between Chartism and international radicalism. Urban distress at home and urban revolution abroad alike seemed to help the Chartist revival.

Inevitably, however, Chartism remained divided. Kydd argued at Sunderland with James Williams over O'Connor's policies. The press campaign against the Land Plan continued in the *Dispatch, Lloyd's Newspaper, Nonconformist, Nottingham Journal, Nottingham Mercury* and, above all, in the *Manchester Examiner,* wherein Somerville ('one who had whistled at the plough') lashed the scheme. Answering Somerville, Hobson charged O'Connor with misappropriating *Star* and Land Plan money. O'Connor bitterly answered the charge at a Manchester rally with three hours of counter-charges. And he demonstrated his old mastery in controlling a crowd. 'Neither pen nor tongue could describe his reception,' declared the *Star*. 'It was not enthusiasm, it was madness, a frenzy that cannot be described.'[1] The Chartist rank-and-file remained trustingly mesmerised by the leader who now took to signing his lengthy epistles 'Feargus Rex'.

The February revolution in Paris provided a further stimulus and was widely hailed by crowded and excited meetings. On 6 March a middle-class rally was called under Charles Cochrane in Trafalgar Square to protest against the Income Tax. Banned by the Home Office, the meeting nevertheless took place under G. W. M. Reynolds, a novelist and republican journalist who secured support for the French Republic and the Charter before a three-day riot developed. On the same day armed riots began in Glasgow and O'Connor addressed 7,000 people at Hanley. A nationwide campaign followed. In the week starting on Sunday the 12th, Kydd and John Shaw aroused the West Riding, O'Connor toured Lancashire, West rallied the North West and Reynolds, Dixon, Fussell, McGrath and Jones addressed enthusiastic London rallies. Town after town held great rallies under the *tricoleur*, to hail the French and the Charter. In the last great surge of Chartist energy, heady oratory was general. 'Before heaven', roared Jones,

> I believe that we stand upon the threshold of our rights. One step, were it even with an iron heel, and they are ours. I conscientiously believe the people are prepared to claim the Charter. Then I say— take it; and God defend the right!... We'll respect the law, if the law-makers respect us. If they don't—France is a Republic!

Such stuff was worthy of O'Connor at his blustering worst. But it found answering responses in Aberdeen, Airdrie, Ayr, Bacup, Barrhead, Bath, Beith, Birmingham, Blackburn, Bradford, Coventry, Crieff, Dalry, Dudley, Dumfries, Dunfermline, Dundee, Edinburgh, Exeter, Glasgow, Gloucester, Greenock, Hamilton, Heywood, Hinckley, Ipswich, Kilbarchan, Leeds, Leicester, Leith, Loughborough, Macclesfield, Mansfield, Manchester, Merthyr Tydfil, Newark, Newport, Northampton, Nottingham, Oldham, Padiham, Paisley, Plymouth, Preston, S. Andrews, South Shields, Sheffield, Southampton, Stalybridge, Stockport, Stroud, Swindon, Tiverton, Trowbridge, Wigan and Wigston. And during the campaign forty-nine delegates were optimistically elected for the last great Convention.[2] Many of them talked of forcing the government to accept the Charter.

I

It was not only Chartists who visualised a British rebellion in the year of revolutions, as thrones toppled throughout Europe and a new dark age seemed about to begin. Queen Victoria, who had been delivered of her sixth child on 18 March, had been alarmed on the 6th when Reynolds's mob broke lamps near Buckingham Palace and on 8 April was glad to escape to Osborne. 'As for general affairs...', wrote Disraeli on 8 March,

all are swamped and merged in the mighty theme of how the devil

Europe, or perhaps England, is to be governed. 6 men shot at Glasgow; here, cockney riots of little boys.

Greville recorded society's surprise at the sequence of events:

In 1789 everybody saw that a revolution was inevitable; in 1830 everybody thought it was probable; but in 1848, up to the very moment at which the explosion took place, and even for a considerable time after it. . . no human being dreamt of a revolution and of the dethronement of the King.

As 10 April, the date for the presentation of the petition, approached, Greville found Graham 'greatly alarmed' and 'uneasy'. But at Apsley House old Wellington, recalled from retirement to protect London, was 'in a prodigious state of excitement':

he had plenty of troops, and would answer for keeping everything quiet if the Government would only be firm and vigorous and announce by a proclamation that the mob should not be permitted to occupy the town.

The Duke brilliantly organised the defence of the capital, taking care to give no military provocation. Oddly, Russell was cool and was only reluctantly persuaded to agree to the preparations.[3]

To many members of the upper classes the world seemed to be falling around them. 'All I know', wrote Lord John Manners to the irresponsible Monckton Milnes,

is that our Colonies are on the verge of Rebellion, our Mills are closed, the Irish starving, the Usurpers gaining millions, the Revenue falling, trade dished, Commerce ruined & Credit annihilated.

'Revolutions go off like pop-guns!' recorded Ashley in March. '. . . We have yet a tumult in store, English Chartists and Irish Repealers are to have their day.' As Disraeli observed to Lady Londonderry, 'Kings and Princes are turned off as we turn away servants— worse, without character—and nobody resists. . . .' 'We get astounding news from the continent,' Cobden told his wife: 'a fresh revolution or a dethronement by every post.' He later thought that 'the Government and the newspapers had made far too much fuss' O'Connor's 'poor dupes' were rightly 'disheartened and disgusted' and would henceforth be 'much more disposed to go along with the middle class'. Bright felt similarly. In March he wrote that

Liberty is on the march, and this year promises to be a great year in European history. . . . We must have another League of some kind, and our aristocracy must be made to submit again.

By April he was sure that[4]

the middle and working classes are beginning to see that united they may win all they require; divided they are a prey to their insatiable enemies.

But the bitter liberals of the Manchester School did not represent the generality of anti-Chartists.

Robert Owen thought it necessary to warn the government on 'practical measures required to prevent greater political changes in Great Britain and Ireland.' His list included freedom of thought, speech and publication; wider representation, the ballot and payment of MPs; Church disestablishment; State education; a graduated property tax; bank nationalisation; paper currency; free trade; and a local militia.[5] Other people raected more robustly to what was thought to be a national emergency. Russell told Prince Albert of the cabinet's plan (drafted by Colonel Rowan, the Chief Commissioner of Police) to allow the Chartists to march to a bridge and halt them there:

[Rowan] thinks this is the only way to avoid a fight. If, however, the Chartists fire and draw their swords and use their daggers, the Military are to be called out. I have no doubt of their easy triumph over a London mob. But any loss of life will cause a deep and rankling resentment.

The Prince also hoped that no 'commotion' would occur, 'as it would shake that confidence which the whole of Europe reposes in our stability at this moment'—and went on to hope that 'economy' would be reconsidered: 'surely this was not the moment for the taxpayers to economise upon the working classes!' Few under-estimated the danger. 'This', Lord Campbell told his brother,

may be the last time I write to you before the Republic is established! I have no serious fears of revolution, but there may be bloodshed.

On 5 April Lord Malmesbury recorded that 'everyone expected that the attack would be serious'; on the 9th 'the alarm . . . was very general all over the town'; and on the 10th his five keepers arrived,

'armed with double-barrelled guns, and determined to use them if
necessary'.[6]

Nervous wives and small children might be sent to the country,
but the aristocrats were determined, if necessary, to fight—aided by
their larger rural retainers. To Lady Palmerston it seemed that

> it is very fortunate that the whole thing has occur'd, as it has
> shewn the good spirit of our middle classes, and almost one may
> say of the whole population of London, as well as the activity
> and courage of the aristocracy. 2 hundred Thousand were sworn
> in special Constables and all higgledy piggledy Peers and Com-
> mons, servants, workmen, and all kinds of people, all hale fellow
> well met, an example of union and loyalty and a determination
> to stand by our constitution, which will have a great effect
> everywhere, in England, in Ireland and in Europe.

Greville found the preparations 'either very sublime or very
ridiculous':

> All the clerks and others in the different offices are ordered to be
> sworn in special constables and to constitute themselves into
> garrisons. I went to the police office with all my clerks, messen-
> gers, &c., and we were all sworn. . . every gentleman in London
> is become a constable, and there is an organisation of some sort
> in every district.

At the Foreign Office Palmerston commanded one garrison, prepared to repel 'foreigners [who] did not show'; but, he told
Normanby,

> the constables, regular and special, had sworn to make an ex-
> ample of any whiskered and bearded rioter whom they might
> meet with, and I am convinced would have mashed them to
> jelly.

Gladstone and his brother John both signed on as special constables; and Frederick Denison Maurice, the Christian Socialist
leader, tried to do so but was rejected as a clergyman. Young
Arthur Pell was sworn in at Marlborough Street station and,
he recalled,

> shared the Testament with a very black coal-heaver. . . . My
> cousin was also sworn in, and so was Louis Napoleon, with
> whom he was put on to patrol Conduit Street. . . . I, with a
> greengrocer, patrolled the Hampstead Road. . . .

The astonishing metropolitan response to a 'patriotic' call quickly put Chartism in its place. The concealed cannon, cavalry and infantry never needed to appear. London's male population of all classes was prepared to defend its city; and, as Pell discovered from Sir James Bathurst, the Army would not act 'so long as a single special constable was alive and on his legs'. Only if the police were resisted and 'likely to be beaten' would the Army move, confirmed Malmesbury—'then the troops are instantly to appear, and the cannon to open with shell and grenades, infantry and cavalry are to charge—in short, they are to be made an example of'.[7] In the event, the police muster alone was enough to make such shrill advocates of violence as Jones quickly lose their nerve. The silent majority had exerted itself.

II

The Convention assembled in the John Street Institution on 4 April, with McGrath as president and Doyle as secretary. Its first problem was to decide whether to accept McCarthy, representing the Irish Democratic Confederation. Despite O'Connor's hostility, McCarthy was accepted, as was the new convert Reynolds. Next, the executive's voting rights were debated. O'Connor, who had recently announced that 'he would rather be taken a corpse from [the] procession' than stay away, resigned his right to vote. O'Brien, however, insisted that Feargus must share the general responsibility for decisions. Delegates proceeded to give regional reports, many of them advocating physical force. O'Connor agreed that they should wait no longer, having collected 5,400,000 signatures; but

> on the faith of that Convention, he should [say] that not one pane of glass nor one pennyworth of property would be injured; that peace and good order would prevail while their grievances were under discussion.

If Parliament rejected the petition they should ask the Queen to call a new pro-Charter cabinet. O'Brien's scoffing doubts were rejected, and on the 6th delegates lengthily debated policy, eventually agreeing to an address on the state of the country and to a statement on future strategy. If the petition were rejected, the Convention would memorialise the Queen 'to dissolve the present Parliament and call to her council such ministers only as will make the People's Charter a cabinet measure'. The memorial would be presented by an elected

National Assembly, which would 'continue permanently sitting until the Charter was the law of the land'; it would be elected on the 21st and meet on the 24th, until which time the Convention would continue.

At extra-conference meetings, enthusiastic Londoners supported the Convention, and on the 4th the Fraternal Democrats under Jones asked the Convention to sit permanently if the petition were rejected. But on the 6th Sir George Grey announced in the Commons that the planned procession to take the petition to Parliament would be prohibited. O'Connor fought against the decision, insisting that the peacefully inclined Convention had no intention of intimidating Parliament; but his case was scarcely helped by the well-reported speeches of such men as Reynolds, who (according to Gammage)

> thought this should be the last Petition to the House, and that its refusal would be a declaration of war against labour. A few drops of blood were as nothing in the scale; and if moral means failed the people were prepared for any means.

Nor was McCarthy's talk of '40,000 Irishmen in London, ready to avenge their brethren' helpful. On the 7th the Convention was appalled by Commissioner Rowan's proclamation against the procession—based on 'a statute passed in the arbitrary reign of King Charles II' and a denial of freedom, which the delegates would ignore. The government meanwhile proceeded with the Crown and Government Security Bill against seditious speeches, which passed through all its stages by the 13th. Convention delegates unanimously resolved to proceed with their rally and march and sent Prater Wilkinson, Reynolds and Clark to tell Grey that *Times* reports that marchers would be armed were untrue; they met Le Marchant, the Home Office under-secretary, and the Attorney General, but achieved no more than did delegations to other politicians.

The Times, that old champion of the anti-Poor Law agitation, was decidedly hostile to the Chartists of 1848. They were 'but tools in the hands of desperadoes', for

> The true character of the present movement is a ramification of the Irish conspiracy. The Repealers wish to make as great a hell of this island as they have made of their own.

There was much evidence to support such assertions. Undoubtedly, Irish militants hoped that Chartist activities would tie down the Army in Britain. Some were more specific: at Liverpool Matthew

Somers declared that action in Ireland would be followed by skies
'reddened with the blaze of the Babylons of England'. O'Brien's
speech at Lambeth on the 9th, announcing his resignation from the
Convention on the ground that other members were moving too
quickly, scarcely improved the image.

At dawn on Monday the 10th, London was hugely garrisoned and
guarded by thousands of police, 8,000 soldiers, 1,500 Chelsea Pensioners, 12 cannon, marines and sailors, armed civil servants and
over 150,000 special constables. The expected Chartist route was
thronged with police; Trafalgar Square and Westminster Bridge
were heavily guarded; excited clerks with their muskets peered over
defences of bound volumes of *The Times* at the Foreign Office. Re-
porters scurried around, gleaning information for hourly newspaper
editions. And special trains arrived with determined country Chartists, to join the London contingents assembling on Stepney Green
and in Finsbury and Russell Squares for ceremonial marches to the
rally on Kennington Common.

At 9 a.m. Reynolds presided over a meeting of the Convention,
when Doyle reported the Commissioner's repeated warning against
a march to Parliament. O'Connor then blamed the militants for provoking the government and warned of plans to shoot Chartist
leaders. He would ask supporters

> in the name of courage...justice and... God, not to hold the pro-
> cession and thus throw their great cause into the hands of pick-
> pockets and scoundrels, and give the Government an opportunity
> of attacking them.

Musing on this latest *volte face*, at 10 a.m. the delegates solemnly left
the hall, to join a decorated cart at the head of a procession to the
Common. At the Land Company office the petition was lifted with
due ceremony into another beflagged cart, pulled by four Chartist
horses from Snigs End. And so the last great roll of signatures was
escorted with maximum ceremony and pageantry to the rally.

The petition and the delegates were ecstatically received on the
Common. By how many voices the cheers were raised remains, as
usual, doubtful. London Chartist cohorts had been supplemented by
provincial contingents and some trades delegates. But many must
have been deterred by the police placards or by sight of official preparations. The estimated attendance varied from 'between 400,000
and 500,000' (O'Connor) through 250,000 (the *Star*), 150–170,000
(Gammage), 'at least 150,000' (the *Evening Sun*), about 20,000,

including bystanders (*The Times*) and an official estimate quoted by West of '15,000 to 20,000' to Russell's report to the Queen of 'about 12,000 or 15,000 persons'. Russell was probably correct.

On arrival at the Common, O'Connor was summoned to Horns Rooms to meet Police Commissioner Richard Mayne, who told him that while the meeting might continue, the procession was banned, that the authorities would forcibly prevent it and that O'Connor would be held responsible for the consequences. While supporters fretted over a rumour that O'Connor had been arrested, Feargus agreed to call off the march. When he returned to the Common, the rally began, under Doyle's chairmanship. The Chartists had marched under brave banners and with recollections of much militant bluster from such leaders as O'Connor, Jones and McCarthy. They had been led to believe that final success was near, that Chartism was about to triumph over the 'base, bloody and brutal Whigs'. Many, no doubt, were uncertain as to how the achievement was to come about. But they had braved ministerial threats to find out from O'Connor.

Alcohol and excitement greatly affected Feargus at this ecstatic period, as hopes rose of 6,000,000 petitioners. 'The government must be met with calm and firm defiance,' Thomas Allsop had told him:

> Violence may be overcome with violence, but a resolute deter-
> mination not to submit cannot be overcome. . . . Precipitate noth-
> ing, yield nothing. Aim not alone to destroy the government,
> but to render a class government impossible. No hesitation, no
> rash impulse, no egotism, but an earnest, serious, unyielding
> progress.

Mayne perhaps reinforced a growing sense of realism. Six sleepless nights and recurring bronchial trouble scarcely helped Feargus to face a dramatic situation. Russell told the Queen that he looked 'pale and frightened' on meeting Mayne, 'expressed the utmost thanks' for the Commissioner's message 'and begged to shake [him] by the hand'. The result of his anguished re-thinking was a curious speech to the assembled 'loyalists'. There was the affirmation of family revolutionaryism—a father tried half a dozen times for high treason, an exiled uncle 'about to be made the first president of the Republic in France', a brother 'Prime Minister and Commander-in-chief of a Republic in South America'. His credentials thus estab-lished, the 'honest father and unpaid bailiff' paternalistically address-ed his 'children', praying that they would not spoil the effect of

5,700,000 signatures by disobeying the police. Constant references to the audience's virtues, his own valour (he had braved his doctor's advice and a hundred threats to be present; he 'would die upon the floor of the House': his 'life was at their command'; 'though he might be stretched on the rack, he would smile terror out of countenance') and a special doubt ('I don't think you could well spare me just now') carried the audience. Ernest Jones agreed, and the rally broke up to hear various orators announce varied schemes. But O'Connor had carried the vast majority. Shortly after 2 p.m. the crowd dissolved, some to scuffle with the police, most to go home. The petition was loaded into three cabs and, refused a quick route by the police, reached Parliament by a roundabout journey.

At 2 p.m. Russell reported to the Queen that the last crowd of 'about 5,000 [was] rapidly dispersing'. O'Connor had visited the Home Office[8]

> where he repeated to Sir George Grey his thanks, his fears and his assurances that the crowd should disperse quietly. Sir George Grey said he had done very rightly, but that the force at the bridges should not be diminished. Mr F. O'Connor—'Not a man should be taken away. The Government have been quite right. I told the Convention that if they had been the Government they never would have allowed such a meeting'.

Later in the afternoon O'Connor presented the petition—signed, he said, by 5,700,000 people—in the Commons.

'The Kennington Common Meeting', as Russell wrote, had 'proved a complete failure'. But the Convention continued. It adopted Jones's proposal to circulate a report of the meeting, Clark's proposal to petition the Commons for the impeachment of the government, Harney's motion to organise the election of an Assembly, Leach's condemnation of any general attack on the middle class, Kydd's denunciation of the Alien Bill and Shirron's appeal for union support—and accepted O'Connor's offer of financial help. In the evening a rally was held in the John Street Institution, at which general optimism prevailed. But in the Commons a different picture was emerging. On the 13th Thornley announced that the alleged 5,700,000 signatures actually totalled 1,975,496, including 'Victoria Rex', Wellington, Peel and Colonel Sibthorp (the arch-Tory MP for Lincoln, who solemnly denied having signed the petition). Other 'signatures' were fictitious or humorous—Pugnose, Punch, Snooks, No Cheese and so on; and there were other words and phrases which, though written in the form of signatures and included in the number reported, [the Committee on Public Petitions] would not hazard offending the House and the dignity and decency of their own proceedings by reporting, though it might be added that they were obviously signatures belonging to no human being.

O'Connor tried to bluster: thirteen lawyers' clerks could not have counted the signatures; the false signatures had been inscribed by government spies; he stood by his original estimate of the number. But the House was unimpressed; figures had never been a strong point with O'Connor and his multiplication of (even forged) signatures was matched by his unnecessary boast of a five-ton petition, which, by official measurement, weighed 5 cwt 84 lb. No Member supported O'Connor, and William Cripps, while defending the Committee, condemned Feargus's veracity. O'Connor stalked out of the House and sent Jones to challenge Cripps to a duel. The Commons acted quickly: the Serjeant-at-Arms arrested O'Connor, who, with Cripps, had to apologise to the House. But any impression which the petition might have made on the Commons had been lost: Chartism, recently so frightening (Wellington had told the Lords that the Kennington rally 'placed all the inhabitants of the metropolis under alarm, paralysing all trade and business') had become a joke.

Denounced in Parliament, O'Connor had little more success in the Convention. Although his cash would be gracelessly accepted, members refused to accept an offer of *Star* profits which would put them under a permanent obligation. The government's supposed triumph, he claimed, 'would only prove evanescent'; but he also blamed some colleagues for the government's precautions—'if strong language had not been used . . . there would have been no resistance to the procession'. And even Convention members could not accept his arguments on petition signatures. The Convention itself became increasingly unrealistic, debating and passing resolutions which were almost meaningless. Members slipped away to address constituents; Leach, Kydd and McGrath were deputed to tour Ireland; of the one hundred seats in the National Assembly, twenty-two would be reserved for trade unionists; and another determined effort was to be made to enlist bourgeois support, following O'Connor's report of 'most kindly and affectionate letters from shopkeepers, tradesmen and others of the middle classes, tendering their hearty cooperation. . . '. But the Assembly was postponed until 1 May—and its future was scarcely aided by O'Connor's assertion that it was illegal. Nevertheless, there was great enthusiasm at meetings throughout the country to select Assembly members; the Convention adjourned on 25 April.[9]

III

The National Assembly met in the John Street Institute on May Day, when the original twenty-nine delegates appointed Dixon as chairman and Shirron as secretary; membership eventually rose to fifty-four. After the usual district reports—including accounts of the formation of a 'National Guard' in Scottish towns—the members turned to future policy. As always, they were divided over physical force, the absent O'Connor, the honesty of *Star* reporting and an alliance with Hume's household suffrage group. McDouall's plan for reorganisation was adopted, establishing a hierarchy of districts, localities, wards and sections. An executive of five would receive £2 weekly, with expenses, and would operate from a London office, aided by twenty commissioners paid similarly. Jones (who had left the *Star* to join the Assembly), Kydd, Leach, McDouall and McCrae were elected to the provisional executive, with James Adams, J. Bassett, Henry Child, Robert Cochran, James Cumming, Daniel Donovan, Andrew Harley, Alexander Henry, David Lightowler, J. Peacock, Richard Pilling, Henry Rankine, Alexander Sharp, John Shaw, James Shirron, Matthew Stevenson, John West and T.M. Wheeler as temporary commissioners. It was proposed to finance the undertaking by a Liberty Fund of £10,000.

Optimism, however, did not last long. As the Londoner W.J. Vernon complained on the 8th, the agitation would die unless the Assembly gave it a real lead. Such feelings were underlined by a message from the associated trades of Glasgow regretting the breach with O'Connor and the Assembly's lack of activity. And O'Connor himself was active in the country, consolidating his personal following and gathering support for a proposed new daily journal, *The Democrat*. But the Assembly rambled through debates against a standing army and the Union with Ireland, on an address on 'the labour question', for Church disestablishment, the employment of paupers on land reclamation, the need for arms and (acrimoniously) over the means of presenting a memorial to the Queen. Members became increasingly disillusioned at their divisions and ineffectiveness. Harley of Glasgow was ordered by his constituents to resign, and on the 13th, after a bitter debate, West and Pilling moved a dissolution. Supporting them, Jones condemned 'the desertion of friends and the invasion of enemies'; 'they must start afresh, start with new power, with new energy, with new confidence'. His claim that 'they had gained two triumphs—first, union, and second, independence'—was ludicrous. The Assembly had achieved next to nothing. It had reorganised the NCA on the basis of the old radical plan of groups of ten members; but it had no authority to do so, as it had no real connection with the declining Association. All the brave talk of marching on Buckingham Palace, all Jones's bluster about the people's leaders asserting their 'right' to put their case to the Queen, all threats of a huge London demonstration to overawe the authorities evaporated as members returned home. The memorial to the Queen was delivered through the post, after a little meeting on Clerkenwell Green.

The obvious fact was that the disappointment over the Kennington Common failure had further weakened and divided the movement. As Gammage observed, O'Connor

> was right in the course he took in abandoning the procession: the people were anything but prepared for a physical encounter with the Government. O'Connor was wrong, not in abandoning the procession, but in having encouraged so long the empty braggarts and enthusiastic but mistaken men of the Convention, and in inducing them, almost to the last moment, to believe that he would head the procession to the House of Commons. The boasting which took place on this subject, and the miserable result, inflicted a wound to Chartism from which it has never recovered.

But Chartism was not dead. Militants allied with Irish Confederates to plot simultaneous risings, on 12 June or 15 August—and ignored O'Connor's uneasy alliance with middle-class reformers.[10]

Support for the ulterior measures which the Assembly was established to frame and which were now more secretly planned—according to Cooper and Frost, with assistance from police agents—was doubtful; but the government took no chances. Action started with the arrest of the Irish extremists. Mitchel's militancy had shocked even Duffy and O'Brien, and in February he, Devin Reilly and John Martin had left the Confederate Council and founded the *United Irishman* as the organ of a radical republicanism. In the spring, the Confederates themselves moved Leftwards and the Lord Lieutenant, the Earl of Clarendon, resolved to act. On 24 May Mitchel was sentenced to fourteen years' transportation for treasonable felony. Smith O'Brien, acquitted of sedition after being beaten up by O'Connellites at Limerick in April, was captured in August and with three others transported for an abortive rising in Tipperary. O'Connor praised 'the noble Irish felon' and offered a week's *Star* profits to his wife:

> What had been John Mitchel's crime? The 'crime' of loving his country and struggling for the rights of the oppressed millions. He is not the first Irishman who has devoted himself ... to the ever defeated but ever glorious struggle to redeem his country from a foreign yoke and the sons and daughters of his native land from slavery; but he is the first man amongst Ireland's modern patriots—sham and real—who has boldly unveiled the hideous vices of Ireland's (anti-) social system and manfully contended for the rights of the labourers and the sons of the soil—their social as well as their political rights.

But, as Greville observed, 'the account of Mitchel's conviction had given great satisfaction' in London. Of O'Brien's capture he commented that[11]

> Some think [it] a good thing and some a bad one; some say he is mad, some are for hanging him, some for transporting, others for letting him go; in short, *quot homines tot sententiae.* He is a good-for-nothing, conceited, contemptible fellow, who has done a great deal of mischief and deserves to be hung, but it will probably be very difficult to convict him.

Starving Irish peasants—most of whom had no interest in O'Brienite policies—were in no position to protest, but some Chartists complained of the sentences.

Next, the authorities turned against militant Chartists. Following May disturbances in Clerkenwell Green, Tower Hamlets, Manchester and elsewhere and reports of insurrectionary plots, police and troops were alerted. On 3 June Greville noted that

> The Government are now getting seriously uneasy about the Chartist manifestations in various parts of the country, especially in London, and at the repeated assemblings and marchings of great bodies of men. Le Marchant told me that ... lately, accounts have been received from well-informed persons, whose occupations lead them to mix with the people, clergymen—particularly Roman Catholic—and medical men, who report that they find a great

change for the worse amongst them, an increasing spirit of discontent and disaffection, and that many who on the 10th of April
went out as special constables declare they would not do so again
if another manifestation required it. The speeches which are made
at the different meetings are remarkable for the coarse language
and savage spirit they display. It is quite new to hear Englishmen
coolly recommend assassination, and the other day a police super-
intendent was wounded in the leg by some sharp instrument.
These are new and very bad symptoms, and it is impossible not to
feel alarm when we consider the vast amount of the population as
compared with any repressive power we possess. The extent and
reality of the distress they suffer, the impossibility of expecting
such masses of people to be eternally patient and forbearing, to
restrain all their natural impulses, and endure tamely severe priva-
tions when they are encouraged and stimulated to do otherwise,
and are thus accessible to every sort of internal and external temp-
tation—all these considerations may well beget a serious
presentiment of danger.

He regretted that the 'sluggish minds' of the majority appeared to be
unconcerned—and went to Ascot for a week.[12]

When Greville returned to London, Grey's long indecision had
ended; his long tolerance of Chartist calls to arms was running out.
London, Bradford and other towns witnessed riots; indeed, Bradford Chartism remained militant to the end. Some local magistrates,
unimpressed by government inaction, might exaggerate dangers,
but risks certainly existed in Yorkshire. In May McDouall told an
enormous crowd at Bradford 'to keep the peace—to respect life and
property—to arm; but to discountenance any premature outbreak'.
While considering the speech seditious, Grey refused to act. 'Bradford was that day in possession of the Chartists', wrote Gammage.
And 'training and drilling went on at Bradford and the several
towns in the district. Three thousand men drilled openly at Wils-
den ... '. Men of diverse views feared violence. In April young W. E.
Forster, a radical Quaker woolstapler and friend of Thomas Cooper,
drew up a middle-class reform document but almost simultaneously
joined some 1,500 other 'respectabilities' in the special constabulary.
'We look forward with some anxiety', he told his father,

to the possibility of a disturbance spreading here from other
places. . . . The feeling in favour of universal suffrage is a very different thing here from what it is with you or in London. It is a

resolute, long-held determination by the large body of the operatives, and they will not rest till they get some great concession;
and, considering the very large proportion they bear here toward
other classes they demand great tact in management.

In May Forster told Cooper of 'night drilling, pike buying, monster
meetings, troops of soldiers and of course a very bitter class feeling'.

Bradford's disturbances diminished after brief clashes between
stone-throwers and constables and eighteen arrests. But from nearby
Bingley the Oastlerite squire W. B. Ferrand reported nightly 'drilling and military exercise among the working classes'; and Grey now
'thought it most desirable that persons drilling should be arrested
and punished under the Statute 60 Geo.3 c.l.'. Ferrand promptly
arrested two men on 26 May; but the prisoners were rescued by a
mob, the magistrates' room in the Brown Cow was attacked, 'the
two men were carried away in triumph and paraded over the Town'
and Ferrand was threatened with murder. General Thorne at
Bradford could spare no soldiers and the county magistrates could
only authorise the raising of two troops of hussar yeomanry. The
threatened squire angrily complained that

> this part of the Country is in a most alarming state and every
> hour is increasing the strength of the organised masses and the
> difficulties of those entrusted with the keeping of the Peace.

'The Government', Ferrand insisted, 'must not be deceived by Mr
Cobden's language into believing the Chartists a small body. They
are an immense body in the manufacturing districts.' At length he
received his soldiers—about 100 Chelsea Pensioners armed with
ancient blunderbusses, one (to local amusement) sporting a wooden
leg. On 31 May they arrested sixteen millworkers and sent them to
York. Further alarms followed Ferrand's victory (on which Grey
and Sir Charles Wood sent congratulations): a dramatic Sunday call
to arms against invading Chartists led to the discovery of a moorland
Primitive Methodist meeting. But the militant backbone was broken.
'I am afraid', wrote Wood,[13]

> that our West Riding people are amongst the most violent dis-
> turbers of the peace in the kingdom, but I trust that judicious firm-
> ness on the part of the Magistrates may keep them in order, and I
> am looking very anxiously for an improvement in trade which will
> do more than anything towards removing their discontent.

This was one of the Chancellor's more realistic predictions.

Massive precautions were taken against Chartist rallies at Birmingham, Blackstone Edge, Bradford, Croydon, Leeds, Leicester, Liverpool, London, Loughborough, Manchester, Newcastle, Nottingham, Sheffield and Toftshaw Moor. But elections proceeded, resulting in the appointment of O'Connor, McCrae, McDouall, Jones and Kydd to the executive, with J.A. Fussell, C. McCarthy, Leach, West, Pilling, Thomas Tattersall, Adams, J. Sweet, Isaac Ironside, Wheeler, Alexander Sharp, Shirron, Lightowler, Vernon, Donovan, William Brook, George White, Joseph Linney, Cuffey and Robert Burrell as commissioners. A measure of Chartist enthusiasm obviously still remained, despite all disappointments and suspicions. Yet there was a fundamental weakness in the divided movement, which no amount of posturing could really hide. The Liberty Fund made little progress and by mid-June the executive had no money. And a series of arrests of national, local and allied Irish leaders further weakened the movement, while the rejection of Hume's reform motion by 351 to 84 in the Commons scarcely raised spirits.

The arrests were soon followed by trials. In July at the Central Criminal Court Mr Justice Wylde sentenced John Fussell, Alexander Sharp, Francis Looney, Ernest Jones, Joseph Williams and W.J. Vernon to 27, 27, 26, 24, 24 and 24 months' imprisonment respectively. On assorted charges—of treason, conspiring to levy war against the Queen, sedition, drilling, riot, assault and misdemeanour—many other Chartists were sentenced. At York two Bradford men were sentenced to 24 months' imprisonment, twelve to 18 months and five to 12 months and three Bingley men to 6, 2 and 1 months. At Lancaster McDouall was imprisoned for 2 years. In London five men—Dowling, W. Cuffey, Fay, Lacey and Ritchie—were transported for life and seventeen were imprisoned for 2 years and three for 18 months. At Chester G.J. Mantle was sentenced for 2 years and sixteen others for shorter periods. At Liverpool sixty-five were charged (including two tried for murder of a policeman) and sentences included five of life transportation, one of 10 years imprisonment, one of 2 years, seven of 1 year and eleven of 3 months upwards. At York eight were sent down for a year, one (Lightowler) for 9 months and others for 4 to 11 months; at Edinburgh two men were sentenced for 4 months.

O'Connor did his best for his colleagues, hiring counsel at considerable expense. But he could not resist recalling his warnings against the Assembly and his anger at attacks upon himself:

I unhesitatingly declare that the base and shameful falsehoods
told by numerous members of that Assembly, as to the state of
preparedness and resolution of their several districts, was treason
and treachery of the rankest kind.

His interests were increasingly Irish, and the *Star* constantly publicised Irish affairs. There was Fr. Thaddeus O'Malley at Dublin
'urging the formation of armed clubs, and stating his intention to
take an active part in their formation.' And there was continued excitement in both Ireland and England. 'In England as well as Ireland', claimed the *Star* in July, 'terror is the order of the day'. But
by October it had to confess that 'popular indifference was never
more clearly manifested than at the present time'.[14] Despite all the
votes of confidence, O'Connor's personal hold was weakening.
Even close disciples were falling away. Jones had preferred to join
the Assembly rather than remain with the *Star*. Harney, who had remained loyal, was soon to fall foul of O'Connor because of his edi-
torial involvement in European affairs and 'the anticipated glories of
republicanism'. In Gammage's recollection, Samuel Kydd emerges
as the most impressive, consistent and thinking of Chartist leaders
at this period. The young Arbroathian, with his active campaigns to
link Chartism with contemporary industrial issues, had few rivals.
When, alarmed by the Attorney-General's assertion that the new
organisation was illegal, the Chartists changed their plan, Kydd became secretary to an executive composed of Clark, Dixon, McGrath,
Ross, Stallwood and Harney. But when he stood as a hustings candidate for a West Riding by-election in December he lost the show
of hands. This was not, however, to be the last blow sustained by
Chartists.

IV

The Land Plan was now entering its last phase. The new company
advertised shares at £5, £7 10s (£7·50p) and £10 for two, three or
four acres, and on 19 February O'Connor raised the legalisation of
the company in Parliament, seeking the protection of the Friendly
Societies legislation. Other matters inevitably prevented O'Connor
from acting quickly, although supporting petitions were again presented. In March he spoke for his Bill, explaining (against some
heckling) the benefits of the plan. But after the Kennington failure
he morosely retired to Snigs End, to consider the ever-declining

state of the company finances and plan a tired visit to Nottingham. At length on 12 May he introduced his Bill to amend the Friendly Societies Acts to cover the company. The hostile Welsh MP Sir Benjamin Hall immediately began to investigate the scheme; and O'Connor was scarcely helped by criticism from some tenants. On the 24th the Commons resolved to appoint a Select Committee on the company, and fifteen members (including Hall, O'Connor, Crawford and Scholefield) were appointed on the 31st, under the chairmanship of William Hayter, the Judge Advocate.

At last, the politicians unravelled the history of the plan. The idle Roberts, who had earned (or at least, taken) £3,823 in fees, appeared in a bad light, while O'Connor (to whom the company owed considerable sums) was proved honest. Chinnery's administration was admittedly weak, but McGrath gave optimistic and impressive testimony to the company's ultimate soundness and McGowan and Price showed that accounts, while rough, were in order. However, John Revans of the Poor Law Board was less sympathetic to schemes which he palpably regarded as impracticable:

> all those who occupy the Land Company's Allotments, with nothing more than the produce of their allotments to depend upon, will fail to obtain a living ... the operations of the Land Company are likely to lead to serious and sudden burthens upon the poor's rates. . . .

And O'Connor himself gave mixed evidence. He could point to the enormous labour which he had personally devoted to the estates and movingly extol the virtues of peasant farming by liberated proletarians; but his proclivity to exaggerate returned as he talked of astounding productivity and prosperity. The government accountant, W.H. Grey, was

> thoroughly satisfied not only that the whole of the money has been honourably appropriated and is fully accounted for, but also that several thousand pounds more of Mr O'Connor's own funds have been applied in furtherance of the views of the National Land Company.

But the company was now desperately short of funds. And, as the barrister Edward Lawes stated, a company to organise a lottery was illegal and ineligible for registration under the Joint Stock Companies Act, while a bank was irrelevant to the Friendly Societies

Act. Furthermore, a total rental of £2,841 was insufficient (and, in any case, was not yet being paid); the plan to mortgage rents and properties and use the money thus raised for further land would not work. Assuming that 70,000 shareholders paid an average of £3 18s (£3 90p) there would be a capital of £273,000. Eighteen mortgages would increase the total to £819,114, sufficient to settle 2,730 people at £300 per head. As the last mortgage would raise only £210, 67,270 paid-up shareholders would receive nothing. O'Connor was lost when faced with such figures and with the estimate that, at the rate of one new estate annually, the company would take seventy five years to settle its members.

The result was inevitable. On 30 July the Committee reported. Registration was impossible: the company was illegal. Records were inaccurate but not fraudulent, O'Connor being owed almost £3,400. Yet the Committee was fair, suggesting that the company might be wound up to evade legal troubles, or even 'that it should be left entirely open to the parties concerned to propose to Parliament any new measure for carrying out the expectations and objects of the promoters of the company'. The Chartists' incapacity was further demonstrated in their reactions to the benevolently hostile report. By mid-August company subscriptions had dropped to £33. Such organisation as there was started to fail. The overworked, brandy-sodden Feargus became alarmed at the rapacity and cowardice of his colleagues. Allottees, some of whom were sub-letting property at considerable profit, organised rent-strikes under T.M. Wheeler at O'Connorville, W.A. How and Patrick O'Brien at Lowbands, James Beattie and John Bradshaw at Charterville and even Henry Cullingham at Snigs End. Roberts started to buy up departing tenants and in August proposed to end the ballots and to provide allotments for cash.[15]

Despite everything, proceedings were protracted. O'Connor solicited rents; tenants refused them. From January 1849, legal attempts began to force registration under the Companies Act and O'Connor, having failed to raise the money for the Mathon estate, took to threatening to sell the properties. In July O'Connor proposed to form a new National Freehold Benefit Friendly Society, selling shares at £15 under the old management; it was hoped to register as a friendly society. At an August conference at Snigs End he explained that he could not grant the long-promised leases until the venture was legalised. But his patience (and perhaps his sanity) was running out. O'Connor's confusion over whether the allottees were to be peasant freeholders (as originally envisaged) or rent-paying tenants with secure leases (as later planned) led to almost universal confusion. In the autumn rents were carefully worked out and retrospective totals were computed; but attempts to levy the money met with refusals and court cases. O'Connor reacted in December. He would no longer pay interest on the mortgages held by Messrs Weaving and Pinnock, which should have been met from the unpaid rents; and in January 1850 he authorised the mortgagees to eject the tenants.

The end of the brave hopes of thousands of trusting workers was approaching. On 30 March O'Connor promised the House to introduce a Winding-up Bill; in June the Queen's Bench supported the Registrar's refusal of registration; in July the company petitioned for a Winding-up Bill. Declining support, widespread slanders (several resulting in expensive legal actions, for which William Rider, the new editor of the *Star*, raised a defence fund), demands from tradesmen and complaints from tenants were O'Connor's rewards for much hard toil. Nottingham remained loyal, despite the attacks of Bradshaw of the *Nottingham Journal*. But the dream closed as a sheriff's officer drove out the Charterville residents. They left peacefully, but, reported the *Oxford Chronicle*,

> many were in a very destitute condition and exclaimed loudly against the scheme, which in the first instance told such a plausible tale of the lasting benefits it would confer on the share-holders, but which had now reduced them to the necessity of returning from whence they came, with little or no means and entirely ruined in their prospects.

The Winding-up Bill was introduced on 10 February 1851, and caused instant consternation; Patrick O'Brien, the Lowbands schoolmaster and a debtor of O'Connor, even demanded compensation for his rent-evading colleagues. The O'Connorville men 'most cheerfully acknowledged [Feargus] as their landlord in trust for their brother shareholders', but several Chartists proposed rival schemes. Wheeler's National Land and Labour Loan Society of April would buy back the estates and (as the National Loan Society) was actually registered by Pratt, but soon disappeared. O'Connor finally determined to avoid any further responsibility. In March he made over his credit with the Land Company to his solicitor, and in May the bank manager announced a closure until the debt was paid. As directors, Dixon, Doyle, Clark and McGrath rejected O'Connor's claim for £3,299 (subsequently raised to £7,000); another batch of old friends was lost. But the Act was passed in August, sparing the promoters, providing for a winding-up by a Master in Chancery (inevitably, a lengthy proceeding), arranging for payments of debts and past rents, organising conveyances to those with title and ultimately preparing a dividend distribution. Amidst continued rows the Land Plan passed away.[16]

V

As the Land Plan collapsed, Chartism itself was further disintegrating. Middle-class aid proved unsuccessful, as usual; Hume's proposal of 'the Little Charter' for household suffrage was ineptly timed on 23 May 1848, the eve of Derby Day. Splits continued to widen. In April Lovett reappeared in Chartist history, to found his People's League, supported by Miall, Epps, Elt, Vincent, Neesom and Lowery. Two days later, Cooper, Hetherington, Watson, Holyoake and Richard Moore founded a rival People's Charter Union. The League, with its plan to align Chartism with an overhaul of the taxation system, soon failed and (with a remnant of the National Association) collapsed in September 1849. The Union soon became involved in reviving the agitation against 'the taxes on knowledge', especially from March 1849, when Moore, J.D. Collett and other PCU leaders formed the Newspaper Stamp Abolition Committee. The NSAC recruited various Chartists and others, including Dr Black, Holyoake, Place and James Stansfeld, and started to lobby sympathetic MPs. In February 1851 it became the Association for the Repeal of the Taxes on Knowledge, under the presidency of Thomas Milner Gibson, MP, backed by Bright, Cobden, Passmore Edwards, William Ewart, Hume and Thornton Hunt. The parent Union had meanwhile disappeared with the failure of Cooper's plan to organise individual petitions.[17]

A continuing reason for the revived interest in the newspaper taxes was the succession of Chartist and radical journals. The *Star*, though now declining, remained the doyen of radical publications. O'Connor also published the monthly *Labourer*, as the organ of the Land Plan in 1847-8. Gammage draws attention to the variety of (generally short-lived) publications from 1848. From his old retreat in the Isle of Man (beyond reach of the newspaper tax, until the government plugged the hole) O'Brien ran *The Reformer*, propounding his individualistic socialist views. He subsequently continued his old campaigns in *The Power of the Pence*. Other unlikely places produced ultra-radical journals. From Uxbridge the young poets J.B. Leno and Gerrald Massey edited *The Spirit of Freedom*, with a republican slant. At Buckingham there was John Small's *Progressionist*, later edited by Gammage. From East Anglia came the Cambridge *Operatives' Free Press* and the Wisbech *Voice in the East*. Other journals included Passmore Edwards' pacifist *Public Good*, Reynolds's immensely successful *Political Instructor*, Cooper's *Plain Speaker* and—in the future—*Cooper's Journal* (1850), *The Leader* (1850-9), Harney's *Democratic Review* (1849-51), *The English Republic* (1851-5), *Reynolds's Weekly Newspaper* (from 1850), Harney's *Red Republican* (1850) and *Friend of the People* (1850-1, 1852) and Jones's *Notes to the People* (1851-2) and *People's Paper* (1852-8). As working-class Chartism declined, Chartist literacy blossomed. But the diversity of (largely bourgeois) Chartist and pseudo-Chartist literary efforts represented an ever-increasing variation of views among the diminishing Chartist ranks. Like many a Protestant sect, in adversity Chartism was ever more splintered over largely personal issues, often disguised in terms of 'theological' deviation from variegated 'norms'. If this attitude was partly an inheritance, it was also one inheritance and curse which Chartism passed on to some of those who regarded themselves as its successors.

The variations inevitably weakened the principal body, the NCA. When Cooper assailed the Land Plan O'Connor replied, in some exasperation, that

> Tom is a most comical genius. He has been protestant, dissenter and infidel; puritan and atheist; total, teetotal, abstemious and boozy. He is the very impersonation of trinity in unity. He has been all things to all men, and God only knows what he may be next.

The description fitted many Chartists—including O'Connor; and it was typical that Feargus was soon professing himself the 'faithful and affectionate friend' of one 'whose works would live when he was no more'. The NCA, indeed, suffered considerably from O'Connor's regular changes of attitude. He was generous enough to spend considerable time and money to improve the harsh conditions of imprisoned allies; but he continued to be vindictive to real and imagined opponents. Similarly, he continued to vacillate

over middle-class alliances. When, in May 1849, Hume, backed by
the National Parliamentary and Financial Reform Association of
March, revived the 'Little Charter' movement in London, he was
supported by Clark and condemned by Feargus. Yet by June Clark
and O'Connor were asking Hume to adopt the Charter. Hume ignored
the advice, but his proposal of household suffrage was easily defeated
by 286 votes to 82 in June. On 3 July O'Connor's own motion for
the Charter was rejected by 224 to 15, and thereafter he again col-
laborated with the bourgeois radicals of Hume's and Lord Nugent's
Household Suffrage Association. Such connections with old enemies
disgusted some loyalists; in particular, the protection-minded Kydd,
a popular lecturer on 'The Labour Question', who was owed £60
and was dismayed by the failing organisation, resigned from the
NCA executive in October.

Pulled in different ways by old loyalties and new enthusiasms—
by the Tory-inclined Christian Socialism of Frederick Denison
Maurice, Charles Kingsley and J.M. Ludlow; by the 'paternalism'
of some protectionists, backed by Ferrand and Oastler; by the successful Manchester liberals, with their varieties of suffrage plans and
financial reforms; and by varied types of socialism—the Chartists
were further divided. 'Chartism in 1850 is a different thing from
Chartism in 1840', Howard Morton asserted in the *Red Republican*.
But in continuing that

> The leaders of the English proletarians have proved that they are
> true Democrats, and no shams, by going ahead so rapidly. . . .
> They have progressed from the idea of a simple *political reform*
> to the idea of a *Social Revolution*.

he deceived few people beyond (perhaps) himself. Alarmed NCA
leaders, headed by Clark, Dixon, Harney, Kydd, McGrath, O'Brien,
O'Connor, Reynolds and D.W. Ruffy tried to revive the movement,
and in December 1849 organised a metropolitan conference of
twenty-eight delegates. There was no national representation, but
the London men proceeded to elect a provisional executive (Clark,
Dixon, Doyle, James Grassby, Harney, Kydd and McGrath) and
to argue over O'Connor's bourgeois connections; Harney joined
Feargus's opponents and was subsequently dismissed from the *Star*.
In January 1850 O'Brien founded his new organisation, which
adopted the style of the National Reform League for the Peaceful
Regeneration of Society in March. This socialistic body would combine the Charter with Poor Law reform, price controls, currency

and taxation reform and nationalisation (particularly of the land and mines).

The NRL policy was anathema to O'Connorite Chartists, but the ubiquitous and ambivalent Reynolds and the latter-day Owenite lecturer Lloyd Jones gave their support. At a London rally in January, under O'Connor, the division widened, after a row between Clark and Harney; and a series of provincial rallies confirmed the split, leading to the resignation of the provisional executive. O'Connor's remaining allies had now lost control of the NCA, as O'Brien triumphantly carried his hybrid socialism into Luke Hansard's National Regeneration Society, and Harney, finally breaking with Feargus, started to carry the principles of the Fraternal Democrats and of their associate, Marx, into the country. In March Clark founded the rival National Charter League, favouring an association with the NPFRA and other middle-class bodies; it soon failed, after heated debates in many towns. O'Connor appears to have kept feet in both camps. Certainly, when, on 11 July, he again raised the Charter in the Commons it was (as West commented) 'with a more than usually socialist preamble'. But he was counted out in a thin House. It was the last time on which the Commons even attempted to debate the issue.

The NCA—now run by a new executive (John Arnott, Thomas Brown, William Davies, Grassby, Harney, Thomas Miles, John Milne, Reynolds and Edward Stallwood)—became increasingly involved in social policies. And, despite the latest parliamentary defeat, the various strands of Chartism maintained considerable activity through the spring and summer. O'Connor had rousing receptions at Hanley, Glasgow, Edinburgh, Paisley, Carlisle and Newcastle; O'Brien, Reynolds and Harney propounded 'socialism' in London and elsewhere; the liberated Jones was tumultuously welcomed on a national tour which included visits to London, Newcastle, Bristol, Leeds, Halifax, Leicester, Bingley, Bradford, Sheffield, Aberdeen, Glasgow and Manchester, as a militant opponent of any bourgeois alliance. Everywhere there was delight with the beating given by Barclay and Perkins' brewery draymen to Marshal Haynau, the notorious woman-flogging Austrian who had savagely repressed the 1848 revolution in the Hapsburg Empire.[18]

Summer optimism, however, scarcely disguised the yawning gulfs between the Chartist leaders. An attempt was made to unite the various groups of supporters of the NCA, NRL, Fraternal Democrats, trade unions and the Social Reform League in a single

National Charter and Social Reform Union; it was a failure. A
basic divider was the new socialism. Chartism, maintained Morton,

> is the cause of the producers, and the battle of this one enslaved
> class is the battle we fight, but it must be fought under the *Red*
> flag. . . .The task given us at present is to rally our brother Pro-
> letarians *en masse* round this flag, by means of a Democratic and
> Social Propaganda; an agitation for 'the Charter and something
> more'.

Jones thought that he sensed a new unity developing on socialist
lines:

> wherever I go, I find the embers of discord still lurking among
> the ashes of party strife and local ambition; but, my friends, they
> are fast expiring and everywhere I find a disposition to fraternise
> among the various sections of the Chartist body . . . the people are
> beginning to unite against their common enemy—THE RICH!
> AYE! THE RICH!

His message again was 'Organise! Organise! Organise!'; but he
now envisaged organisation on purely class lines against capitalism
and all its works and opposed any deviation—co-operative, unionist, Christian Socialist, republican or teetotal. But Jones was (as
usual) over-optimistic. His hard-line socialism was to repel many
potential allies. Harney, Thornton Hunt, Holyoake, Augustus Dela-
force of the London Trades, O'Brien and others could never agree
on the NCSRU. And O'Connor, still determined not to abdicate, provoked division by calling a Manchester conference to organise 'a
perfect union'. Local reformers decided that the meeting should be
held on 1 January 1851, but Jones, the executive and a West Riding
conference were hostile. O'Connor nevertheless pressed ahead, securing the support of a Manchester rally on 17 November. The row
flared. O'Connor now turned against his allies of the NPFRA,
presumably in order to show himself as 'progressive' as the new
socialists. When the new executive was elected in December,
O'Connor joined it, but only as the fifth member. The executive
soon demonstrated their new mood:

> We desire to rally all social reformers in one phalanx, and we
> desire to do so not by breaking up, altering or weakening our
> association but by showing them that *we, too, are social reformers,*

like themselves, but that we understand the only way of obtaining social reforms and political power is through Chartist organisation.

And they urged Chartists not to support the O'Connorite meeting at Manchester. Jones was the principal opponent of the Manchester men's alleged 'attempt . . . to uphold the perishing spirit of faction in our ranks, by meetings, cheers, rhetoric and clap-trap'; but he took care not to offend the still-influential Feargus. He bitterly attacked the Manchester men's association with retail co-operation: 'they would have the Charter pure and simple, and in the very next line they tacked the grocery business to it.'[19] At the basic level the division was between 'the Charter pure and simple' and 'the Charter and something more'; but the issue was complicated by many cross-currents.

The Manchester conference of 26 January, consisting of eight delegates, achieved nothing, although both O'Connor and Jones attended to make their case. 'On both sides, petty intrigues, much retailing of scandal, which consoles one for a good deal of unpleasantness in London,' Engels told Marx. 'On Jones's side, a superior declamatory talent. Leach, on the other hand, is extraordinarily imperturbable, but at times horribly absurd. Donovan is a vulgar intriguing local celebrity.' Jones confessed himself 'a red replubican and a supporter of the nationalisation of landed property, while Leach presented himself as in all things the representative of the co-operative societies, even to the extent of their repudiation of all political agitation. These societies seem now to be very numerous in Lancashire, and Jones and his friends are afraid that if they form some sort of an alliance with the Chartists, thay may get the Chartist movement into their hands.' To Engels, 'the O'Connor Conference . . . turned out to be pure humbug.' But the NCL of McGrath, Leach, Dixon, Clark and Doyle continued and sundry other groups grew. According to Gammage, Jones now acted with 'only the prudence of the hypocrite', publicly professing loyalty to Feargus while 'in secret he hated [him] and would have used any means to crush him'—including O'Brien, who refused to help. Much of this argument probably developed from Gammage's personal dislike of Jones.

Even the eight delegates contrived to disagree. Mantle and North (representing Manchester and Bradford), dismayed by the small attendance, proposed an instant dissolution. Clark and Leach proposed the expected resolution for collaboration with other reformers, but O'Connor deserted them and his own recent policies:

> They must rely solely on themselves. The Financial Reformers would use them for their own purposes .... The aim of these men was to juggle for their own benefit. He told them. . .to place no confidence on any other class of the community but the working class.

Clark naturally protested that O'Connor had been a staunch ally of the Financial Reformers and eventually the debate ended in compromise. The gathering called for the Charter pure and simple, but went on to advocate co-operation. And it finally broke over Mantle's motion to attend the forthcoming NCA Convention, which O'Connor, North and Lawson of Lower Warley supported, against Clark, McGrath and Leach. A subsequent NCL-led Manchester meeting rejected the last motion.

While O'Connor toured the cotton towns, the NCA executive and London meetings condemned his reported explanation that Harney had been dismissed for advocating murder. But Feargus now threw in his lot with the larger NCA. The executive initially advocated a moderate programme, mainly devoted to improving partnership law to protect co-operative members. O'Brien and others at the John Street Institute caused a row by denouncing such a meagre production and undoubtedly influenced some delegates to the Convention who started to assemble in the Parthenium Rooms in St Martins Lane on 31 March. Many districts could no longer afford to send delegates and the NCA was weakened by sizeable desertions and by such new organisations as the NCL, the Political and Social Propagandist Society and others. The result was that only thirty of the planned forty-nine delegates appear to have turned up, largely (thought West) from 'the *petite bourgeoisie* of the movement, and generally undistinguished.[20] Scotland had five representatives' Yorkshire and London four each and Lancashire three.

Despite its general lack of experience—or perhaps because of it—the Convention gradually adopted the most extreme of Chartist policies, and the one most pleasing to contemporary and later Marxists. The 'nothing but the Charter' school was defeated; any alliance with the NPFRA was opposed; a new petition was to be organised; Chartist candidates were to contest the next elections, nationally and locally; organisation was to be extended among the unions, various working groups and the Irish. These decisions represented

unjustified hopes rather than new departures. But the Convention
went on to adopt a new social programme: Chartism should

> stand forward as the protector of the oppressed—each suffering
> class should see in it the redresser of its several wrongs—it ought
> to be the connecting link that draws together on one common
> ground the now isolated bodies of the working classes. . . .

The interest in class led to 'socialist' policies. Land, as 'the inalien-
able inheritance of all mankind', should be nationalised (by purchase gradually, as opposed to Harney's expropriating plan). The
Church should be disestablished and its 'temporalties . . . declared
national property' (apart from voluntary gifts). 'Education should
. . . be national, universal, gratuitous and, to a certain extent
[except in "its higher branches"] compulsory.' Labour laws should
free the worker from 'wages slavery' and develop 'the co-operative
principle'; 'until the complete re-adjustment of the labour question',
workers' co-operatives should be given state aid, on a national
basis, for

> The co-operative principle is essential for the well-being of the
> people; the centralisation of wealth ought to be counteracted by
> a distributive tendency; its accumulation in the hands of isolated
> clubs is an evil second only to that of its monopoly by
> individuals. . . .

The Poor Law must be reformed; to work was every man's duty
and right; while the State should maintain the aged and sick, it
should provide for the able-bodied, preferably on the land; and
'where the State cannot find work for the unemployed it is bound to
support them until labour is provided'. 'All taxation ought . . . to be
levied on land and accumulated property.' The National Debt, 'having been contracted for class purposes, cannot be considered as legally
contracted by the people' and should be 'liquidated by the money
now annually paid as interest being forthwith applied as repayment
of the capital'. Some 'change of currency laws was absolutely necessary to the welfare of the producers' and should be explained.
Although 'standing armies were contrary to the principles of Democracy and dangerous to the liberties of the people', the Convention
accepted such forces until 'suitable changes in our colonies and at
home' made them unnecessary; meanwhile, the essentially pacific
delegates made some modest proposals on enlistment terms, pro-
motion, floggings, courts martial and (oddly) on the need for private

billets instead of barracks for soldiers and sailors. 'Every male of sound mind and body over 15 years of age should be afforded the opportunity of military training' in the militia. Finally, 'absolute freedom of thought and expression being one of the primary and most sacred of the rights of man', the 'unjust and iniquitous' restrictions on the press should end.

The claims made for such a re-statement of so many old-style radical aims and dreams are rather surprising; but the policy was, in its way, a notable reassertion of Chartist social policies, weakest on those points which were least understood—finance and the armed services. It was not passed, however, without some opposition; Graham of Dundee, in particular, opposed the State credit fund for co-operative bodies and several delegates disliked the State education scheme. The second week was spent on opposing capital punishment, advocating the return of the 'Welsh martyrs' of 1839 and reviving the NCA. Convention dissolved on 10 April, leaving the executive to re-state policy. The brave new world was not to be. With only around 4,000 divided members, the NCA was scarcely in a position to revive an increasingly moribund movement. O'Connor was now breaking down mentally, worn out by alcoholic (and perhaps sexual) excess, the worries of the Land Plan, the desertion of old allies, the thought of (allegedly) £130,000 spent in the cause and by sheer hard work. The Convention denounced his warnings that foreign visitors to the Great Exhibition were plotting a revolution. And arguments continued, not only between Feargus and his Judases but between the Judases.

Harney's *Red Republican*, started on 22 June 1850, had proved rather too strong for both newsagents and readers. Its sub-heading of 'Liberty, Equality and Fraternity', its publication of the first English version of the *Communist Manifesto* and its unstamped nature alike gave offence, and it ceased publication on 30 November. In its place Harney published *The Friend of the People* (edited initially by Holyoake and Jones), which ran from 14 December to 26 July 1851. He now bitterly assailed O'Connor over the Land Plan investigation:

O'Connor alienated from himself the affections of all honest men, surrounded himself with none but sycpohants and traffickers, and now he begins to meet his well-merited reward.

He next took up the claims of the directors (Clark, Dixon, Doyle and McGrath)—so recently disappointed by O'Connor's rejection of NCL policies—that Feargus's claims about the company and bank were inaccurate, transcribing *Daily News* and *Lloyd's Weekly Newspaper* reports and correspondence. 'We are bound, in justice to ourselves,' said the directors, 'to expose the falsity of the ostentatious bounty of O'Connor.' Harney would not let old enemies off so lightly:[21]

> the more they succeed in blackening [O'Connor's] character, the lower they sink themselves in the slough of infamy. They shared the spoil with him when the money came rolling in, and now they must share with him the execration of their long-confiding, but at last enlightened, dupes and victims.

The new leaders continued to produce papers. Harney revived his *Friend* between 7 February and 24 April 1852. And Jones started his *Notes to the People* on 3 May 1851, following it from 8 May 1852 with *The People's Paper*, which lasted until 1858. Jones's message was clearly socialist, and Marx gave close support. Jones saw 'only three great movements having anything like extended power and cohesion: THE CHARTER, THE TRADES UNIONS and SHORT TIME. These three organisations were noble, salutary and needful'—but the first was the most important. Attempts to establish industrial arbitration machinery were 'a Tory factory lords' Protection dodge', for 'political power could alone give protection—and real protection could alone consist in Social Rights'. Ferrand's Labour League of 1853 was wrong to advocate protection:

> No! no! the fault lies not in Trade's being *free*—but in labour's being *enslaved*—the remedy lies not in Trade's being fettered, but in labour's being freed. . . . The protection of labour is to set it free—so that it will want no artificial protection at all! Free Trade, Free Land, Free Labour—founded on and guarded by the FREE VOTE—these are the securities for our future and the redeemers of our present.

'Welcome brutality', wrote Jones,

> but Heaven preserve us from 'kind masters'. Brutal slavery can enslave the body, but brutal kindness does worse, it enslaves the mind. . . . 'Duty to your employers'. Your duty is to have no employers at all, but to employ yourselves. . . . IT IS YOUR INTEREST TO RUIN THEM AND IT IS THEIR INTEREST TO RUIN YOU.

In order to maintain the class purity of the proletarian 'Social War', middle-class alliances were rejected and the 'aristocratic' aloofness of the craft unions regularly condemned. For years to come Jones campaigned energetically, brilliantly and hopelessly to create a mass, class-conscious socialist Chartism.

Jones headed the poll in the winter election to the NCA executive in 1851. But the polling figures demonstrated the movement's decline: Jones 900, Arnott 720, O'Connor 600, Wheeler 566, Grassby 565, Shaw 502, Linton 470, Beezer 456 and Holyoake 336. Jones was appalled by his colleagues and 'could not consent to sit on an Executive constituted like the present'; Linton resigned because he favoured a bourgeois alliance and Wheeler because he disliked Arnott and was insulted by Holyoake. The remaining members insulted Arnott by giving his secretarial duties to Grassby. The office was given up, and five members meeting at Grassby's house in Lambeth devoted themselves to paying off a debt of £37. At least one of the five could give little help. O'Connor, white-haired and mumbling to himself, was rapidly degenerating mentally. Jones had apparently attacked him in his novel *The History of the Democratic Movement*, serialised in his *Notes*, under the character of de Brassier—and other old allies were deserting him. Feargus had long been eccentric. In 1849 he had addressed the Queen as his 'Well-Beloved Cousin', signing himself 'Feargus, Rex, by the Grace of the People'. Victoria can scarcely have been amused. Now it was the turn of Chartists to be embarrassed. His 'old-fashioned' clothes were forgivable. But in October 1851 his behaviour at London receptions for the Hungarian nationalist Louis Kossuth caused concern. He misbehaved in Parliament and in Chancery during the Land Company hearings. He could no longer write semi-coherent letters for the *Star*. Justin McCarthy saw him in Covent Garden, 'his eyes gleaming with the peculiar, quick, shallow, ever-changing glitter of Madness'. In December a *Star* writer suggested that O'Connor should rest until he 'recovered from the shock' delivered by opponents of the Land Plan. But O'Connor's collapse was complete. His Irish estate at Fort Robert was ruinously mortgaged, and the *Star* was now almost worthless; it was sold to G.W.M. Fleming and Dougal McGowan, the editor and printer, in January 1852 for only £100. In February O'Connor had a fight at the Lyceum and spent seven days in Coldbath Fields gaol for hitting a constable. Friends now thought of committing him, while others tried to relieve his financial worries but raised only £32. Feargus escaped to America in April, furtively avoiding his detractors. In New York he chatted oddly to store-girls, still trying to exercise the old charm which had led him to be the father of several illegitimate children. New York was not amused. By June O'Connor was back in England. On the 8th he hit an MP in the Commons and apologised to the Speaker. Next day he attacked another Member and was promptly arrested. His sister Harriet secured his release on the 16th, for his removal to the Chiswick asylum of Dr Harrington Tuke.[22]

The remaining Chartists rapidly proceeded to fall further apart. Fleming and McGowan had replaced the O'Connorite Rider on the *Star*, which gradually lost its Chartist posture. The *Northern* prefix was dropped. Chartism's greatest journal became the *Star and National Trades' Journal* and from 20 March *The Star of Freedom,* under Harney's control. Now even the 'Left' started to divide, as Harney and Jones launched bitter attacks on each other, over allegations of 'dictatorship'. In the end Jones's cheaper journal helped to end the *Star*, in November; by then Jones was a socialist and Harney a radical. Chartism itself had evaporated. Yet it took a long time to face the fact of its demise. From late 1851 Jones favoured the abolition of the nine-member NCA executive and the creation of a committee of three paid full-time organisers, though other leaders opposed the plan, sensing in it Jones's hope of dominating the movement. But Jones, with a power base of sorts in the revived Metropolitan Delegate Council, was determined to defeat both the angry Harney and the remnant of the NCA executive (which was still divided over collaboration with the Financial Reformers). He therefore backed the call for a convention to reorganise the movement.

Eight delegates, representing six localities, attended Jones's conference in Manchester from 17 to 21 May 1852. They arranged a constitution under which executive power should be held by three men (paid 30s [£1·50] weekly), initially appointed for three months and thereafter elected at six-monthly intervals by paid-up members. R. G. Gammage, James Finlen and Jones (with seeming reluctance) were chosen. The old executive (which, at the end, consisted of Arnott, Beezer, Grassby, Holyoake, Hunt, LeBlond, Linton and Shaw) inevitably fought back, but the little meetings in London and elsewhere generally supported the conference decisions, despite Harney's mockery. And the new men campaigned actively. At their first real election, Gammage received 922 votes, Finlen 839 and Jones 739; William Grocott of Manchester was appointed secretary. 'It was on this election of the Executive that Gammage began to see the real design of Jones', who broke many promises by accepting nomination and whose dictatorial intentions were further suspected. Gammage had a further grouse. *The People's Paper* gobbled up Chartists' money; the Charter Fund received only £27 in its first quarter, of which £13 was paid to Grocott—'and all that Gammage got for his three months' hard work was little more than two weeks' salary'. But the executive members continued to travel widely, trying to raise a further petition from ever-declining audiences.

Jones's campaign to dominate what was left of the movement came to a head from the winter of 1853, when he urged working-class unity in support of the Preston cotton strikers and started to advocate a labour parliament to head an allegedly reviving Chartism. The parliament, with about forty members, met in Manchester on 6 March 1854 and adopted the policy which Jones had rashly and over-optimistically planned for it. A weekly subscription of $1\frac{1}{4}$d from all workers would raise a weekly income of £100,000, to be spent on industrial disputes and massive land and industrial co-operatives. Before the meeting dissolved on the 18th, a 'Mass Movement' had been planned, a detailed programme worked out and an executive (Finlen, Abraham Robinson, James Williams, Joseph Hogg and George Harrison, with Jones as an honorary member) established.[23] It was all pathetically over-optimistic, and the scheme was soon in ruins; by August Robinson pointed out that 'the Mass Movement seemed, so far as the mass of the people were concerned, a failure'. Furthermore, as Gammage commented, it represented a major policy change and a reversal of Jones's previous attitudes. 'Gammage's surprise ... as well as his disappointment was great, when Jones propounded a scheme of co-operation in land and manufactures, in utter opposition to the views laid down by him in the discussions with Lloyd Jones, and on many other occasions.'

Gammage had another difference with the arrogant, inconsistent Jones. A Newcastle meeting which he had addressed passed resolutions suggesting that another editor should join Jones, 'to make the *People's Paper* a paying organ' and suggesting O'Brien. Jones furiously attacked Gammage, O'Brien and John Days of the National Reform League as conspirators against him. He gained revenge by using some sharp practices to eject Gammage from the executive at the March election. Jones, Finlen and Gammage were originally elected (with 759,637 and 435 votes to John Shaw's 361, Williams's 194 and Royall's 28). Mysterious additional votes arrived after the poll, adding 183 to Jones's list, 192 to Finlen's, 66 to Gammage's, 159 to Shaw's (who thus became the third member) and 1 to Williams's.[24] Several districts henceforth refused to recognise the executive, and what remained of Chartism was still further divided. Shaw virtually left the executive, and Jones and Finlen addressed an ever-decreasing audience. Blinded by delusions of leading a proletarian host, Jones founded and joined a plethora of short-lived organisations. In July 1855 he ran another executive election, announcing that he, Finlen and Robinson had succeeded 'by large majorities', though there was only a handful of voters. Jones and Finlen henceforth became dictators. By January 1856 Jones made the situation explicit:

> If you so confide to our hands, you must expect no explanations, and no long-worded programmes from us. If we say 'organise', you must organise—'assemble', you must assemble....A thousand times sooner give me the worst Dictatorship than the blabbing squabbles of contending factions in our ranks.

Such stuff scarcely pleased those Chartists who believed that their cause was concerned with democracy. When Manchester men protested against the denial of authority to Robinson, they were told that Jones and Finlen 'would decline to associate in their plans any one they had not first tried and deeply tested' and that the best plan would be for two leaders 'in office on good behaviour, with no polling lists, no show of strength or weakness'. The final stage of the dictatorship was reached when Finlen retreated to Glasgow and planned to produce a new *Northern Star*, with Gammage.

Jones contested Nottingham in the election of March 1857, as a Chartist with a typically 'radical' programme, but was easily defeated by two Liberals. Now he reversed another policy by again exploring the possibility of a middle-class alliance for manhood suffrage, while retaining a Chartist organisation, as 'one of the safest guarantees for keeping the middle classes honest'. To decide the question he called a conference in St Martin's Hall, London, on 5 February 1858. Frost—recently returned from Australia—refused to preside, and many others rejected Jones's latest switch of plan; indeed arguments continued throughout 1857. But Jones, despite his poverty and lack of support, pressed on, meeting various middle-class reformers and insisting that 'every proposition short of Manhood Suffrage should be opposed'.[25]

Forty-one delegates eventually assembled for the last Convention; they represented (according to the anti-Jones *Reynold's Newspaper*) only about 500 people, as membership had been 'arranged'. The first chairman was the unionist Benjamin Lucraft of Finsbury, the second Thomas Livesey of Rochdale. An alliance with bourgeois reformers was accepted, despite the dying Owen's advice 'in favour of the whole of the Charter'. A one-man executive (Jones) was appointed. Samuel Morley's Parliamentary Reform Association was greeted. And—through a committee decision—a Political Reform League was established, under the presidency of Joseph Sturge, to forward the new policy. The result was further failure. Despite Jones's appeals, the PRL would go no further than manhood suffrage, the ballot, abolition of property qualifications, triennial parliaments and adjusted boundaries. Furthermore, it took over the *People's Paper* in May; the *Paper* closed in September, followed in November by Jones's *London News*. And men like Wheeler, William Slocombe, J. B. Leno, William Taylor and Finlen, discontented with the new NCA policy, founded the National Political Union for the Obtainment of the People's Charter, publishing a monthly paper, *The National Union*, from May to December. The NPU embarrassed the NCA and its new allies by regularly proposing Chartist motions at other organisations' meetings. And the PRL was regularly divided, particulary over the continued existence of the NCA; it collapsed in December, being succeeded by Jones's London Manhood Suffrage Demonstration Committee, for which his new *Cabinet Newspaper* of November became a mouthpiece. Throughout this period Jones was constantly attacked by *Reynolds's Newspaper*, which specialised in scandal and alleged financial dishonesty on Jones's part. When, at the Nottingham election of April 1859 Jones's vote fell from 614 to 151, he blamed Reynolds and successfully sued him for libel. This was, however, the only cheering news. The *Cabinet* failed in February 1860 and Jones's plans for further journals collapsed.[26]

Chartism, at last, was dead.

9 Epilogue

The old comradeship of the great days of Chartism had evaporated long before the movement withered away in 1860. Throughout its history it was constantly weakened by bitter personal disputes among its leaders. The leadership's quarrels compounded the weakness caused by the variety of policy divisions. Chartism, as Carlyle diagnosed it in 1839, 'meant the bitter discontent grown fierce and mad, the wrong condition, therefore, of the Working Classes of England. It was a new name for a thing which had many names, which would yet have many.' But the discontent varied and the suggested remedies were confusingly numerous. All the sacrifices and labour were in vain—at least, in the short term. Chartism appeared to disappear almost without trace. The halls, churches, co-operatives, farms, journals and schools passed almost from memory. Yet there was much truth in Harney's prophecy of 1852 that 'Chartism itself will survive the wreck of parties and the ruin of politicians. Apparently it has fallen into contempt, and is nearly consigned to oblivion; but in truth its spirit has begun to exercise an influence over the country's politics; and all parties have come to acknowledge the potency of that democratic opinion. . . .'[1]

I

The lives of prominent Chartists and their allies varied widely. Poor, demented Feargus resided in Tuke's asylum, convinced that he was a State prisoner, until, epileptic and incurable, he was taken to his sister's house in Notting Hill in August 1854, where he died a year later.[2] His old associate Oastler lived to see the success of factory reform, to work as a protectionist speaker to working-class meetings and to edit a Tory-Christian journal, *The Home*, in 1851–5.

He died, while returning to visit old Yorkshire friends, in August
1861.[3] Stephens continued to preach in his chapels around Ashton,
was a militant speaker during the cotton famine and died in February 1879.[4] Jones became a prosperous Manchester barrister, a
leader of Lancashire radicalism, a vice-president of the Reform
League of 1865 and such a supporter of Gladstone and Bright that
he had wide Liberal support at the 1868 Manchester election. He
died of pleurisy in January 1869.[5] Lovett became owner of the
National Hall in Holborn and continued to propound those 'moral
force' and educational policies which he had once sought to force
on Chartism. He published his autobiography in 1876, still convinced of the virtues of self-help: 'the industrious classes . . . would do
well . . . to resolve to do their work themselves.' He died in the
following year.[6] Vincent, the western 'Demosthenes', greatly changed by his prison experience, became a temperance advocate and a
liberal Christian lecturer with considerable fame in Britain and
America. He married John Cleave's daughter and, asserted Holyoake, 'never returned again to the dark valley of unseeing faith, but
dwelt on the hills of orthodoxy, where some light of reason falls'.
He died in 1878.[7] Cooper lived until 1892, becoming a considerable
author; 'poems, novels, essays, sermons are departments of literature in which he has been distinguished,' noted Holyoake. 'As he
had changed from piety to rationalism,' observed Adams,

> so he changed from rationalism to piety again. And the rest of his
> long and active life was spent in preaching the Gospel to all the
> earth that he could reach.

The irritable but intensely generous preacher kept up a constant
flow of publications, including his distinguished autobiography,
and shortly before his death at the age of eighty-eight was awarded
a State grant of £200, at the instance of a former convert, A. J.
Mundella.[8]

Attwood, the Anglican and first parliamentary champion of
Chartism, retired from the House which he had so often bored in
1839 and died in 1856.[9] 'Honest John' Fielden was defeated at Oldham in the 1847 election, just after carrying the Ten Hours Bill,
and died in May 1849. His campaign for factory reform was continued by his sons and son-in-law (Cobbett's son, John) from Tory
positions.[10] Several Chartists subsequently became businessmen,
though rarely on the scale of Attwood and Fielden. One consequence of the 'Mass Movement' scheme of 1854 was the formation

of the United Brothers' Industrial, Sick Benefit and Life Assurance Company. It followed a variety of similar ventures. In 1831 John Shaw, a London undertaker, had founded the Friend-in-Need Benefit and Burial Society, which was revived in 1853, with Wheeler (who died in 1862) as a director. Wheeler was also London manager of the British Industrial Association of 1852. His friend Clark (who, like Shaw, died in 1857) founded the National Assurance Friendly Society, which Shaw's concern took over. McGrath apparently worked in insurance in London, Doyle in Birmingham and Dixon at Wigan.[11]

In America some Chartists prospered enormously. Allan Pinkerton, who died in 1884 at the age of sixty-five, was a powerloom dresser who helped to form the militant Glasgow Democratic Association of 1839 to 'carry the People's Charter, peaceably if we may, forcibly if we must'. As a prominent 'physical force' advocate, he thought it essential to emigrate in 1842 and moved to Illinois, later settling in Chicago. The son of a policeman, he later founded the famous detective agency, so often used against American trade unionists. William Carnegie, a moderate, anti-Corn Law handloom weaver at Dunfermline, sold his four looms in 1848 and moved to Pittsburgh, where he died, aged seventy-one, in 1872. He took with him his radical son Andrew, a bobbin boy who was to become a multi-millionaire steelmaster—and employer of Pinkerton's men during the famous Homestead strike of 1892.[12]

Few of those who emigrated to America shared such prosperity. Several who fled to the democratic New World with high hopes of republican egalitarianism were soon disillusioned by experience of the reality. The Paineite Thomas Brothers who stayed in the USA from 1824 to 1838 returned 'most reluctantly obliged to acknowledge the fallacy of self-government'; his *The United States of North America as They Really Are* (1840) was intended as 'a cure for radicalism'. The radical Dr John Smyles (a cousin of Samuel Smiles) confessed that 'the greatest evil into which the American people had fallen, was that of having allowed wealth an undue influence'. He regretted that

> This country, or rather a residence in this country of some years, often changes the political opinions of old country radicals. One sees so little of real practical republicanism that some are apt to become disgusted, and because of a little disappointment, almost become tory. . . .

His friend Lawrence Pitkeithley of Huddersfield visited the States in the summer of 1842, 'to ascertain how far the much-reduced and unwillingly idle artisans of this country could improve their condition by removing there'; but he soon returned home. The fact was that as Smyles had written, 'a people may be given all the rights of freemen, and yet not maintain themselves such'.[13] The lesson was to be learned by several Chartists.

Peter Bussey of Bradford started hopefully in New York as proprietor of a boarding house in 1840, becoming a New Jersey farmer in 1842, a New York boarding-house owner in 1843, and around 1848, a street-hawker. The militant tavern-keeper changed his views as his luck changed. 'This government is not what it is cracked up to be,' he told the equally disillusioned William Brown, a Leeds cloth finisher who lived in America from 1841 to 1845:

> and I believe if I were to go back to England with my present experience, I should then become as great an advocate for Tory measures as ever I was for those of the Chartists.

Bussey did return, to become a publican in Horsforth from 1854; he died in September 1869.[14] John Alexander, an O'Brienite communitarian, was more quickly disillusioned; a few months' experience convinced him that America was 'in a hopeless condition as regards either moral, political or intellectual progression', in 1848–9. Several other Chartists shared this view of the promised land at least sufficiently to return to Britain. William S. Brown of Glasgow, who was about to commence a Glasgow *Weekly Democratic Circular*, was imprisoned in April 1848 for publishing a poster on 'Threatened Revolution in London'. Two years later he emigrated to Boston and found that universal suffrage was 'not producing many of the fruits predicted of it.' William Ashton of Barnsley emigrated to America in 1842, apparently with official assistance, but seems to have followed Bussey back to Yorkshire.[15]

Some Chartist sympathisers settled happily in America. The mild Methodist secessionist minister and journalist Joseph Barker of Wortley, editor of *The Christian* (1844–8) and *The People* (1848–51)—who had for long advocated emigration—lived with his brother on an Omaha farm in 1851–60 and returned to America in 1865; he died in Nebraska in 1875.[16] Others became prominent in American labour movements. The Yorkshire miner John Bates founded a pioneer miners' union in Schuylkill County, Pennsylvania. John Siney of Wigan became an official of the Workingmen's

Benevolent Association and the first president of the Miners' National Association in 1873; he died in 1880. The Staffordshire miner Thomas Lloyd was president of the earlier American Miners' Association founded in Illinois in 1861; he died in 1896. His secretary was his Staffordshire friend Daniel Weaver, who died in 1899. The AMA's organ, the *Weekly Miner*, was edited by the Bradford tailor and lawyer John Hinchcliffe, a notable 'eight hours' campaigner whose weaver brother Robert supported the Lancashire weaver Robert Bower in organising workers at Lawrence, Massachusetts. Richard Trevellick, a Southampton carpenter, was a currency reformer, eight hours agitator and a leader of the National Labour Union, of which he was president in 1869; he died in 1895. John Campbell, the Mancunian Irish leader of the NCA, regularly attacked Republican abolitionists and founded the Social Reform Society in 1844 at Philadelphia, where he died in 1874, as a bookseller and legal publisher. The Glasgow weaver John Cluer was a leader of the National Reform Movement and of the New York 'ten hours' agitation. The Sheffield shoemaker Thomas Phillips was a pioneer of retail co-operation at Philadelphia in the 1860s and president of the Boot and Shoe Workers' Union in 1889; and the Stockport shoemaker James Dillon became a leader of the mechanics of Lynn, Massachusetts, in the 1850s. Richard Hinton, a Lancashire weaver who emigrated to Boston in 1848, became a civil war colonel, a prominent abolitionist and a socialist; and Matthew Trumbull, a London labourer who moved in 1846, became a brigadier-general and radical lawyer, dying in 1894. John Samuel, a Swansea glassblower, founded a glass workers' union at Philadelphia in 1857 and later became a co-operative leader. Andrew Cameron, son of a Berwick printer, published the *Workingman's Advocate* from 1864 to 1880 and was prominent in Typographical Union affairs before his death in Chicago in 1890. And the tradition continued; Thomas Morgan, the son of a Birmingham Chartist nailmaker, was the first president of the Brassworkers' Union in 1874, and Samuel Fielden, son of a Todmorden Chartist, was an organiser of the teamsters and was imprisoned after the anarchist affray in the Chicago Haymarket in 1886.[17]

Thomas Ainge Devyr, the Irishman who worked on the *Northern Liberator* staff in 1838–9 and was associated with some violent plotters in the Newcastle district, fled to New York in 1840. He edited a Williamsburg journal and the Fenian *Irish People*. 'He was', wrote W.E. Adams, a Nationalist in Ireland, a Chartist in England, a kind of revolutionist even in America. Anyway, he had only scorn and contempt for the politicians of America. 'Democrats?' he said to me: 'they call themselves Democrats, but they are all thieves'.

Arriving with a capital of 1s 3d (7p) and the Newcastle druggist John Rewcastle, Devyr became a Democratic politician, a leader of the tenant farmers' agitation and a founder of the National Reform Party. He published his curious memoirs in 1882 and died five years later in Brooklyn.[18]

John Francis Bray, whose writings influenced some socialistic Chartists, was born in Washington but moved to Leeds at the age of thirteen in 1822. He made his plea for the right of the labourer to retain the whole produce of his labour in his *Labour's Wrongs and Labour's Remedy, or the Age of Might and the Age of Right* in 1839; hitherto, 'the workmen had given the capitalist the labour of a whole year, in exchange for the value of only half a year'. Disappointed by the reception of his work, Bray returned to America in 1842, becoming a socialist printer, anti-abolitionist, philosopher and farmer. This pioneer of American socialism died in Detroit in 1897.[19] But Chartist socialists, as Jones and others discovered, were numerically weak. Real Chartist revolutionaries were even more sparse.

The leaders of the Newport rising for long remained in Van Diemen's Land; indeed, Zephaniah Williams and William Jones lived there until their deaths in 1874. The energetic Williams spent two years in chains at Port Arthur, became a constable in New Norfolk, a servant at Launceston, a miner and eventually a coal owner; he received a free pardon in 1857. Jones apparently acted as a government informer. The London 'revolutionary' William Cuffey, transported in 1848 at the age of sixty one, worked as a tailor until his death in 1870, when he was remembered as an advocate of improved labour legislation. Frost returned to Britain in 1856, ignored contemporary Chartists and died in 1877, a 93-year-old Spiritualist. Other Chartists voluntarily moved to Australia. Young W.E. Adams's hero at Cheltenham, the Paineite blacksmith J. P. Glenister (a delegate in 1848) emigrated with apparent success. Beezer (briefly an NCA executive member) followed him in 1852. McDouall was apparently drowned off Australia in 1853, and George Binns died of consumption in New Zealand.[20]

Some Chartists remained active in public life. George Edmonds became town clerk of Birmingham. James Williams, a Sunderland printer and bookseller, served on the local town council, becoming an alderman. The tea merchant James Moir became a Glasgow councillor, police commissioner, bailie, and (with Robert Cranston) a promoter of the Scottish National Reform League of 1866; he died in 1880. Robert Cochran was a councillor at Paisley and provost in 1885. Cranston became an Edinburgh councillor and bailie; James McPherson was elected to Aberdeen council. James Sweet, a Chartist bookseller, served on Nottingham council and there were Chartist groups on other councils, notably at Leeds and Sheffield. Many Chartists continued to support suffrage extension through a plethora of organisations in the fifties and sixties, and periodically assembled for 'reunions'. Perhaps the last such assembly was Ben Wilson's meeting at Halifax in 1885 to thank Gladstone for the third Reform Act. But even reunions could occasionally revive controversy: not all Dundee veterans favoured the choice of a temperance hotel for their meeting in December 1873.[21]

Harney, a latter-day leader, 'at last abandoned the now hopeless business'. He claimed that thousands of Chartists voluntarily emigrated to America; among them was his acolyte Charles Keen (who left in 1849). Unlike some former colleagues, Harney felt strongly on the slavery issue; in 1862 he resigned his seven-year editorship of the *Jersey Independent* rather than support the Confederates. He moved to Boston, Massachusetts, in 1863, became increasingly disenchanted with American democracy and returned to Britain in 1888. Until his death in 1897 he wrote regularly for the *Newcastle Weekly Chronicle,* slanging Gladstone as 'The Grand Old Mountebank'.[22] 'Penury was the lot ... of one of the best known of the Chartist officials,' wrote Adams, who saw John Arnott begging in the Strand in about 1865. Ben Wilson of Halifax (who died in 1887) recalled that other Chartists were also very poor: 'there was not a worse paid lot of men in the country.' While lecturing in West Yorkshire, Harney 'sent for a Mr Burns, a tailor, to mend his trousers whilst he remained in bed', Kydd sat 'in a shoemaker's shop ... whilst his shoes were repaired' and during a visit by Jones 'we had to buy him a new shirt and front before he could appear at the meeting'. But both Kydd and Jones were to become lawyers, and Kydd, after speaking for Ferrand's new protectionist movement in the early fifties, was the first historian of factory reform.[23]

Several Chartists devoted themselves to literature and journalism. W. J. Linton became a distinguished poet and wood engraver; he died in 1898. George Reynolds, who died in 1879, was the highly successful proprietor of the popular and sensational *Reynold's Weekly Newspaper*. G.J. Holyoake became author of radical and secularist works—and a raconteur of (not always accurate) reminiscences—until his death in 1906. R. K. Douglas edited the *Birmingham Journal*. William Hill became editor of the *North British Weekly Express* at Edinburgh from 1847. R. K. Philp moved from Bath to become a London publisher. James Leach—to Engels 'an upright, trustworthy and capable fellow'—remained a printer at Manchester and Joshua Hobson at Huddersfield; R.J. Richardson became a Manchester bookseller. Quaker Sturge died in 1859, after a career of business success and pioneering philanthropy.[24]

Dr A. S. Wade, the radical Warwick priest, died in 1845. Of other 'clerical' Chartists, Patrick Brewster lived until 1859 and Arthur O'Neill ministered for many years in a Birmingham Baptist chapel. Matthew Fletcher practised as a Bury surgeon until his death in 1878. R. G. Gammage became a medical practitioner in Newcastle and Sunderland and in 1854 published the first Chartist history; he died in 1888. Lawrence Pitkeithley became a merchant in Manchester, where he died in 1858. His old Huddersfield associates in Oastlerite and Chartist agitations followed varied careers. John Leech, who died in 1871, was a general dealer who became a Conservative. John Hanson also 'embraced all shades of politics, from communism up to conservatism'; the former Owenite atheist died in 1878, as a convinced Tory, Anglican and Imperialist. Joshua Hobson, the self-taught weaver, printer, editor and councillor, followed a similar path, with a 'somewhat chequered political career, beginning with chartism and ending with conservatism'. He edited local Conservative journals and patronised Conservative Working Men's Associations until his death in 1876. Many West Riding associates in the factory agitation had followed the Huddersfield men into Chartist involvement. At Halifax there were the weaver Benjamin Rushton and carpenter Robert Wilkinson; at Dewsbury the operative Mark Crabtree; at Keighley the grocer and spiritualist David Weatherhead (who died in 1875), his fellow Urquartite Francis Butterfield, the workman-poet Abraham Wildman, who died in poverty in 1870, and the itinerant dealer Joseph Firth, who died in 1872.[25]

On the other side of the political spectrum, Robert Owen, who had advised Chartists both to stand by their demands and 'as a matter of expediency to accept what the middle classes offered. . . .', had become increasingly eccentric. By the 1850s he was consulting a spiritualist medium—who apparently agreed with his messages to the world. Owen died in 1858. Meanwhile, others had followed the tragic ends of Beaumont and O'Connor. John Collins of Birmingham, 'sank into physical weakness and imbecility, and died [Gammage believed] in 1850'. James Shirron, the enthusiastic young Aberdeen leader died in 1848, 'a victim to his own honesty and to the fickleness of the multitude'. Salt and Attwood both 'died from failure of mental power'.[26]

The brave old campaigners against the 'taxes on knowledge' gradually passed away. Cholera killed Henry Hetherington in 1849. The Owenite publisher 'made no parade, no defiance, but was immovable. He did for the unstamped press what Carlile did for Free thought works.' His colleagues, the 'rotund, energetic, Radical publisher' John Cleave and the 'straightforward and defiant' James Watson (aided in old age by Holyoake) died in 1847 and 1874. Edward Truelove, an Owenite London bookseller, survived to be imprisoned in 1878 for publishing Dale Owen's birth-control tract *Moral Physiology*: he died in 1899.

'For George White,' recalled Holyoake, 'I had as much regard as for any Irish leader among the Chartists. He was so frank, generous and brave.' Gammage wrote similarly:

> He was noted for his inflexible perseverance and determination in everything which he undertook to perform. He was ever ready for whatever kind of work fell to his lot. . . . In battering the head of a policeman he was quite at home, and if circumstances had favoured he would just as readily have headed an insurrection. . . . George's chief talent as a speaker lay in his ready wit and poignant sarcasms, which were launched forth in language anything but classical. . . .

This 'personification of energy, physical and mental' organised the defence of socialist meetings, 'like other Chartists, took money from the Tories, the better to enable him to destroy the Whigs' and died in Sheffield infirmary perhaps (as Holyoake thought) 'dreaming of pies to come' from Mrs Holyoake. Holyoake considered Stephens 'the greatest orator on the Chartist side', for 'on the platform he was a master of assemblies' and 'in conversation he excelled all men [Holyoake] had known'. But 'the most volcanic voice in the Chartist movement was that of G. J. Mantle. . . . His sentences seemed shot from a culverin. His throat opened like the mouth of a tunnel'.

To Holyoake, Bronterre O'Brien 'excelled all the Chartist leaders in passion of speech and invective' and was 'the only Chartist who comprehended fully how large a share, social, financial and commercial error contributed to the suffering of the people'. The splenetic and changeable journalist-philosopher died in 1864.[27]

Thousands of humbler Chartists died unnoticed. A few, like Ben Wilson of Halifax, left memoirs demonstrating why they had joined the movement:

> It may be said now that we were fools, but you have no idea what we had to endure. . . . From 18 to 24 years old I should not average nine shillings a week wages, and things were very dear. I have been a weaver, a comber, a navvy on the railway, a bearer in the delph, and claim to know something of the condition of the working classes, and well remember talking with an old friend lately, who was making bullets in the cellar in 1848, hungry and sad, for he had a wife and five children depending on him, and had no work, and little chance of getting any.

Some certainly lived bleak lives. William Armitage of Honley was a poor weaver who was dismissed for radical activities in the Huddersfield district; in 1888 W. R. Croft dedicated his *History of the Factory Movement* to the 75-year-old veteran. Mark Crabtree, the Dewsbury doorkeeper at the 1839 Convention, became Fielden's Yorkshire agent in the factory campaign. John Avison became the 'Fieldenite' organiser in Lancashire and later a popular schoolteacher at Saddleworth and Stalybridge.[28] But gradually the majority of the Chartist host disappeared from public view.

II

In the short term, inevitably, the first working-class party failed. But over the years its political aims (with the exception of annual parliaments) have gradually been implemented. And, in any case, much depends upon the criterion by which success or failure is measured. As Julius West wrote:

> The Chartist movement with its derivations, its appeals to 'blistered hands and fustian jackets', its actual tenets of class antagonism, its association with industrial unrest, and its inability to accept the advances of middle-class sympathisers, was the first organised effort to stir up class consciousness on a national scale.

The movement's failures lay in the direction of securing legislation, or national approbation for its leaders. Judged by its crop of statutes and statues, Chartism was a failure. Judged by its essential and generally overlooked purpose, Chartism was a success. It achieved not the Six Points, but a state of mind.

Lovett had accepted this broader aim from the start. In previous radical movements, he wrote,[29]

> A lord, an MP, or an esquire was a leading requisite to secure a full attendance and attention. . . . They were always looking up to leadership of one description or another. . . . In fact, the masses, in their political organisations, were taught to look up to 'great men'. . . . We wished, therefore, to establish a political school of self-instruction among them, in which they would accustom themselves to examine great social and political principles, and by their publicity and free discussion help to form a sound and healthful public opinion throughout the country.

O'Connor, with his assertion 'to the fustian jackets, blistered hands and unshorn chins, 'I am your father, and you are my children', was of course the great menace to Lovett's vision. Nevertheless, in its efforts to enhance the dignity and self-respect of working people by means of self-help, Chartism had considerable success. The succession of Chartist journals, the Chartist churches, temperance societies and co-operatives provide remarkable evidence of the vitality of the movement.

If the 'six points' proved unattainable in the 1840s—and though personal hatreds among the leadership regularly made the position worse—Chartism was not without influence. Successive governments might fear the movement but were also led to ameliorate conditions as part of their response, as they gradually realised that foul living standards lay at the root of much agitation. 'Carlisle is a bad place, and always has been,' Ashley noted in 1839. 'Handloom weavers here, as elsewhere, are the stock-in-trade for agitators to work with.' Much of Chartism was, indeed, 'bitter discontent grown fierce and mad'. The consequence was that when the causes of discontent were removed, Chartism languished. 'Chartism is dead in these parts,' Ashley told Russell from Manchester in 1851. 'The Ten Hours Act and cheap provisions have slain it outright.' O'Connor had the same experience at Nottingham: 'when trade was bad,' he complained in 1850, 'the operatives cried out to be led: but when trade improved . . . they became indifferent to politics at the very time when they were best able to maintain agitation.' As Jones commented in 1847, '*Contentment* is the best *Police*'.[30]

Chartism undoubtedly 'trained' many working people for further participation in public life. Members entered the Liberal and Conservative parties and various radical agitations. They continued and extended working-class involvement in international affairs. And they left traditions which were to influence later British socialism. A few even survived to participate in the founding of Henry Hyndman's Democratic Federation of 1881, and Chartist memories were revived by Yorkshire pioneers of the Independent Labour Party of 1893.[31] But many recent studies underline the regional and local differences in the movement. Chartism failed in Cornwall—where the miners 'laboured . . . sorrowed . . . suffered; but . . . patiently endured',—because of Methodist and temperance hostility. 'I don't think there can be much love of liberty here,' the missionary Duncan reported: 'it's too full of Methodist chapels.'[32] In the North, however, Methodism could co-exist with Chartism, and class-consciousness (however loosely defined) overturned lingering elements of social deference. In religious South Wales, despite the impression created by the risings of 1839, such men as the miner William Miles and the weaver David Ellis of Methyr created a 're-spectable', predominantly nonconformist movement.[33] Chartism was always multi-contoured, its policies were always shaped by local experiences, traditions and personalities.

Groping for a class-based philosophy which would unite a movement embracing such diverse groups as Oastlerite Yorkshire operatives, half-starved handloom weavers, Primitive Methodist Durham miners, rationalist London craftsmen, Presbyterian Glasgow tradesmen, radicals from the declining West-Country woollen towns, the shopkeepers of Bristol and the cobblers of Aberdeen inevitably proved a difficult task. Chartists' theoretical and philosophical deficiencies have disturbed many historians. Engels was too optimistic in seeing 'Chartism [as] the compact form of [proletarian] opposition to the bourgeoisie . . . in Chartism it is the whole working-class which arises against the bourgeoisie. . .'; and he was simply inaccurate in thinking that the Charter was published in 1835. Indeed, the founding fathers of modern socialism, Marx and Engels, are doubtful authorities on the movement because of their own preconceptions and sparsity of contact with working people. Chartism was a typically British movement, largely unconcerned with the dialectics of continental philosophers.

The nature of Chartism, its real strength and ethic, is not to be found in word-chopping exercises. It is to be found rather in the courage of ordinary, grass-root supporters. 'They have cast you among thieves, they themselves being wholesome robbers,' Pitkeithley told James Duffy in his unpleasant cell at Northallerton, in 1840,[35]

> and I assure you the time is not far distant when the ruffians shall expiate their crimes, when tyranny shall be swept from the land and when their victims shall become the legislators of the country. They are preparing for havoc and have gone so far as to leave it impossible to retract, and blood will flow in greater floods than it did in the worst days of Robespeare in France. . . .

It is to be found in the assertion of the Finsbury Chartists in 1839 that

> the possession of the franchise is the only difference between a freeman and a Russian serf, who is sold with the land and the cattle, as part of the farm stock—or the slave of South Carolina, where it is punishable to teach a slave to read: it is the only security against bad laws and for good government, and while the exclusive few have a profitable interest in bad laws, there will be no barrier to tyranny and corruption but the fear of resistance on the part of the enslaved many.

It lies behind North-Eastern protests at the arrest of Harney in 1839:

> MEN OF DURHAM AND NORTHUMBERLAND. Your oppressors have set the majesty of the people at utter defiance. They have determined that you shall live a life of toil and die a death of hunger when you can toil no more. If you do not submit to this they will consign you to a bloody grave by the grand old argument 'the bayonet, the bullet, the halter'.

And it rests within a vast and largely unexplored working-class literature, of which Thomas Wilson's song of 1842 may be taken as representative:[36]

> The purse-proud have joined in the effort to quell
>   The determined and resolute shout,
> Which the universe echoes as tyranny's knell—
>   'Tis the voice of the banded and stout;
> For the people will rise with the might of the just,
>   And pride and oppression shall sink to the dust.

Notes

1 *The Antecedents*

1. W. F. Monypenny, *The life of Benjamin Disraeli, Earl of Beaconsfield*, II (1912), 87-8.

2. See Sir C. H. Firth (ed.), *Clarke Papers*, I (Camden Soc., 1891), 315; S. R. Gardiner, *The Constitutional Documents of the Puritan Revolution, 1625-1660* (1900 edn), 316-26; J. R. Tanner, *English Consitutional Conflicts of the Seventeenth Century, 1603-1689* (Cambridge, 1948 edn), 146-9; Christopher Hill, *Puritanism and Revolution* (1965).

3. E. and A. G. Porritt, *The Unreformed House of Commons*, I (Cambridge, 1903), 166; Sir C. G. Robertson, *Select Cases, Statutes and Documents . . . 1660-1832* (1949 edn), 138-9, 200-3; Sir Lewis Namier, *The Structure of Politics at the Accession of George III* (1957 edn), A. S. Turberville, *The House of Lords in the Eighteenth Century* (Oxford, 1927), J. H. Philbin, *Parliamentary Representation, 1832. England and Wales* (New Haven, Conn., 1965), *passim*.

4. See Robertson, 440-55, 473-9; Sir D. L. Keir, *The Constitutional History of Modern Britain* (1948 impr.), 310-11, 341-3; G. S. Veitch, *The Genesis of Parliamentary Reform* (1948 impr.), 25-34; George Rudé, *Wilkes and Liberty* (Oxford, 1962), *passim. Cf.* Caroline Robbins, *The Eighteenth-Century Commonwealthman* (Cambridge, Mass., 1959), J. P. Carswell, *The Old Cause* (1954), C. Hibbert, *King Mob* (1958), I. R. Christie, *Wilkes, Wyvill and Reform* (1962), C. Chevenix Trench, *Portrait of a Patriot* (1962).

5. Veitch, 27-51; Alexander Stephens, *Memoirs of John Horne Tooke* (2 vols, 1813); F. D. Cartwright, *The Life and Correspondence of John Cartwright* (2 vols, 1826).

6. Sir D. L. Keir, 'Economical Reform, 1779-1787', *Law Quarterly Rev.*, i (1934); I. R. Christie, 'Economical Reform and the "Influence of the

NOTES

Crown", 1780', *Cambridge Hist. J.*, xii (1956); A. G. Olsen, *The Radical Duke* (1961), *passim*.

7. See Herbert Butterfield, 'The Yorkshire Association and the Crisis of 1779–1780', *Trans. R. Hist. Soc.*, 4s., xxix (1947); I. R. Christie, 'The Yorkshire Association: a Study in Political Organisation', *Hist. J.*, iii (1960), 'Sir George Saville, Edmund Burke and the Yorkshire Reform Programme, February 1780', *Yorks. Arch. J.*, xl (1961); N. C. Phillips, 'Burke and the County Movement', *English Hist. Rev.*, lxxvi (1961), 'County against Court. Christopher Wyvill, a Yorkshire Champion', *Yorks. Arch. J.*, xl (1960); E. C. Black, *The Association, 1769–1793*; (Cambridge, Mass., 1963).

8. Veitch, 71–5; J. Disney, *The Works of John Jebb* (3 vols, 1787).

9. I. R. Christie, *The End of North's Ministry, 1780–1782* (1958); John Norris, *Shelburne, and Reform* (1963); Peter Brown, *The Chathamites* (1967).

10. Veitch, 78–97; P. A. Brown, *The French Revolution in English History* (1918), 15–23; J. P. W. Ehrman, *The Younger Pitt: The Years of Acclaim* (1969); John Cannon, *The Fox-North Coalition: Crisis of the Constitution, 1782–1784* (Cambridge, 1969).

11. C. Wyvill, *Political Papers*, IV (6 vols, York, 1794–1802), 14–15, 60; J. Holland Rose, *William Pitt and National Revival* (1911), 197–8; Brown, 23.

12. Veitch, 103–6.

13. Price's discourse is partly reprinted in Alfred Cobban (ed.), *The Debate on the French Revolution, 1789–1800* (1950) and S. MacCoby, *The English Radical Tradition, 1763–1914* (1966 edn).

14. *Cf.* Cobban, *passim*; S. MacCoby, *English Radicalism, 1786–1832* (1955), ch. 2; G. Woodcock, *William Goodwin* (1946.)

15. Veitch, ch. 6; F. O'Gorman, *The Whig Party and the French Revolution* (1967).

16. Veitch, ch. 8; C. Grey, *Life and Opinions of Charles, 2nd Earl Grey* (1861), 11; Peter Mackenzie, *Memoir of Thomas Hardy* (1832); Brown, 51–7; Mary Thale (ed.), *The Autobiography of Francis Place, 1771–1854* (Cambridge, 1971), *passim*.

17. Brown, 66–9; Veitch, 243–52; Lord Cockburn, *Life of Francis, Lord Jeffrey* (2 vols, Edinburgh, 1852).

18. Veitch, ch. 11; Brown, ch. 4.

19. See H. G. Graham, *The Social Life of Scotland in the Eighteenth Century* (1969 edn); T. C. Smout, *A History of the Scottish People, 1560–1830*

(1969), *passim*; Peter Mackenzie, *Life of Thomas Muir* (Glasgow, 1831); T. B. and T. J. Howells, *A Complete Collection of State Trials*, xxiii (1817), 124, *seq.*; Veitch, 255–8; Brown, 95–9; Frank Clune, *The Scottish Martyrs* (Sydney, 1969), chs 1–2; W. Ferguson, *Scotland, 1689 to the Present* (Edinburgh, 1968), ch. 8.

20. *Narrative of the Sufferings of T. F. Palmer and W. Skirving* (Cambridge, 1797); William Norrie, *Dundee Celebrities of the Nineteenth Century* (Dundee, 1873), 9–14; Veitch, 259–61; Howells, XXIII, 238, *seq.*; H. W. Meikle, *Scotland and the French Revolution* (1912).

21. *Memoirs and Trials of the Political Martyrs of Scotland* (1837); Veitch, ch. 12; Brown, ch. 5; Howells, XXIII, 391–471, 486–8, 542–6, 553–5, 619–22, 649–53, 683, 715–16, 720–2, 803 *seq.*; MacCoby, *Radicalism*, 71–6; M. Roe, 'A Radical in Two Hemispheres', *Bull. Inst. Hist. Res.*, xxxi (1958)—on Margarot.

22. Veitch, ch. 13; Brown, ch. 6; Howells, XXIV, 205, *seq.*, XXV, 10, *seq.*; *Life of John Thelwall*, I (1837), 235–6; MacCoby, *Radicalism*, 76–87; E. Fearn, 'Henry Redhead Yorke—Radical Traitor', *Yorks. Arch. J.*, xlii (1970).

23. Veitch, ch. 14; Brown, ch. 8; MacCoby, *Radicalism*, chs 5–7; B. Dobree and G. E. Manwaring, *The Floating Republic* (1937); T. Pakenham, *The Year of Liberty* (1969).

24. See N. C. Miller, 'John Cartwright and Radical Parliamentary Reform, 1808–1819', *English Hist. Rev.*, lxxxiii (1968).

25. Graham Wallas, *The Life of Francis Place* (1898, 1951); *cf.* M. W. Patterson, *Sir Francis Burdett and his Times* (2 vols, 1931), G. D. H. Cole, *The Life of William Cobbett* (1947 edn), *passim*.

26. See Denis Gray, *Spencer Perceval, The Evangelical Prime Minister, 1762–1812* (1963); Michael Roberts, *The Whig Party, 1807–1812* (1939).

27. Cole, 150–9; Robertson, 499–511; Betty Kemp, *King and Commons, 1660–1832* (1957), 107, *seq.*; Richard Pares, *King George III and the Politicians* (1953). On the King's troubles, see Ida Macalpine and Richard Hunter, *George III and the Mad Business* (1969) and, on early Whig hopes, J. W. Derry, *The Regency Crisis and the Whigs, 1788–1789* (Cambridge, 1963).

28. Brown, ch. 10; R. J. White, *Waterloo to Peterloo* (1968 edn), ch. 11 and, on a longer period, *The Age of George III* (1968). *Cf.* Cartwright, II, 24, *seq.*

29. See J. L. and B. Hammond, *The Town Labourer, 1760–1832* (1949 edn), Arthur Aspinall, *The Early English Trade Unions* (1949), *passim*; *cf.* E. P.

Thompson, *The Making of the English Working Class* (1968 edn), 537–45, 598–645 *et passim*; M. I. Thomis, *The Luddites* (Newton Abbot, 1970); 'The Luddites in the Period 1779–1830', *Our History* (1956), reprinted in L. M. Munby (ed.), *The Luddites and Other Essays* (Edgeware, 1971), 33–56.

30. MacCoby, *Radicalism*, ch. 17–18; D. G. Barnes, *History of the English Corn Laws from 1660 to 1846* (1930), *passim*; Samuel Bamford, *Passages in the Life of a Radical*, I (1841, 1894, 1968), 6.

31. See W. R. Brock, *Lord Liverpool and Liberal Toryism* (1941), C. J. Bartlett, *Castlereagh* (1966), P. J. V. Rolo, *George Canning* (1965), H. Twiss, *Life of Lord Eldon* (1844), P. Ziegler, *Addington* (1965), Lady Longford, *Wellington. The Years of the Sword* (1969), N. Gash, *Mr Secretary Peel* (1961); C. R. Fay, *Huskisson and his Age* (1951).

32. J. T. Ward, *The Factory Movement, 1830–55* (1962), *The Factory System*, II (Newton Abbot, 1970), *passim*; J. F. C. Harrison, *Robert Owen and the Owenites in Britain and America* (1969); J. Butt (ed.), *Robert Owen, Prince of Cotton Spinners* (Newton Abbot, 1971).

33. Bamford, I, 38; *Political Register*, 3 Nov. 1816; S. T. Coleridge, *Two Addresses on Sir Robert Peel's Bill* (1818); Jack Simmons, *Southey* (1945), 154. *Cf.* R. J. White (ed.), *Political Tracts of Wordsworth, Coleridge and Southey* (1953), Max Beer, *A History of British Socialism*, I (1929), ch. 9; White, *Waterloo*, ch. 6; Harold Perkin, *The Origins of Modern English Society, 1780–1880* (1969), ch. 6.

34. G. D. H. Cole, *Socialist Thought: The Forerunners* (1953), ch. 3; Beer, I, pt. 2; Max Morris, *From Cobbett to the Chartists* (1948), *passim*; T. L. Jarman, *Socialism in Britain* (1972); R. K. P. Pankhurst, *William Thompson, 1775–1833* (1954).

35. On Pentrich see R. J. White, 'The Pentrich Revolution, 1817', *History Today*, v (1955) and *Waterloo*, ch. 11; *cf.* Thompson, 723–5. On Oliver see A. F. Fremantle, 'The Truth about Oliver the Spy', *English Hist. Rev.*, xlvii (1932), White, *Waterloo*, ch. 13; *cf.* J. L. and B. Hammond, *The Skilled Labourer* (1919), ch. 12; Thompson, 711–36; *Political Register*, 16 May 1818; *Leeds Mercury*, 14 June 1817.

36. G. Pellew, *Life and Correspondence of . . . Sidmouth*, III (1847), 199; White, *Waterloo*, ch. 15; Donald Read, *Peterloo, The Massacre and its Background* (Manchester, 1958), 39 *et passim*.

37. Read, 102–5; Hammonds, *Skilled Labourer*, 94–121; Thompson, 706–7 *et passim*.

38. Read, 47–54, 106-7, 210–16; *Manchester Observer*, 23 Jan. 1819.

39. *Leeds Mercury* 30 Oct. 1817.

40. For varied accounts, see Bamford, ch. 33–4; F. A. Bruton, 'The Story of Peterloo', *Bull. John Rylands Library*, v (1919), *Three Accounts of Peterloo by Eyewitnesses* (Manchester, 1921); Archibald Prentice, *Historical Sketches and Personal Recollections of Manchester* (Manchester, 1851 edn); Read, ch. 8; Thompson, ch. 15, pt 5; G. M. Trevelyan, 'The Number of Casualties at Peterloo', *History*, vii (1923); Robert Walmsley, *Peterloo: The Case Re-opened* (Manchester, 1969); White, *Waterloo*, ch. 15.

41. Arthur Aspinall, *Lord Brougham and the Whig Party* (1927), 276–7.

42. More sympathetic accounts are given in John Stanhope, *The Cato Street Conspiracy* (1962) and P. B. Ellis and Seumas Mac a'Ghobhainn, *The Scottish Insurrection of 1820*; *cf.* A. Smith, 'Arthur Thistlewood: a Regency Republican', *History Today*, iii (1953); Ferguson, 284; F. A. Sherry, *The Rising of 1820* (Glasgow, 1969).

2 *The Background*

1. See W. O. Henderson, *Industrial Britain under the Regency* (1968); Ward, *Factory System*.

2. Asa Briggs, 'The Language of "Class" in Early Nineteenth-Century England', in A. Briggs and J. Saville (eds), *Essays in Labour History* (1967 edn); Perkin, *passim*; W. A. Mackinnon, *On the Rise, Progress and Present State of Public Opinion . . .* (1828), 2.

3. PP. 1874, lxxii; 1876, lxxx; John Bateman, *The Great Landowners of Great Britain and Ireland* (1883 edn; repr. Leicester, 1971, intr. David Spring).

4. See Barnes, *passim*; L. G. Johnson, *General T. Perronet Thompson* (1957); A. E. Musson, 'The Ideology of Early Co-operation in Lancashire and Cheshire', *Trans. Lancs. and Ches. Antiq. Soc.*, lxviii (1958); Sidney Pollard, 'Nineteenth Century Co-operation: From Community Building to Shopkeeping', in Briggs and Saville. Owenite literature is vast; see the bibliography in Harrison. The latest studies are Butt, *op. cit.* and S. Pollard and J. Salt (ed.), *Robert Owen: Prophet of the Poor* (1971).

5. *The Book of Fallacies: from Unfinished Papers of Jeremy Bentham* (1824), 389–90.

6. See Arthur Aspinall, *Politics and the Press, c. 1780–1850* (1949); Donald Read, *Press and People, 1790–1850* (1961); J. F. C. Harrison, *Learning and Living, 1790–1960* (1962); Mabel Tylecote, *The Mechanics Institutes of Lancashire and Yorkshire before 1851* (Manchester, 1957); R. K. Webb, *The British Working-Class Reader* (1955).

7. N. Gash, 'English Reform and French Revolution in the General Election of 1830', in R. Pares and A. J. P. Taylor (eds), *Essays Presented to Sir Lewis Namier* (1956); J. T. Ward, *Sir James Graham* (1967), 87.

8. *Speeches of the Rt. Hon. T. B. Macaulay, M.P.* (1854), 73, 75–6, 74–5.

9. See J. L. and B. Hammond, *The Village Labourer, 1760–1832*, II (1948 edn), 41–128; G. Rudé, 'English Rural and Urban Disturbances on the Eve of the First Reform Bill, 1830–1831', *Past and Present*, 37 (1967); E. J. Hobsbawm and G. Rudé, *Captain Swing* (1969).

10. Ward, *Graham*, 104; [Sir] Edward Baines, *The Life of Edward Baines* (1859 edn), 138–9; Thompson, 897; Briggs 'Language'. *The Poor Man's Guardian* (1831–5) has been reissued (1969).

11. G. A. Williams, *Rowland Detrosier, A Working-Class Infidel* (York, 1965), 20; C. M. Wakefield, *Life of Thomas Attwood* (1885), 179; *Poor Man's Guardian, passim*.

12. On local features see Asa Briggs, 'Thomas Attwood and the Economic Background of the Birmingham Political Union', *Cambridge Hist. J.*, ix (1948), 'The Parliamentary Reform Movement in Three English Cities', ibid., x (1952); H. Ferguson, 'The Birmingham Political Union and the Government', *Victorian Studies*, iii (1960); W. Ferguson, 'The Reform Act (Scotland) of 1832: Intention and Effect', *Scottish Hist, Rev.*, xlv (1966); G. P. Jones, 'The Reform Movement in Sheffield'. *Trans. Hunter Arch. Soc.*, iv (1958); J. M. Main, 'Working Class Politics in Manchester . . . 1819–32', *Hist. Studies, Australia and New Zealand*, vi (1955); L. S. Marshall, 'The First Parliamentary Election in Manchester', *American Hist. Rev.*, xlvii (1942); A. Temple Patterson, *Radical Leicester* (Leicester, 1954); Donald Read, *The English Provinces* (1964); A. S. Turberville and Frank Beckwith, 'Leeds and Parliamentary Reform, 1820–1832', *Publ. Thoresby Soc.*, xli (1943).

13. The course of the Bill's history is traced by J. R. M. Butler, *The Passing of the Great Reform Bill* (1914, 1964); D. G. Southgate, *The Passing of the Whigs* (1962) and G. M. Trevelyan, *Lord Grey and the Reform Bill* (1920). The results are examined in N. Gash, *Politics in the Age of Peel* (1953). Aspects of the question are discussed in Élie Halévy, *The Triumph of Reform* (1950); Joseph Hamburger, *James Mill and the Art of Revolution* (New Haven, Conn., 1963); D. C. Moore, 'The Other Face of Reform', *Victorian Studies*, v (1961), 'Concession or Cure: The Sociological Premises of the First Reform Act', *Hist. J.*, ix (1966). Attitudes are summarised in W. H. Maehl, *The Reform Act of 1832* (New York, 1967) and Derek Fraser, 'The Agitation for Parliamentary Reform', in J. T. Ward (ed.), *Popular Movements, c. 1830–1850* (1970), ch. 1.

14. See Cecil Driver, *Tory Radical. The Life of Richard Oastler* (New York, 1946); J. T. Ward, 'Two Pioneers in Industrial Reform', *Bradford Textile Soc. J.* (1963–4), 'Some Industrial Reformers', ibid. (1962–3); *Leeds Mercury*, 16 Oct. 1830, seq., *Halifax and Huddersfield Express*, 12 Mar. 1831, *The Home*, 6 Mar. 1852, *Leeds Intelligencer*, 20 Oct. 1831.

15. PP. 1831–2, xv; *Leeds Mercury*, 8 Sept. 1832; on Sadler see *Memoirs of the Life and Writings of M. T. Sadler* (1842), J. T. Ward, 'M. T. Sadler', *Univ. of Leeds Rev.*, vii (1960).

16. *Poor Man's Advocate*, 31 Mar. 1832; *Poor Man's Guardian* 11 Apr. 1832; Cavie Richardson, *Address to the Working Classes of Leeds and the West Riding* (Leeds 1831), 7; *Leeds Intelligencer*, 21 June 1832; Ralph Taylor and John Hannam, *To the Public* (Leeds, 1832); *Fleet Papers*, 13 Feb. 1841.

17. Richard Oastler, *Facts and Plain Words on Everyday Subjects* (Leeds, 1833), 3–4, 13–14, 19–20, 46–7, 55; *British Labourer's Protector*, 22 Feb. 1833. On Bull, see J. C. Gill, *The Ten Hours Parson* (1959) and *Parson Bull of Byerley* (1963); on Ashley, Sir Edwin Hodder, *Life and Work of the Seventh Earl of Shaftesbury, K.G.* (3 vols, 1886).

18. Richard Oastler, *Infant Slavery* (Preston, 1833), 4–7; PP. 1833, xx. The agitation is traced in detail in 'Alfred' [Samuel Kydd], *The History of the Factory Movement* (2 vols, 1857) and Ward, *Factory Movement*.

19. See M. D. George, 'The Combination Laws Reconsidered', *Economic Hist.*, i (1927); J. L. Gray, 'The Law of Combination in Scotland', *Economica*, vii (1928).

20. S. and B. Webb, *The History of Trade Unionism* (1950 impr.), *passim*; J. T. Ward, 'A Great Bradford Dispute', *Bradford Textile Soc. J.* (1961–2); W. E. S. Thomas, 'Francis Place and Working-Class History', *Hist. J.*, v (1962); D. J. Rowe (ed.), *London Radicalism, 1830–1843* (1970); George Howell, *A History of the Working Man's Association* (1900; intr. D. J. Rowe, Newcastle, 1972).

21. G. D. H. Cole, *Attempts at General Union, 1818–1834* (1953); Henry Pelling, *A History of British Trade Unionism* (1963 edn), ch. 3; W. H. Oliver, 'Robert Owen and the English Working Class Movement', *History Today*, viii (1958), 'The Consolidated Trades Union of 1834', *Economic Hist. Rev.*, 2s., xviii (1964); W. H. Fraser, 'Trade Unionism', in Ward, *Popular Movements*, ch. 4. and 'Robert Owen and the Workers' in Butt, ch. 4.

22. *The Martyrs of Tolpuddle* (1934), *passim*.

23. See C. D. Collett, *History of the Taxes on Knowledge* (1933); W. H. Wickwar, *The Struggle for the Freedom of the Press* (1928); Patricia Hollis, *The Pauper Press* (Oxford, 1970); J. H. Wiener, *The War of the Unstamped* (1970).

24. See S. and B. Webb, *English Poor Law History*, pt ii (1963 repr.), *English Poor Law Policy* (1963 repr.); J. D. Marshall, *The Old Poor Law* (1968); Mark Blaug, 'The Myth of the Old Poor Law and the Making of the New', *J. Economic Hist.*, xxiii (1963), 'The Poor Law Report Re-examined', ibid., xxiv (1964); G. B. A. Finlayson, *England in the Eighteen Thirties* (1969), 50–64; J. J. and A. J. Bagley, *The English Poor Law* (1966).

25. John Walter, *A Letter to the Electors of Berkshire* (1834), 23; *Political Register*, 16 Aug. 1834; Richard Oastler, *Eight Letters to the Duke of Wellington* (1835), 102–3.

3 *The Foundations*

1. Oastler, *Letters*, 34.

2. See Ward, *Factory Movement*, ch. 7; N. C. Edsall, *The Anti-Poor Law Movement, 1834–44* (Manchester, 1971) and M. E. Rose, 'The Anti-Poor Law Movement in the North of England', *Northern History*, i (1966), 'The Anti-Poor Law Agitation', in Ward, *Popular Movements*, ch. 3 and *The English Poor Law, 1780–1930* (Newton Abbot, 1971).

3. Richard Oastler, *Damnation. . .* (1837), 20, 22; M. Fletcher, *Migration of Agricultural Labourers* (Bury, 1837), 4; *Leeds Intelligencer*, 11 Mar., 20 May, *Manchester and Salford Advertiser*, 25 Nov., 2 Dec., 1837.

4. *Manchester and Salford Advertiser*, 29 Sept. 1838; *Northern Star*, 5 Jan. 1839.

5. Place Papers (British Museum Add. MSS 27,791) *ff.* 280–1.

6. On Benbow, see A. J. C. Ruter's reprint of *Grand National Holiday* (1832), in *International Rev. Social Hist.*, (1936); Alfred Plummer, 'The General Strike during One Hundred Years', *Economic Hist.*, i (1927).

7. *Poor Man's Guardian* 27 Apr. 1833; W. Lovett, *The Life and Struggles of William Lovett in his Pursuit of Bread, Knowledge and Freedom* (1876; intr. R. H. Tawney, 1920, 1967), 59.

8. See, for instance, Edouard Dolléans, *Le Chartisme* (2 vols, Paris, 1912), I, 26–9.

9. Quoted in D. J. Rowe, 'The London Working Men's Association and the "People's Charter" ', *Past and Present*, 36 (1967). Dr Rowe's work is vital to the study of London Chartism. *Cf.* Place MSS 27, 819, *f.* 31.

10. Lovett, 75 and ch. 5, *passim*.

11. *The Radical*, 17 Apr. 1836; Place MSS 27,835, *f.* 98; Rowe, appendix; *Address and Rules of the Working Men's Association* (1836). The last document is reprinted in Mrs Dorothy Thompson's valuable collection of

documents *The Early Chartists* (1971), 50–4; *cf.* D. Thompson, 'Chartism as an Historical Subject', *Bull. Soc. Study of Labour Hist.*, 20 (1970).

12. See the interesting argument advanced in D.J. Rowe, 'Chartism and the Spitalfields Silk-Weaver's, *Economic Hist. Rev.*, 2s., xx (1967); *cf.* D. J. Rowe, 'The Failure of London Chartism', *Hist. J.*, xi (1968) and I. Prothero, 'Chartism in London', *Past and Present*, 44 (1969).

13. *Morning Chronicle*, 20 Jan. 1840, quoted in Rowe, 'Chartism'.

14. This account is largely based on Mark Hovell, *The Chartist Movement* (Manchester, 1943 repr.), ch. 4 and Rowe, 'The LWMA'; *cf.* I. Prothero's comments and D. J. Rowe's rejoinder, *Past and Present*, 38 (1967).

15. The prospectus is reprinted by Mrs Thompson, 55–6; on Harney see A. R. Schoyen, *The Chartist Challenge* (1958); *cf.* Rowe, 'Failure'.

16. This period is covered by Donald Read and Eric Glasgow, *Feargus O'Connor. Irishman and Chartist* (1961), ch. 6.

17. *Manchester and Salford Advertiser*, 12 Dec. 1835.

18. See Hovell, 65-6.

19. Julius West, *A History of the Chartist Movement* (1920), 76; see W. H. Maehl, 'A. H. Beaumont: Anglo-American Radical (1798–1838) *International Rev. Social Hist.*, xiv (1969).

20. *London Mercury*, 4 Mar. 1837; Lovett, 84,311–14; Hovell, 69–70.

21. Conrad Gill, *History of Birmingham*, I (Oxford, 1952), *passim*; *cf.* T. R. Tholfsen, 'The Artisan and the Culture of Early Victorian Birmingham', *Univ. of Birmingham Hist. J.*, iv (1954); *Report of the Proceedings of the Birmingham Political Union* (Birmingham, 1830).

22. *Poor Man's Guardian*, 10 Nov. 1832.

23. *Report of the Town's Meeting in Support of Parliamentary Reform* (Birmingham, 1832), quoted in Asa Briggs (ed.), *Chartist Studies* (1965), 18–19; Hovell, 99.

24. *Birmingham Journal*, 12 Nov. 1836; Place MSS 27,819, 94, 99; Hovell, 101–2.

25. Wallas, Rowe, *London Radicalism*, *passim*.

26. *The Times*, 31 July 1837; C. C. F. Greville, *A Journal of the Reign of Queen Victoria from 1837 to 1852*, I (1885) 26.

27. Peel to Graham, 21 Nov. 1837 (Graham MSS); Place MSS 27,819,153.

28. *Address to Reformers* (1837); Lovett, 164–72.

29. West, 5, 78–9; Hovell, 73; Lovett, 168–9; Briggs, 24; Place MSS 27,835, 126; Rowe, 'The LWMA' and 'Rejoinder', *loc. cit.*

30. The 'Charter' is largely reproduced in N. Gash, *The Age of Peel* (1968), 91–4. The revised (1842) version is given in Lovett, 315–30.

31. Part of the petition is reprinted in G. D. H. Cole and A. W. Filson, *British Working Class Movements. Select Documents, 1789–1875* (1951), 349–51, 353–5.

32. *Bronterre's National Reformer*, 15 Jan. 1837.

4 *Emergence*

1. R. G. Gammage, *History of the Chartist Movement* (1894 edn), 11–12. See William Dorling, *Henry Vincent, A Biographical Sketch* (1879).

2. Oastler, *Damnation*, 4; Read and Glasgow, 51; *The Times*, 16–19 May, *Leeds Intelligencer*, 19 May 1837.

3. *The Times*, 8 July 1837; Alexander Wilson, *The Chartist Movement in Scotland* (Manchester, 1970), 37; *cf.* Driver, 337–9; Ward, *Factory Movement*, ch. 7.

4. *Northern Star*, 18 Nov. 1837. This account is based on *Manchester Examiner*, 19 Oct., 6 Nov. 1847; E. L. H. Glasgow, 'The Establishment of the *Northern Star* Newspaper', *History*, xxxix (1954); Read and Glasgow, ch. 7. On Hill, see Alexander Paterson, 'Feargus O'Connor and the *Northern Star*', *Leeds Mercury*, 24 Feb. 1900 and on Hobson, *Huddersfield Weekly News*, 13 May 1876.

5. *Leeds Times*, 2 Jan. 1836. The development of Leeds Chartism is best examined in J. F. C. Harrison, 'Chartism in Leeds', in Briggs, *Chartist Studies*, ch. 3.

6. *Leeds Times*, 2, 23 Sept. 1837, 9 June 1838. Mr K. Geering of Sussex University is preparing a study of White.

7. *Leeds Times*, 31 Jan. 1835, 9, 23 Jan. 1836, 15 Sept. 1838; *Bradford Observer*, 7 June, 13 Sept. 1838; *Northern Star*, 15 Sept. 1838. See A. J. Peacock, *Bradford Chartism, 1838–1840* (York, 1969); William Cudworth, *Histories of Manningham, Heaton and Allerton* (Bradford, 1896), *Round About Bradford* (Bradford, 1876). On Bussey, see P. Bussey, *Address to the Working Men of England* (Bradford, 1838); *Yorkshire Observer*, 12 Feb. 1902; J. T. Ward, 'Old and New Bradfordians in the Nineteenth Century', *Bradford Textile Soc. J.* (1964–5).

8. *Leeds Mercury*, 20 Nov. 1830; *Halifax and Huddersfield Express*, 19 Mar. 1831; *Leeds Intelligencer*, 9 Mar. 1832; *Halifax Guardian*, 23 Jan. 1838. See

Benjamin Wilson, *The Struggles of an Old Chartist* (Halifax, 1887); Frank Peel, *Spen Valley, Past and Present* (Heckmondwike, 1893); G. R. Dalby, 'The Chartist Movement in Halifax and District', *Trans. Halifax Antiq. Soc.* (1956).

9. J. C. Symons, *Arts and Artisans at Home and Abroad* (1839), 125; Edwin Chadwick, *Report on the Sanitary Condition of the Labouring Population of Great Britain* (1842; Edinburgh, 1965, intr. M. W. Flinn), 97.

10. *The Loyal Reformers' Gazette*, 1 Feb., 29 Mar., 2 Aug., 1 Nov. 1834, 31 Jan., 28 Mar., 2 May., 29 Aug., 26 Sept. 1835; Peter Mackenzie, *Exposure of the Spy System* (Glasgow, 1832); *Trial for Libel ... A. B. Richmond v. Simkin & Marshall* (Glasgow, 1835); *cf.* A. B. Richmond, *Narrative of the Conditions of the Manufacturing Population* (1835); W. M. Roach, 'Alexander Richmond and the Radical Reform Movements in Glasgow in 1816–17', *Scottish Hist. Rev.*, li (1972).

11. On the general background see A. Wilson, chs. 1–2. Quotations are taken from *Glasgow Argus*, 13 Nov. 1837; Gammage, 57; *Northern Star*, 13 Jan. 1838, 23 Dec. 1837. On Taylor, see 'John Taylor, Esq. M.D., of Backhouse, Ayrshire (1805–42)', *Ayrshire Arch. & Nat. Hist. Collections*, 2s., i (1947–9).

12. Archibald Swinton, *Report of the Trial of Thomas Hunter and other Operative Cotton Spinners* (Edinburgh, 1838); James Marshall, *The Trial of ... the Glasgow Cotton Spinners* (Glasgow, 1838); PP. 1837–8, viii, 'Report of S. C. on Combinations of Workmen'; Sir Archibald Alison, *Some Account of My Life and Writings* (Edinburgh, 1883), *passim*. Mr G. Z. Brassay of Strathclyde University is preparing a new study of these events.

13. *Scotch Reformers' Gazette*, 14 Apr. 1838. Attwood's letter was issued as a leaflet, reproduced in A. Wilson, 48.

14. Gammage, 20–2; *Northern Star*, 7–28 July 1838.

15. A. Wilson, 56–7; Patrick Brewster, *Seven Chartist and Military Discourses* (Glasgow, 1843); *Dundee Advertiser*, *passim*; *Memoranda of the Chartist Agitation in Dundee* (Dundee, n.d.); S. D. McCalman, 'Chartism in Aberdeen', *Scottish Labour Hist. Soc. J.*, 2 (1970).

16. J. K. Edwards, 'Chartism in Norwich', *Yorkshire Bull. of Economic and Social Research*, xix (1967); R. Young, 'The Norwich Chartists', A. F. J. Brown, 'The Chartist Movement in Essex' and H. Fearn, 'Chartist Activity in Suffolk', in *Chartism in East Anglia* (Cambridge, 1951); H. Fearn, 'Chartism in Suffolk' in Briggs, *Chartist Studies*, ch. 5.

17. John Cannon, *The Chartists in Bristol* (Bristol, 1967), 1–2; R. B. Pugh, 'Chartism in Wiltshire', *Wilts. Arch. & Nat. Hist. Mag.*, liv (1952) and 'Chartism in Somerset and Wiltshire', in Briggs, *Chartist Studies*, ch. 6.

18. See A. H. John, *The Industrial Development of South Wales* (Cardiff, 1950); A. H. Dodd, *The Industrial Revolution in North Wales* (Cardiff, 1951 edn); D. J. V. Jones, 'Welsh Chartism', *Bull. Soc. Study of Labour Hist.*, 23 (1971); David Williams, *John Frost* (Cardiff, 1939; repr. 1969), *The Rebecca Riots. A Study in Agrarian Discontent* (1955) and 'Chartism in Wales', in Briggs, *Chartist Studies*, ch. 7; W. Ll. Davies, 'Notes on Hugh Williams and the Rebecca Riots', *Bull. Board of Celtic Studies*, ii (1945).

19. Peter Searby, *Coventry Politics in the Age of the Chartists* (Coventry, 1964), 3–18; *Coventry Standard*, 18 Feb., 22 July 1842; Gammage, 36–40; G. Barmsby, *The Dudley Working-Class Movement, 1832–1860* (Dudley, 1967); *cf.* John Prest, *The Industrial Revolution in Coventry* (Oxford, 1960), 139; V. E. Chancellor, *Master and Artisan in Victorian England* (1969). Mr Searby's researches on Coventry politics continue.

20. See *The Life of Thomas Cooper. Written by Himself* (1872); Patterson, *Radical Leicester*; J. F. C. Harrison, 'Chartism in Leicester', in Briggs, *Chartist Studies*, ch. 4; R. A. Church, *Economic and Social Change in a Midland Town—Victorian Nottingham* (1966), 123, 128–57; Peter Wyncoll, *Nottingham Chartism* (Nottingham, 1966); A. C. Wood, 'Nottingham, 1835–65', *Trans. Thoroton Soc..*, lix (1955); R. Barnes, 'The Midland Counties Illuminator: A Leicester Chartist Journal', *Trans. Leics. Arch. & Hist. Soc.*, xxxv (1959).

21. *Manchester and Salford Advertiser*, 25 Mar., 29 Apr., 9 Dec. 1837, 29 Sept. 1838. See Donald Read, 'Chartism in Manchester', in Briggs, *Chartist Studies*, ch. 2.

22. *Twopenny Dispatch*, 13 Feb., *Leeds Times*, 30 Apr. 1836; *Northern Star*, 13, 20 Jan., *seq.*, 4 July, *Northern Liberator*, 27 July 1838.

23. *The Times*, 19 May, *Leeds Intelligencer*, *Leeds Mercury*, 20 May., 11 Nov. 1837; H. Cockburn, *Journal* (Edinburgh, 1874), 155; *Northern Star*, *London Dispatch*, 8 Jan., *Northern Star*, *The Examiner*, 10 Feb., *Northern Star*, 9 June., 16 Oct., 10 Nov. 1838. See also H. L. Jephson, *The Platform, Its Rise and Progress*, II (2 vols, 1892) *passim*, which is still a useful collection of extracts from speeches.

24. *Northern Star*, 13 Oct., 31 Mar., 17 Nov., *Wigan Gazette* 16 Nov. 1838; Place MSS 27, 820, 141.

25. Gammage, 22–8, 31–6, 42; *Northern Liberator*, 30 June, *Northern Star*, 17 Nov. 1838. See also W. H. Maehl, 'Chartist Disturbances in North-eastern England, 1839', *International Rev. Social Hist.*, viii (1963); Norman McCord, 'The Implementation of the 1834 Poor Law Amendment Act on Tyneside', ibid., xiv (1969); D. J. Rowe, 'Some Aspects of Chartism on Tyneside', ibid., xvi (1971); Brian Harrison and Patricia Hollis,

'Chartism, Liberalism and the Life of Robert Lowery', *English Hist. Rev.*, lxxxii (1967); R. L. Galloway, *Annals of Coal Mining*, II (1898), ch. 14; Schoyen, 41–2, *seq.*

26. *Birmingham Journal, Northern Star*, 11 Aug. 1838; Gammage, 41–6; Wakefield, 327.

27. *Northern Star*, 22 Sept, *The Sun*, 18 Sept. 1838; Gammage, 46–53; West, 103–4; Hovell, 75–6. Actual attendance was probably around 15,000: *cf. London Dispatch*, 11 Nov. 1838.

28. *Manchester and Salford Advertiser, Manchester Times, Northern Star*, 29 Sept., *Manchester Guardian*, 26 Sept. 1838; Gammage 59–63; Read and Glasgow, 70–5.

29. *Leeds Times*, 20 Oct., *Northern Star*, 16 Oct. 1838; Gammage, 63–4.

30. *True Scotsman, Northern Star*, 27, *Birmingham Journal*, 24 Nov. 1838, *seq.*; see A. Wilson, 59, *seq.*

31. *True Scotsman, Northern Star, Birmingham Journal*, 8, 15 Dec. 1838; Gammage, 59–70; A. Wilson, ch. 4.

32. *Northern Star*, 12 May 1838, 5 Jan. 1839; *cf.* Hovell, 66, *seq.*; West, 103, *seq.*

33. See R. M. W. Cowan, *The Newspaper in Scotland* (Glasgow, 1946); A. Wilson, *passim* and 'The Scottish Chartist Press', *Scottish Labour Hist. Soc. J.*, 4 (1971).

34. *Northern Star*, 10, 17, 24 Nov., 1, 15, 29 Dec.; *Birmingham Journal*, 24 Nov. 1838; Place MSS 27, 820, 327, *seq.*; *cf.* Hovell, 110–14; Read and Glasgow, 79–80; Schoyen, 41.

35. *The Times*, 1 Jan., *Northern Liberator, Northern Star*, 5 Jan. 1839; Henry Goddard, *Memoirs of a Bow Street Runner* (1956 edn), 154–61; J. T. Ward, 'Revolutionary Tory: The Life of Joseph Rayner Stephens of Ashton-under-Lyne (1805–1879)', *Trans. Lancs. & Cheshire Antiq. Soc.*, lxviii (1958). On reactions to the arrest, see *Northern Star*, 5, 12, 19, 26 Jan., 16 Feb., 9, 16 Mar. 1839.

36. *Northern Star*, 5, 12, 19 Jan. 1839. On Deegan's views, see ibid., 23 Feb. 1839.

5 *Physical and Moral Force*

1. *Ayr Observer*, 11 Dec., *True Scotsman, Northern Star*, 15, 22, 29 Dec., *Scotch Reformers' Gazette*, 12 Dec. 1838.

2. *Northern Liberator, Northern Star, True Scotsman*, 5, 12, 19 Jan. 1839.

3. *The Operative*, 10 Feb. 1839. The 'good man' was Oastler (*Northern Liberator*, 27 July 1838).

4. *Northern Star*, 5, 26 Jan., 9 Mar. 1839.

5. See Hovell, 122–4; West, 106–8; A. Wilson, 70–1; Gammage, 91, 105, *seq.*

6. Place MSS 34, 245, *passim*; *Northern Star*, 9, 16 Feb, *The Charter*, 10, 14, 17 Feb. 1839.

7. Place MSS 35, 151; Norman McCord, *The Anti-Corn Law League, 1838–1846* (1958) ch. 1, *Free Trade. Theory and Practice from Adam Smith to Keynes* (Newton Abbot, 1970), 63–6; Archibald Prentice, *History of the Anti-Corn Law League* (1853; intr. W. H. Chaloner, 1968), 1, 116; *Northern Star*, 2, 23 Feb. 1839.

8. Place MSS 27, 821, *passim*; *The Charter*, 17, 24 Feb., *Northern Star*, 16, 23 Feb. 1839. The *Star* hopefully maintained that 'one remarkable consequence of this debate will be to disabuse the minds of the Irishmen in their country, and through them the Irish nation in general, of the erroneous notions they entertain regarding the feelings of their British brethren towards them. . .'.

9. *Northern Star*, 2, 9, 16 Mar. 1839; Place MSS 34, 245 B. See D. J. Rowe, 'The Chartist Convention and the Regions', *Economic Hist. Rev.*, 2s., xxii (1969).

10. *The Charter*, 10, 24, 31 Mar., 7, 14 Apr., *The London Democrat*, 23 Mar. 1839.

11. *The London Democrat*, 7, 20, 27 Apr., *Morning Chronicle*, 19 Mar., *The Charter*, 31 Mar. 1839; M. Fletcher, *Address to the People of Bury* (Bury, 1839).

12. Hovell, 129–31; Pugh in Briggs, *Chartist Studies*, 182–4; *Northern Star*, 13, 27 Apr., *True Scotsman*, 13 Apr., 18, 25 May 1839; A. Wilson, 71–4; Place MSS 34, 245 A.

13. *The Charter*, 28 Apr., 5, 12 May, *Northern Star*, 11 May 1839. See G. D. H. Cole, *Chartist Portraits* (1941; repr. 1965, intr. Asa Briggs), 128–9, 232.

14. *Northern Star*, 11 May, *The Charter*, 12 May 1839; Lovett, 214–15.

15. *Northern Star*, 10 Feb., 8 Sept., 27 Oct., 10 Nov. 1838.

16. *The Times*, 9 Oct. 1838, 1 Jan., 26 Mar. 1839, *seq.*, *Northern Liberator*, 5 Jan., 11, 18 May *Bolton Free Press*, 5 Jan. 1839; Hovell, 136–42; F. C. Mather, *Public Order in the Age of the Chartists* (Manchester, 1959), *passim*, and 'The Government and the Chartists', in Briggs, *Chartist Studies*, ch. 12;

Goddard, 154–61; Sir William Napier, *Life and Opinions of Sir C. J. Napier*, II (1857), *passim*; Gammage, 92, *seq.*

17. *The Charter*, 28 Apr., 19 May, *Northern Star*, 18 May, 1839; Hovell, 144–9; West, 116–18; Gammage, 109–11.

18. *The Charter*, 12, 19, 26, *The London Dispatch*, 12 May 1839; Edward Hamer, *A Brief Account of the Chartist Outbreak in Llanidloes* (Llanidloes, 1867) *cf.* Williams, *Frost*, 156–8; Napier, II, *passim*; Gammage, 112–13.

19. Gammage, 113–23; Napier, II, 29, *seq.*; *Manchester and Salford Advertiser*, 11 May, *The Times*, 28 May, *Northern Star*, *Leeds Times*, *Northern Liberator*, 25 May, *True Scotsman*, 15 June 1839, *seq.*; Ward, 'Revolutionary Tory', *loc. cit.*

20. *Manchester and Salford Advertiser*, 11 May, *Northern Star*, *True Scotsman*, 25 May, *The Charter*, 16 June, *Northern Star*, *True Scotsman*, 20, 27 June, *The London Dispatch*, *The Charter*, 7 July, *Northern Star*, 7 Sept. 1839.

21. *Northern Star*, 2 July, 24, 31 Aug., *True Scotsman*, 24 Aug., *Manchester and Salford Advertiser*, 11 May, 29 June 1839.

22. Place MSS 27, 821; *The Charter*, 7 July 1839; Hovell, 156–8.

23. Taylor quoted in Rowe, 'Failure', *loc. cit.*; *The Times*, 1 Jan, *Northern Liberator*, 5 Jan.; Hamer, *passim*; *The Charter*, *The London Democrat*, 12 May, *The Times*, 11 May, *Manchester and Salford Advertiser*, 6 July, *Leicester Chronicle*, *Leeds Times*, 27 July 1839; *Northern Star*, Hovell, West, Briggs, Mather, *passim*.

24. Napier, II, 6, 40, 43, 9, 62. Macerone's *Defensive Instruction to the People* was published in 1832 and 1834. Alexander Somerville, a former trooper in the Scots Greys, who became famous after a monstrous military flogging for protesting against orders to disperse Birmingham reformers in 1832, countered Macerone's views with his *Warnings to the People on Street Warfare* (1838). Somerville subsequently became an Anti-Corn Law League lecturer. See A. Somerville, *The Autobiography of a Working Man* (1848; repr. 1951, intr. John Carswell), *The Whistler at the Plough* (1852).

25. *Hansard*, 3s., xlix, 220–78; *Northern Star*, 20, 27 July, 3 Aug., *The London Dispatch*, 21, 28 July, *The Charter*, 12, 21, 28 July, 11 Aug. 1839; Place MSS 34, 245 B. On Newcastle, see A. Jenkin, 'Chartism and the Trade Unions', *Our History* (1963, repr. Munby, 75–91); R. Challinor and B. Ripley, *The Miners' Association: A Trade Union in the Age of the Chartists* (1968); Rowe, 'Chartism on Tyneside', *loc. cit.*

26. *Northern Liberator*, 21 July, 3 Aug. 1839; Hovell, 165–6, 169; D. Thompson, 131–4.

27. *Manchester Guardian*, 3, 7, 10, 14, 17 Aug., *Northern Liberator*, 3 Aug. 1839; Gammage, 151–6; H. U. Faulkner, *Chartism and the Churches* (New York, 1916; repr. 1970), 35–41; *Northern Star*, 10 Aug., *Manchester and Salford Advertiser*, 17 Aug. 1839.

28. *Manchester and Salford Advertiser*, 28 Sept., *Northern Star*, 19 Oct. 1839; *cf. Fleet Papers*, 3 Dec. 1842.

29. *Northern Star*, 5, 19 Oct. *seq.* 1839; Lovett, 238–41; Williams, *Frost, passim; cf.* R. Davies, 'A Drop of Dew: William Price of Llantrisant', *Wales*, ix (1949); Earl Stanhope, *Notes of Conversations with the Duke of Wellington, 1831–1851* (1886, 1888, 1938, 1947), 195.

30. Gammage, 262–7; J. Watkins, *Impeachment of Feargus O'Connor* (1843); F. O'Connor, *Reply to Mr Watkins's Charges*(1843); Williams, *Frost*, 199–203. On Ashton's account, see *Northern Star*, 3 May 1845. Frost never attacked O'Connor, and O'Connor's biographers believe that he visited Ireland to deal with estate affairs and (unsuccessfully) to establish Chartist societies in Cork. (Read and Glasgow, 88).

31. *Northern Liberator*, 21 Feb., 31 Oct. 1840; *Diplomatic Review*, Jan., July 1873; T. Frost, *Forty Years' Recollections* (1880), 102, *seq*. On Urquhart see also Asa Briggs, 'David Urquhart and the West Riding Foreign Affairs Committees', *Bradford Antiquary*, n.s., xxxix (1958).

32. Hovell, ch. 11, *passim*; Lovett, 238–41; Peel, 313, *seq*.; Peacock, 28, *seq*.; B. Wilson, Dalby, T. A. Devyr, *The Odd Book of the Nineteenth Century* (New York, 1882), *passim*.

33. *Northern Liberator*, 18, 24 Jan., *Northern Star*, 4, 11, 18 Jan., *Leeds Mercury, Leeds Times, Halifax Guardian*, 18 Jan., *True Scotsman*, 22 Feb. 1840; *Northern Star*, 3 May 1845; Lovett, 209. An important corrective to older accounts is given in Peacock, 28–46.

34. Hovell, 187; Gammage, 164–82; *Northern Star, passim*.

35. *Northern Star*, 8, 15 Feb., 14, 21 Mar. 1840; Gammage, 167, 170; Napier, II, 40, 77; *Ashton Chronicle*, 29 Apr. 1848.

36. *Northern Star*, 2 May, 18 July, *Northern Liberator*, 2 May, 11 Apr. 1840. Along with a vast amount of other papers, Philp produced a *Vindication of his Political Conduct*.

37. *Northern Liberator*, 21 Mar., *Scottish Patriot*, 7 Mar. 1840; A. Wilson, 101 *et passim*; *Northern Star*, 2, 9, 16, 30 May 1840, 16 Jan. 1841; Faulkner, *passim*.

38. *Northern Star*, 20 June, 18 July, 3 Oct. 1840; G. J. Holyoake, *Sixty Years of an Agitator's Life*, I (1906 edn), 104; William Lovett and John Collins, *Chartism; A New Organisation of the People* (1840, 1841; intr. Asa

Briggs, Leicester, 1969) 1, 24–6, 27, *seq.*, 124. Lovett's scheme is discussed in Professor Brigg's introduction; *cf.* Hovell, 203–8, West, 150–3; Gammage 195–6.

39. *Northern Star*, 25 July, 1 Aug. 1840, 27 Feb. 1841; Lovett, 252; Place to Collins, 27 Feb. 1841 (West, 162–3); Hovell, 196–9; Gammage, 183–4; *English Chartist Circular*, 46.

6 *The New Chartism*

1. *Northern Liberator*, 28 Nov. 1840, *Northern Star*, 9, 16 Oct., 13 Nov., 4, 11 Dec. 1841.

2. Gammage, 184–90; Faulkner, *passim*; Holyoake, I, 104; *Leicestershire Mercury*, 26 Sept. 1840 (quoted by Harrison in Briggs, *Chartist Studies*, 108); *Northern Star*, 9 Jan., 27 Mar., 10 July 1841; G. J. Barmsby, 'Chartism in the Black Country, 1850–1860', *Our History* (1966) (Munby, 93–114); Lovett, *Life and Struggles*, ch. 13; Cole and Filson, 380–1.

3. *Northern Star*, 8 May, 5 June 1841; West, 164; Hovell, 211. 'Chartism and sobriety are going hand in hand', it was reported at Shaw in December (*Northern Star*, 8 Jan. 1842). *Cf.* Brian Harrison, *Drink and the Victorians* (1971).

4. *Freeman's Journal*, 14 Dec. 1838, 26 Jan. 1839, 25 Jan., 6 Apr. 1841; *Liverpool Mercury*, 28 June 1839; *Northern Star*, 19 Dec. 1840–23 Jan. 1841; *Leeds Times*, *Leeds Mercury*, 23 Jan. 1841; W. J. Fitzpatrick (ed.), *Correspondence of Daniel O'Connell*, II (1888), 156. See Read and Glasgow, 92–3; R. O'Higgins, 'The Irish Influence in the Chartist Movement', *Past and Present*, 20 (1961); J. H. Treble, 'O'Connor, O'Connell and the Attitudes of Irish Immigrants towards Chartism in the North of England, 1838–1848', in J. Butt (ed.), *The Victorians and Social Protest* (Newton Abbot, 1973).

5. *Freeman's Journal*, 11 May 1841; *Northern Star*, 29 May, 3, 10 July 1841, 1, 8, 15, 22 Jan. 1842; Cockburn, I, 297; *Fleet Papers*, I, 30; *Glasgow Chronicle*, 6 Sept., *Scotch Reformers' Gazette*, 7 Aug. 1841.

6. *Northern Star*, 25 Apr., 16 May, 18 July 1840, 16, 30 Jan., 28 Aug. 1841. O'Connor's poem is quoted in Hovell, 222.

7. Place MSS 27, 820, 3; Cooper, 179; *Northern Star*, 24 Apr.–29 May, 21, 28 Aug., 4, 11, 25 Sept., 9, 16, 23 Oct., 13, 27 Nov., 4, 11 Dec., *Glasgow Chronicle*, 18, 25 Oct., 3, 5 Nov. 1841.

8. *Northern Star*, 4, 11 July 1840, 27 Mar., 17, 24 Apr., 1, 8, 22, 29 May 1841; West, 159–60; Lovett, 251.

9. *Northern Star*, 17 Apr., 29 May, 19, 26 June, 3, 10, 24, 31 July, 14 Aug., 16 Oct., 20 Nov. 1841, 12 Nov. 1842; *cf.* Gammage, 192–5; Hovell, 236–40; West, 168–70; *McDouall's Chartist and Republican Journal*, 22 May, 19 June 1841 [P. W. Slosson, *The Decline of the Chartist Movement* (New York, 1916) 157].

10. See Asa Briggs, 'Ebenezer Elliott, The Corn Law Rhymer', *Cambridge J.* (1950); Lucy Brown, 'The Chartists and the Anti-Corn Law League', in Briggs, *Chartist Studies*, ch. 11; G. M. Trevelyan, *The Life of John Bright* (1913), 62; McCord, *League*, 51–2; Prentice, I, 116–20.

11. *Northern Star*, 23 Jan., 9 Oct. 1841, 19 Feb., 9 Apr. 1842; *Leeds Times*, 8 June, 1839, 15 Jan. 1841; West, 165–6; Harrison in Briggs, *Chartist Studies*, ch. 3. A delegate meeting at Burnley proposed to publish a 'North Lancashire Chartist and Teetotal Letter Bag', which appears to have been still-born (*Northern Star*, 1 Jan. 1842).

12. Hovell, 241; *Freeman's Journal*, 14 Sept. 1841; *Northern Star*, 4 July 1840, 5 June 1841, 1 Jan., 30 July 1842; *Northern Liberator*, 10, 23 May 1840.

13. McCord, *League*, 51; Gammage, 102–4; John Buckley (ed. J. C. Buckmaster), *A Village Politician* (1897), 137; Fitzpatrick, 204. Even Lovett 'remembered' in May 1840 that 'the agitation for the alteration of the Corn Laws did not commence till after the people were actively engaged in contending for the suffrage. . ., knew that a vast number of those who talked of giving the people cheap bread spurned the idea of giving them the suffrage [and] very much doubted the sincerity of their professions' (Hovell, 204). On Chartist 'takeovers' of League meetings, see *Northern Star*, 2 Feb. (Barnoldswick), 9 Feb. (Huddersfield, Rochdale), 16 Feb. (Halifax, Rochdale, Bradford) 1839, 29 Jan. (Hull), 26 Feb. (Sheffield), 4 June (Rochdale) 1840. *Cf. English Chartist Circular*, ii, 59 (1842).

14. *The London Dispatch*, 13 Apr. 1839; *Northern Star*, 3 Oct., 3 Nov. 1840, 30 Mar., 16 Oct. 1841, 22 Jan. 1842; J. Campbell, *An Examination of the Corn and Provision Laws* (Manchester, 1841); J. Leach, *Stubborn Facts from the Factories* (1844); Gammage, 216; Ward, *Factory Movement*, 302–3.

15. *Manchester Times*, 22 May, 2 Oct. 1841, 8 Jan., 12 Mar., 2 Apr. 1842; *Northern Star*, 3 Nov. 1840, 2 Oct. 1841, 8, 22, 29 Jan., 12, 26 Feb., 12, 19, 26 Mar., 2, 9 Apr., 16 July 1842; *Manchester Times, Manchester and Salford Advertiser*, 12, 19, 26 Mar. 1842. See [Sir] E. Watkin, *Alderman Cobden of Manchester* (1891), *passim*; McCord, *League*, 98–103; Read and Glasgow, 93–4; Lucy Brown in Briggs, *Chartist Studies*, ch. 11.

16. L. Faucher (trans. J. P. Culverwell), *Manchester in 1844* (1844) *Northern Star*, 6 Jan., *The League*, 10 Aug. 1844; Gammage, 254–5.

17. *Northern Star*, 16 Oct., 27 Nov., 24 Dec. 1841, 8, 15, 22, 29 Jan., 5, 19, 26 Feb., 16, 23, 30 Apr., 7, 14, 21 May, 18 June, 12 Dec. 1842; *Hansard*, 3s., lxiii, 13–91.

18. *Report of Proceedings of the Middle and Working Classes at Birmingham, April 5, 1842 and Following Days* (1842); *Brief Sketches of the Birmingham Conference* (1842); H. Richard, *Memoirs of Joseph Sturge* (1864); Henry Sooly, *These Eighty Years* (1891); Philp, *passim*; Hovell, 240–50; West, 172–9; A. Wilson, ch. 13 and 'Chartism' in Ward, *Popular Movements*, ch. 5; Briggs *Chartist Studies*, *passim*; *The Nonconformist*, 13, 20 Apr., *British Statesman*, 16, 24 Apr., *Northern Star*, 1 Jan., 5, 12, 26 Mar., 2, 9, 16 Apr., 21, 28 May, 18 June, 2, 23 July, 1842; Stephen Hobhouse, *Joseph Sturge* (1919); Lovett, *Life and Struggles*, ch. 15; Place MSS 27, 810, 152.

19. *Northern Star*, 4 June–13 Aug.; *Nottingham Review*, *The Times*, 5 Aug.; *Fleet Papers*, 3 Dec. 1842; Church, 141–3.

20. *Blackburn Standard*, 4 May 1842; *Annual Register*, lxxxiv, ii, 102; *Northern Star*, *passim* (on 16 Apr. it reported reductions of up to 8s for Manchester mechanics and on 16 July noted a 'further' 15 per cent reduction for Stockport spinners).

21. Gammage, 213–16; Schoyen, 113–14; *Northern Star*, 25 June 1842, 10 Feb. 1844; *Fleet Papers*, 7 May, 6, 13, 27 Aug., 3, 17 Sept. 1842; Ward, *Factory Movement*, 244–8.

22. *Bolton Chronicle*, *Manchester Courier*, *Morning Chronicle*, 13 Aug., *Stockport Advertiser*, 12 Aug., *Blackburn Standard*, 17 Aug., *Manchester Times*, *Manchester and Salford Advertiser*, 20 Aug., *Northern Star*, 13, 20, 27 Aug., *Halifax Guardian*, *Leeds Intelligencer*, *Leeds Mercury*, 6–27 Aug., *Illustrated London News*, 27 Aug., *Manchester Guardian*, 3, 10, 13, 17, 27 Aug., 7, 22 Sept., *The Times*, 12, 15, 19, 22, 23, 26, 27 Aug., 1 Sept., *Fleet Papers*, 13 Aug., 3, 17 Sept. 1842; *Quarterly Review*, lxxi (1842). *Cf.* T. E. Ashworth, *An Account of the Todmorden Poor Law Riots* (Todmorden, 1901); William Cudworth, *Rambles round Horton* (Bradford, 1886), 24–9; Dalby, *loc. cit.*; Friedrich Engels, *The Condition of the Working Class in England* (1845; Oxford, 1971 edn, trans. and ed. W. O. Henderson and W. H. Chaloner), 263–5; Hovell, 259–67; Mather, *passim*; Peel, *Spen Valley*, 324–6, *Risings of the Luddites, Chartists and Plugdrawers* (Heckmondwike, 1888, 1895; intr. E. P. Thompson, 1969), 339–49; Slosson, 67–9; West, 188–93; G. Kitson Clark, 'Hunger and Politics in 1842', *J. Modern Hist.*, xxv (1953); A. G. Rose, 'The Plug Riots of 1842 in Lancashire and Cheshire', *Trans. Lancs. & Cheshire Antiq. Soc.*, lxvii (1958); John Miller, 'Songs of the Labour Movement', *Our History* (1963; Munby, 115–42).

23. *Glasgow Argus*, 11, 18 June, 23 July, 27 Aug., *Dundee Advertiser*, 26

Aug. 1842; *Memoranda of the Chartist Agitation in Dundee*, 33-45, 59-65; James Myles, *Rambles in Forfarshire* (Dundee, 1850); A. Wilson, ch. 14.

24. *Northern Star*, 27 Aug., 24 Sept., 8 Oct. 1842; Graham MSS (Ward, *Graham*, 189-93); *cf*. Mather, *passim*, and in Briggs, *Chartist Studies*, ch. 12.

25. *Northern Star*, 20, 27 Aug., 3, 10, 17, 24 Sept., 1, 8, 22 Oct., 3, 10 Dec. 1842, 7 Jan., 11, 18 Mar. 1843; *British Statesman*, 26 Nov. 1842; *Annual Register*, lxxxiv, ii, 163; William Lovett, *Address to the Working Classes* (1842); Gammage, 228-31, 242.

26. *Northern Star*, 10, 17, 24, 31 Dec. 1842, 7, 14, 21 Jan. 1843, 3 Feb. 1844; *The Nonconformist, Birmingham Journal*, 31 Dec. 1842; *The Times*, 1 Feb. 1844; Cooper, 222-44; Gammage, 242-7, 230-1; *Hansard*, 3s., lxix, 530.

27. The point is made, in rather exaggerated fashion, in J. L. Tildsley, *Die Enstehung und die Okonomischen Grundsatze der Chartistenbewegung* (Jena, 1898), 52. Tildsley does, however, show the importance of the Factory Movement to Northern Chartist development ch. 3, especially 21-2); *cf.* Theodore Rothstein, *From Chartism to Labourism* (1929), 71-7; Christopher Thorne, *Chartism* (1966), ch. 2; H. T. N. Gaitskell, *Chartism* (1929), ch. 2; F. C. Mather, *Chartism* (1962), *passim*. Neil Stewart, *The Fight for Charter* (1937), 92-3, 197-8, is much less perceptive.

7 New Directions

1. On the development of the Plan, see Read and Glasgow, 108-9; Joy MacAskill, 'The Chartist Land Plan', in Briggs, *Chartist Studies*, ch. 10; A. M. Hatfield, *The Chartist Land Company* (Newton Abbot, 1970), ch. 1; *Northern Star*, 11 July 1840, 10 July-7 Aug. 1841, 23, 30 Apr. 1842.

2. Pollock to Graham, 9 Oct. 1842 (Graham MSS); Mather, *Public Order*, *passim* and in Briggs, *Chartist Studies*, 391-3; *Northern Star*, 25 Feb., 11, 18 Mar. 1843; *The Trial of Feargus O'Connor and 58 Others at Lancaster* (1843); *Personal Remembrances of Sir Frederick Pollock*, I (1887), 204-5.

3. *Northern Star*, 27 Nov., 25 Dec. 1841, 1 Jan., 7 May 1842; Feargus O'Connor, *The Land and Its Capabilities* (Manchester, 1842). On similar Tory ideas, see W. B. Ferrand, *Allotment of Waste Lands. Speech... March 30, 1843* (1843); *The Times*, 31 Mar. 1843; J. T. Ward, 'Young England at Bingley', *Bradford Textile Soc. J.* (1965-6).

4. *Northern Star*, 11, 25 Mar., 1, 15 Apr.-27 May, 3, 10, 17, 24 June, 1 July, 19, 26 Aug., 9, 16 Sept., *Bradford Observer*, 30 Mar., 6 Apr., 18 May, *Sheffield and Rotherham Independent*, 1 Apr., *Leeds Mercury*, 4, 11, 18, 25 Mar., 1, 15, 22, 29 Apr., 6, 20 May, 17 June, *Manchester Guardian*, 22, 29 Apr.,

7, 14 June 1843; Gammage, 247–51; West, 204. On the 1843 Factory Bill, see J. T. Ward, 'A Lost Opportunity in Education, 1843', *Researches and Studies*, 20 (1959) and J. T. Ward and J. H. Treble, 'Religion and Education in 1843', *J. Ecclesiastical Hist.*, xx (1969).

5. *Northern Star*, 15 July, 5 Aug., 9–30 Sept., 4, 18 Nov., 2, 19 Dec. 1843; Gammage, 252; A. Wilson, 205–6.

6. Gammage, 252–3; R. J. Conklin, *Thomas Cooper The Chartist* (Manila, 1935), 208; Fearn in Briggs, *Chartist Studies*, 211–12; *Northern Star*, 27 Jan., 3–17 Feb., 30 Mar., 20, 27 Apr., 7, 14, 21, 28 Sept., 5, 12, 19, 26 Oct., 2 Nov. 1844, 10, 17 May 1845.

7. *Manchester Times*, 16 Mar. 1844; *Leeds Times*, 4 Jan. 1840, 4 Nov. 1843, 2 Nov. 1844, 1 Nov. 1845; *Northern Star*, 8 Jan., 30 July 1842, 10, 17, 24 Feb., 2, 9, 23, 30 Mar., 6, 13, 20, 27 Apr., 11, 18 May 1844; Harrison in Briggs, *Chartist Studies*, 86–92 and 'James Hole and Social Reform in Leeds', *Pub. Thoresby Soc.*, Monograph iii (1954); Michael Brook, 'Joseph Barker and *The People*', ibid., Miscellany, xiii (1963).

8. A. Wilson, 208–11; *Northern Star*, 20 Apr., 5 Aug., 19 Oct., 23 Nov., 7, 28 Dec., 1844, 4, 11, 18, 25 Jan. 1845.

9. Graham MSS 52a; Webbs, *Trade Unionism* (1950 impr.), 176–9, 187, *seq.*; A. J. Taylor, 'The Miners Association of Great Britain and Ireland', *Economica*, xxii (1955); Challinor and Ripley, *passim*; *Northern Star*, 26 Mar., 14, 21 May, 4 June 1842, 6, 13, 20 Jan., 10, 17 Feb., 2, 30 Mar., 6, 13, 20 Apr., 4, 11, 18, 25 May, 1, 22, 29 June, 6, 13, 20, 27 July, 3, 10, 24, 30 Aug., 16, 23 Nov. 1844, 8, 29 Mar., 2 Aug., 11 Oct. 1845, 6, 13 June 1846.

10. *Northern Star*, 29 Mar., 1 Nov. 1845, 24 Aug. 1846, 25 Jan., 17, 24 May, 26 July 1845.

11. *Northern Star*, 26 Apr., 3 May, 7, 21, 28 June, 12 July, 2, 30 Aug., 20, 27 Sept., 11 Oct. 1845; O'Brien quoted in Slosson, 88; *National Reformer*, 9 Jan. 1847.

12. *Northern Star*, *passim*; West, 208–9; Cooper, 273–4.

13. *Northern Star*, 6, 13, 20 Dec., 7 June 1845; Joy MacAskill, in Briggs, *Chartist Studies*, ch. 10; Mrs Hadfield, ch. 1.

14. *Northern Star*, 11 Jan., 14 Mar., 30 May 1846 and *passim*. Examples of Jones's poetry are given in John Saville, *Ernest Jones, Chartist* (1952) and Y. V. Kovalev, *An Anthology of Chartist Literature.* (Moscow, 1956) Translations of the Russian introduction are provided by W. H. Chaloner in *Victorian Studies*, ii (1958) and by Joan Simon in Munby, *op. cit.*, 57–73.

15. *Northern Star*, 16 May, 6 June, 11 July, 1, 8 Aug. 1846; Kovalev, 135–40.

16. *Northern Star*, 22 Aug. 1846; 3 Feb., 10 Aug. 1844, 4 Mar. 1843, 20 Jan., 2, 9, 23 Mar., 25 May 1844, 12, 19 Apr., 10 May, 20, 27 Dec. 1845, 31 Jan., 4 July 1846.

17. *The League*, 23 Mar. 1844, 11 Nov., 23, 30 Dec. 1843, 23 Mar. 1844, 13 June 1846.

18. Holyoake, I, 85; Gammage, 270–1; *Northern Star*, 25 July 1845.

19. *Manchester Guardian*, 9 Aug. 1845; Ward, *Factory Movement*, ch. 13; *Northern Star*, 17 Jan., 7 Feb. 1846.

20. *Northern Star*, 27 Dec. 1845, 3, 17, 31 Jan. 1846.

21. *Northern Star*, 13 July, 1, 8 Aug., *seq.*, 26 Sept., 31 Oct., 12, 19, 26 Dec., 22 Aug. 1846.

22. *Northern Star*, 23 Oct. 1847, 7 Mar., 19 Dec. 1846, 13 Feb. 1847; Jones's diary, 8 Oct. 1846.

23. *Northern Star*, 12 June, 8 May, 21, 28 Aug., 4 Sept., 13 Nov., 24, 31 July, 7 Aug. 1847; T. H. Duncombe, *Life and Correspondence of T. S. Duncombe*, I (1868), 373; *The Nation* 15 Aug. 1847.

24. *Northern Star*, 7 Aug., 25 Sept., 30 Oct., 20 Nov., 4, 18 Dec. 1847, 8 Jan., 19 Feb. 1848; *Manchester Examiner*, 12 Feb. 1848; *Journal of the House of Commons*, ciii (1848), *passim*. See J. H. Treble, 'The Irish Agitation', in Ward, *Popular Movements*, ch. 7.

25. See R. D. Edwards and T. O. Williams (eds), *The Great Famine* (1956), 183–4; Cecil Woodham-Smith, *The Great Hunger* (1962), *passim*; Read and Glasgow, ch. 13; *Northern Star*, 11 Dec. 1847, 11, 18, 25 Mar. 1848.

26. On the depression, see W. W. Rostow, *British Economy of the Nineteenth Century* (Oxford, 1948), 118–20; C. N. Ward-Perkins, 'The Commercial Crisis of 1847', *Oxford Economic Papers*, ii (1950); R. C. O. Matthews, *A Study in Trade-Cycle Theory* (Cambridge, 1954), *passim*.

27. *Northern Star*, 25 Dec., *Manchester Guardian*, 20 Feb. 1847; *Northern Star*, 8 Apr., 18 Mar., 1 Apr. 1848.

28. *Weekly Dispatch*, 9 June 1844; West, 227, *seq.*; Ward, *Graham*, 208–11; Lovett, *Life and Struggles*, 297–8; *Northern Star*, 11 Aug., 15 Nov. 1845, 21, 28 Mar., 18 July 1846, 11 Dec. 1847, 18, 25 Mar. 1848; Saville, *Jones*, 21; Schoyen, *passim*; Thomas Frost, *Forty Years' Recollections* (1880), 125; *cf.* Henry Weisser, 'Chartist Internationalism, 1845–1848', *Hist. J.*, xiv (1971).

29. *The Scotsman*, 8, 11 Mar., *Northern Star*, 4, 11 Mar., *Manchester Examiner*, 14 Mar., *Northern Star*, 26 Feb. 1848. A pioneer study of Chartist interest in the Land is Fritz Bachmann, *Die Agrarreform in Chartistenbewegung* (Bern, 1928). *Cf.* J. Salt, 'Isaac Ironside and the Hollow Meadows Farm Experiment', *Yorkshire Bull. Economic & Social Research*, xii (1960).

8 *Finale*

1. Gammage, 286–90; *cf.* Joshua Hobson, *Land Scheme of Feargus O'Connor* (Manchester, 1848); *Manchester Examiner, Northern Star, passim.*

2. *Northern Star*, 4 Mar., *seq.* 1848.

3. See Lady Longford, *Victoria, R. I.* (1964), 195–8; W. F. Monypenny and G. E. Buckle, *The Life of Benjamin Disraeli, Earl of Beaconsfield,* III (1914), 95; Greville, III, 133, 160, 162; C. D. Yonge, *The Life of Arthur, Duke of Wellington* (1891), 488–9; Spencer Walpole, *A History of England from the Conclusion of the Great War in 1815,* V (1890), 194–6; Earl Russell, *Recollections and Suggestions, 1813–73* (1875), 252–3.

4. J. Pope-Hennessy, *Monckton Milnes. The Years of Promise* (1949), 276; Hodder, *Shaftesbury* (1887 edn), 393; Lady Londonderry, *Frances Anne* (1958), 238; John Morley, *The Life of Richard Cobden* (1910 edn), 484–5; Trevelyan, 183.

5. *Northern Star*, 25 Mar. 1848.

6. A. C. Benson and Viscount Esher (eds), *The Letters of Queen Victoria . . . 1837–1861,* II (1908), 167–8; West, 245; Lord Malmesbury, *Memoirs of an Ex-Minister,* I (1855), 223, *seq.*

7. Sir Tresham Lever, *Letters of Lady Palmerston* (1957); Greville, III, 164–5; Jasper Ridley, *Lord Palmerston* (1970), 339; John Morley, *Life of W. E. Gladstone,* I (1903), 358; F. Maurice, *The Life of F. D. Maurice,* I (1885), 472; Thomas Mackay (ed.), *The Reminiscences of Albert Pell* (1908), 148–9.

8. *Northern Star,* 1, 8, 15 Apr., *Evening Sun,* 10 Apr., *The Times,* 10, 11 Apr. 1848; *Annual Register,* xc, ii, 50–4; Gammage, 301–16; West, 241–9; Hovell, 288–91; Benson and Esher, 168–9; Frost, 136–41.

9. *Hansard,* 3s., xcviii, 284–301; *Northern Star,* 15, 22, 29 Apr. 1848; Gammage, 317–24; *Annual Register,* xc, ii, 50.

10. Gammage, 324–31; *Northern Star,* 6, 13, 20 May 1848; West, 253–4; Hovell, 292; Read and Glasgow, 137–8.

11. Cooper, *passim;* Frost, 143–65; *Northern Star,* 3 June 1848; Greville, III, 182, 215–16.

12. Greville, III, 188–90.

13. Gammage, 332–3; Mather, *Public Order, passim* and in Briggs, *Chartist Studies,* 397; Sir T. W. Reid, *Life of the Rt. Hon. W. E. Forster,* I (1888), 167–9, 216–27, 245; *Leeds Intelligencer,* 3 June 1848; Ferrand to Grey, 25, 27, 28, to Lord Harewood, 26, Grey to Ferrand, 25, 27, John Rand,

27 May, Grey, Wood, 1 June 1848 (Ferrand MSS); Harry Speight, *Chronicles and Stories of Bingley and District* (1904), 232–7; E. E. Dodd, *Bingley* (Bingley, 1958), 111.

14. Gammage, 332–45; *Northern Star*, 8, 15 July, 15 June, 9 Sept., 1, 22 July, 28 Oct., *The Times*, 8 June 1848, *seq.*

15. *Northern Star*, 19, 26 Feb., 18, 25 Mar., 29 Apr., *seq.*, 1, 15, 22 July, 12, 19, 26 Aug. 1848; *The Labourer, passim*; PP. 1847–8, xix; *cf.* W. H. G. Armytage, 'The Chartist Land Colonies, 1846–48', *Agricultural Hist.*, xxxii (1958); Mrs Hadfield, chs. 4–5; Joy MacAskill, in Briggs, *Chartist Studies*, ch. 10; P. Searby, 'Great Dodford and the Later History of the Chartist Land Scheme', *Agricultural Hist. Rev.*, xvi (1968).

16. *Oxford Chronicle*, 23 Nov. (quoted Joy MacAskill, *op. cit.* 333), *Northern Star*, 31 Aug. 1850, 17 May, 1851, *seq.*; Mrs Hadfield, *passim*.

17. Lovett, *Life and Struggles*, 279–92; Collet, *passim*; *cf.* Hovell, 297; West, 258–9.

18. *Northern Star, passim*; *Red Republican*, 22 June; *Reynolds's Weekly Newspaper*, 14, 21 July 1850; Cole and Filson, 406–11; *cf.* Charles Kingsley in *Politics for the People*, 13 May 1848.

19. *Red Republican*, 13 July, *Northern Star*, 14 Sept., 26 Oct., 7 Dec., 20 July, 10 Aug., 5 Oct., 21, 28 Dec. 1850, 4 Jan. 1851. Davies soon left the executive, being succeeded by Thornton Hunt (who, with Linton and others, had been rejected by the electors); Owen, Cooper, O'Brien, Kydd and Gerald Massey had refused nomination. The successful candidates, Reynolds, Harney, Jones, Arnott, O'Connor, Holyoake, Davies, Grassby and Milne, received respectively 1,805, 1,774, 1,757, 1,605, 1,314, 1,021, 818, 811 and 709 votes.

20. Engels to Marx, 8, 29 Jan. 1851 (Saville, *Jones*, 232); Gammage, 359, *seq.*; *cf.* Saville, 248–56; *Northern Star*, 1 Feb., *seq.*, 5 Apr. 1851.

21. *Northern Star*, 5, 12 Apr., 12 June, *The Times*, 3 May, *Friend of the People*, 24, 31 1851.

22. *People's Paper*, 13 Nov. 1852, 8, 15 Oct. 1853; *Northern Star*, 28 July 1849, 13 Dec. 1851, 3, 10 Jan. 1852; *The Times*, 26 May 1852; West, 267–8; Gammage, 361–6; W. Tinsley, *Random Recollections of an Old Publisher*, I (1900), 44; J. McCarthy, *Reminiscences*, II (1899), 259; Read and Glasgow, 140–3; *Hansard*, 3s., cxix, 252; Gammage, 377–8, 390.

23. *Northern Star*, 13, 20 Nov. 1851, 10, 24 Jan. 1852; *Friend of the People*, 24 Apr. 1852; *People's Paper*, 22, 29 May 1852, 2 July, 12 Nov. 1853, *seq.*, 11, 18, 25 Mar., 1 Apr. 1854; Gammage, 386–94; Saville, *Jones*, 264–73.

24. *People's Paper*, 26 Aug. 1854; Gammage, 394, *seq.*

25. *People's Paper*, 1 Sept. 1855, 26 Jan., 22 Mar., 5 Apr. 1856, 14 Mar., 16 Apr., 2, 9 May, 5 Dec. 1857.

26. *Reynolds's Newspaper*, 14, 21, *People's Paper*, 13, 20, 27 Feb. 1858; Saville, *Jones*, 255–6. On this period, see also Reg Groves, *But We Shall Rise Again: A Narrative History* (1938); Rothstein, *passim*; A. M. Lehning, 'The International Association', *International Rev. Social Hist.*, iii (1938); Fr. de J., 'Ernest Jones and Chartism, c. 1856', *Bull. International Inst. Social Hist.*, 5 (1950), 'An Open Letter from Ernest Jones to Weydemeyer', ibid., 7 (1952); 'Diary of Ernest Jones', *Our History*, 21 (1961); *cf.* J. Saville, 'Some Aspects of Chartism in Decline', *Bull. Soc. Study of Labour Hist.*, 20 (1970).

9 *Epilogue*

1. Thomas Carlyle, *Chartism* (1839, 1870 edn), 3; Schoyen, *passim*.

2. *The Times*, 1, 11 Sept. 1855; Read and Glasgow, 143; W. J. O'N. Daunt, *A Life Spent for Ireland* (1896), 127.

3. *The Times, Leeds Mercury, Leeds Intelligencer*, 24 Aug. 1861; Driver, 519.

4. F. Boase, *Modern English Biography*, III (Truro, 1901), 732; G. J. Holyoake, *The Life of J. R. Stephens* (1881), 237; Ward, 'Revolutionary Tory', 116.

5. *The Times*, 27 Jan. 1879; Saville, 81.

6. Lovett, *Life and Struggles*, 239 *et passim*; G. D. H. Cole, *Chartist Portraits* (1941; intr. Asa Briggs, 1965), ch. 1.

7. Holyoake, *Sixty Years*, I, 104.

8. Holyoake, *Sixty Years*, I, 104; W. E. Adams, *Memoirs of a Social Atom* (1903), 215–16; Cooper, *Life, Thoughts at Fourscore* (1885), *passim*; Cole, *Chartist Portraits*, ch. 7; D. L. Hobman, 'Thomas Cooper, Chartist and Poet', *Contemporary Rev.* (1948).

9. Wakefield, *Attwood*; Cole, *Chartist Portraits*, ch. 4. A much-needed new biography is being prepared by Canon J. C. Gill.

10. *Preston Guardian*, 9 June 1849; *Annual Register*, xcii, 243–4; Ward, intr. to John Fielden, *The Curse of the Factory System* (1836; repr. 1969) xxxvii, *seq.*

11. West, 282–3; Gammage, 402.

12. A. Wilson, 94, 151, 258; Ray Boston, *British Chartists in America, 1839–1900* (Manchester, 1971), 93, 90, 96; Philip Taft, *Organised Labor in American History* (New York, 1964), 139–45, 73; J. G. Rayback, *A History of American Labor* (New York, 1966 edn), 195–6.

13. Boston, 37–8; John Smyles, *Emigration to the United States* (1842); *Northern Star*, 8 Apr. 1843; Ward, 'Industrial Reformers'; Michael Brook, 'Lawrence Pitkeithley, Dr Smyles and Canadian Revolutionaries in the United States, 1842', *Ontario Hist.*, lvii (1965).

14. *Northern Star*, 6 June 1840, 29 Apr. 30, Sept. 1843; William Brown, *America: Four Years' Residence in the United States and Canada* (Leeds, 1849); *Yorkshire Observer*, 12 Feb. 1902; Ward, 'Bradfordians', *loc. cit.*

15. *The Reformer*, 26 May 1849; A. Wilson, 224 and in Briggs, *Chartist Studies*, 281, n.3; Boston, 42–3, 24–5; *cf.* Thompson, 294.

16. J. T. Barker (ed.), *The Life of Joseph Barker, written by himself* (1880); Brook, 'Barker', *loc. cit.*

17. See Taft, Rayback, Brook and C. K. Yearley, *Britons in American Labor* (Baltimore, 1957), *passim.*

18. Adams, 178–83; Boston, 49–56 68–70; Harrison, *Owen*, 64–5; T. A. Devyr, *The Odd Book of the Nineteenth Century*, *passim.*

19. J. F. Bray, *Labour's Wrongs . . .* (Leeds, 1839 edn), 49; *cf.* M. F. Lloyd Pritchard, intr. to J. F. Bray, *A Voyage from Utopia* (1957).

20. Asa Briggs, 'Chartists in Tasmania', *Bull. Soc. Study of Labour Hist.*, 3 (1961); Williams, *Frost*, *passim*, and 'Zephaniah Williams. A Note', *Bull. Soc. Study of Labour Hist.*, 5 (1962); Adams, 168–70; Gammage, 401–2; Cole, *Chartist Portraits*, ch. 5.

21. Gammage, 401–2; Holyoake, *Sixty Years*, I, 106; A. Wilson, 258, 264; Briggs, *Chartist Studies*, 292–3; S. Pollard, *A History of Labour in Sheffield* (Liverpool, 1959), 47–9; Lamb Collection (Dundee City Library).

22. Adams, 161, 223–7; Schoyen, *passim*; Gammage, 401–2; *cf.* Cole, *Chartist Portraits*, ch. 10, Peter Cadogan, 'Harney and Engels', *International Rev. Social Hist.*, x (1965). On a predecessor in the North East see Maehl, 'Beaumont', *loc. cit.*

23. Adams, 161–2; B. Wilson, 20; Ward, *Factory Movement*, *passim.*

24. Holyoake, *Sixty Years*, I, 238; Hovell, 299; A. Wilson, 216; Gammage, 401–21; Engels, 152; Cole, *Chartist Portraits*, ch. 6; Joseph McCabe, *Life and Letters of G. J. Holyoake* (1908); W. J. Linton, *Memories* (1895); T. Frost, *Reminiscences of a Country Journalist* (1886), *passim.*

25. Ward, *Factory Movement*, 410–11, 'Industrial Reformers', *loc. cit.*; Speight, 396–7.

26. *People's Paper*, 13 Feb. 1858; Owen, *Life* I, xxxiii, *seq.*; Gammage, 401; A. Wilson, 234; Holyoake, *Sixty Years*, I, 103.

27. Holyoake, *Sixty Years*, I, 102, 104–5, 107, II, 161, 267; Harrison, *Owen*, 253; Gammage, 154; Cole, *Chartist Portraits*, ch. 9; W. J. Linton, *Memoir of James Watson* (1879); A. G. Barker, *Henry Hetherington* (n.d.).

28. B. Wilson, *op. cit.*; D. F. E. Sykes, *Huddersfield and its Vicinity* (Huddersfield, 1898), 301; Ward, 'Industrial Reformers', *loc. cit.*, 'The Factory Movement in Lancashire, 1830– 55', *Trans. Lancs. & Cheshire Antiq. Soc.*, lxxv–lxxvi (1966); *cf.* T. P. Newbould, *W. H. Chadwick, The Last of the Manchester Chartists* (1910); Henry Solly, *James Woodford, Carpenter and Chartist* (1881).

29. West, 294–5; Lovett, *Life and Struggles*, I, 93–4.

30. See Mather, *Public Order* and *Chartism*, *passim*; Hodder, *Shaftesbury*, I, 262; G. P. Gooch (ed.), *Later Correspondence of Lord John Russell*, I (1925), 214; *Nottingham Review*, 6 Sept. 1850 (Church, 151); E. Jones, 'The Factory Town' (1847); Rothstein, 71.

31. See E. P. Thompson, 'Homage to Tom Maguire', in Briggs and Saville, 287–9; Henry Pelling, *The Origins of the Labour Party* (1954), ch. 1; Kira Tatarinova, 'Soviet Historians on Chartism', *Bull. Soc. Study of Labour Hist.*, 5 (1962).

32. See E. J. Hobsbawm, 'Methodism and the Threat of Revolution in Britain', in *Labouring Men* (1964); John Rule, 'Methodism and Chartism among the Cornish Miners', *Bull. Soc. Study of Labour Hist.*, 22 (1971); R. F. Wearmouth, *Methodism and Working-Class Movements, 1800–1850* (1937), *passim*.

33. See D. Thompson, 'Notes on Aspects of Chartist Leadership', *Bull. Soc. Study Labour Hist.*, 15 (1967); *cf.* D. J. V. Jones, 'Welsh Chartism', ibid., 23 (1971), W. T. Morgan, 'Chartism and Industrial Unrest in South Wales', *Nat. Library of Wales J.*, x (1957), R. N. Soffner, 'Attitudes and Allegiances in the Unskilled North, 1830–1850', *International Rev. Social Hist.*, xi (1965).

34. Engels, *Condition* (1892 trans. by Mrs F. K. Wischnewetzky; repr. Moscow, 1953, in *Karl Marx and Frederick Engels On Britain*), 263; *cf.* the improved translation in the Henderson and Chaloner edition (1971), 258.

35. Pitkeithley to Duffy, 5 Sept. 1840 [North Riding Record Office, Northallerton; printed in Fred Singleton, *Industrial Revolution in Yorkshire* (Clapham, 1970), 182–3].

36. *The Question 'What is a Chartist?' Answered* (1839); Devyr, 180; *Northern Star*, 29 Oct. 1846.

Author Index

General Index